TRANSGRESSIVE CITY-MAKING AND GOVERNANCE

Studies in Critical Social Sciences Book Series

Haymarket Books is proud to be working with Brill Academic Publishers (www.brill.nl) to republish the *Studies in Critical Social Sciences* book series in paperback editions. This peer-reviewed book series offers insights into our current reality by exploring the content and consequences of power relationships under capitalism, and by considering the spaces of opposition and resistance to these changes that have been defining our new age. Our full catalog of *SCSS* volumes can be viewed at https://www.haymarketbooks .org/series_collections/4-studies-in-critical-social-sciences.

Series Editor
David Fasenfest (York University)

New Scholarship in Political Economy Book Series

Series Editors
David Fasenfest (York University)
Alfredo Saad-Filho (Queen's University, Belfast)

Editorial Board
Kevin B. Anderson (University of California, Santa Barbara)
Tom Brass (formerly of SPS, University of Cambridge)
Raju Das (York University)
Ben Fine ((emeritus) SOAS University of London)
Jayati Ghosh (Jawaharlal Nehru University)
Elizabeth Hill (University of Sydney)
Dan Krier (Iowa State University)
Lauren Langman (Loyola University Chicago)
Valentine Moghadam (Northeastern University)
David N. Smith (University of Kansas)
Susanne Soederberg (Queen's University)
Aylin Topal (Middle East Technical University)
Fiona Tregenna (University of Johannesburg)
Matt Vidal (Loughborough University London)
Michelle Williams (University of the Witwatersrand)

Transgressive City-Making and Governance

Housing Struggles, Occupations and Evictions in the Lisbon Metropolitan Area

SAILA-MARIA SAARISTO

Haymarket Books
Chicago, IL

First published in 2025 by Brill Academic Publishers, The Netherlands
© 2025 Koninklijke Brill NV, Leiden, The Netherlands

Published in paperback in 2026 by
Haymarket Books
P.O. Box 180165
Chicago, IL 60618
773-583-7884
www.haymarketbooks.org

ISBN: 979-8-88890-801-3

Distributed to the trade in the US through Consortium Book Sales and
Distribution (www.cbsd.com) and internationally through Ingram Publisher
Services International (www.ingramcontent.com).

This book was published with the generous support of Lannan Foundation,
Wallace Action Fund, and the Marguerite Casey Foundation.

Special discounts are available for bulk purchases by organizations and
institutions. Please call 773-583-7884 or email info@haymarketbooks.org for more
information.

Cover design by Jamie Kerry and Ragina Johnson.

Printed in the United States.

Library of Congress Cataloging-in-Publication data is available.

Contents

Acknowledgements

This book has evolved significantly from its original conception as a doctoral dissertation for the Universities of Helsinki and Coimbra. Yet its seeds were undoubtedly planted as early as 2016 when I began my doctoral studies in Global Development Studies at the University of Helsinki, and in 2017 when I initiated my collaboration with CES – Centro de Estudos Sociais at the University of Coimbra.

I would first like to express my deepest gratitude to my three supervisors for their exceptional support during my PhD journey. Anja Nygren guided me with patience and dedication through theoretical debates, focus adjustments, and thesis editing. Barry Gills and Giovanni Allegretti provided invaluable encouragement and insights, with Giovanni specifically sharing his expertise on Portuguese housing and governance sectors.

The research presented in this book owes much to the collaboration with the Habita association and the Stop Despejos collective, whose debates greatly enriched my understanding of politics, activism, and social theory. I am profoundly grateful to the families who shared their challenging stories on housing struggles in Lisbon and Loures; their experiences are at the heart of this study. Thanks also to the Lisbon and Loures City Council officials, especially former City Councillor Paula Marques, for their valuable insights and openness to my work's critical approach.

Transforming a doctoral dissertation into a book has been an entirely new journey. I am especially grateful to Miguel Martínez, whose comments and encouragement during and after my thesis examination were invaluable. The pre-examiners Susanne Soederberg and Rita Ávila Cachado engaged thoroughly with my manuscript and provided avenues to develop my work further. In Portugal, I am indebted to my Care(4)Housing project colleagues, Joana Pestana Lages, Ana Carolina Farias, and Sebastião Santos, for their essential support. I also thank Alfredo Saad-Filho for highlighting the opportunity to publish in this book series and David Fasenfest for his patient guidance throughout the process. I would also like to express my gratitude to the Portuguese FCT (Foundation for Science and Technology) for funding my work from 2022 to the present through the grants 'Care(4)Housing: A Care Through Design Approach to Address Housing Precarity' [PTDC/ART-DAQ/0181/2021] and 2023.07870.CEECIND.

Last, my infinite thanks to my closest family: Bruno, Aaron, Luana, Antti, Pilvi, Pihla, Elias, Helena, Rute, and Laura.

This book is dedicated to my late mother, Milja Annikki.

Figures and Tables

Figures

Tables

Abbreviations

AUGIS	Áreas Urbanas de Génese Ilegal (Urban Areas of Illegal Genesis)
BNA	Balcão Nacional de Arrendamento (National Rental Desk)
CERD	UN Committee on the Elimination of Racial Discrimination
EAC	European Action Coalition for the Right to Housing and the City
ECHR	European Convention on Human Rights and Fundamental Freedoms
ETHOS	European Typology of Homelessness and Housing Exclusion
FEANTSA	European Federation of National Organisations Working with the Homeless
ICESCR	International Covenant on Economic, Social and Cultural Rights
INE	Instituto Nacional de Estatística (Statistics Portugal)
IHRU	Instituto da Habitação e da Reabilitação Urbana (National Institute for Housing and Urban Renewal)
LAA	Lei do Arrendamento Apoiado (Law for Subsidised Renting)
LMA	Lisbon Metropolitan Area
NGO	Non-governmental organisation
NGPH	Nova Geração de Políticas da Habitação (New Generation of Housing Policies)
NRAU	Novo Regime do Arrendamento Urbano (New Urban Rental Regime)
OHCHR	UN Office of the High Commissioner for Human Rights
PIMP	Programa de Intervenção a Médio Prazo (Medium-Term Intervention Programme)
PER	Programa Especial de Realojamento (Special Resettlement Programme)
PREC	Processo Revolucionário em Curso (Portuguese revolutionary period)
RMDH	Regulamento Municipal do Direito à Habitação (Municipal Regulation for the Right to Housing)
RRAHM	Regulamento do Regime de Acesso à Habitação Municipal (Regulation of Access to Municipal Housing Regime)
SAAL	Serviço de Apoio Ambulatório Local (Mobile Service for Local Support)

CHAPTER 1

From Old to New Housing Struggles

1   Occupations as a Form of Making the City

One day in 2018, I was in one of the council housing estates in Lisbon, together with activists from the Habita and Stop Despejos collectives, demanding that the eviction of Tita[1] and her children should be stopped. Three months earlier, Tita had decided to occupy an apartment that she had identified as vacant in one of the social housing blocks. During the 1.5 years that I was part of the Habita collective, participating in their activities in the Lisbon Metropolitan Area (LMA), I met many families like Tita's, who had reached the conclusion that their only viable housing alternative was to occupy one of the abandoned apartments in the social housing estates. The representatives of the City Councils of Lisbon and Loures – the councils that I worked with the most – referred to these forms of inhabiting as *ocupações abusivas*, "abusive/unjust/illegal occupations". I was personally struck by the high number of occupations, as well as by the fact that single mothers constituted a clear majority of these occupiers. I became curious as to why these occupations take place. This curiosity led to the research presented in this book.

Moreover, the council housing estates in question are resettlement neighbourhoods, originating from the resettlement of residents of 'informal' neighbourhoods, neighbourhoods promoted by the residents themselves. This meant that these families, who were now inhabiting these homes 'abusively', were often daughters or sons of families that had been resettled earlier, having had their previous homes demolished. They had thus faced eviction previously and, as I discovered, they also often faced eviction and homelessness later on for different reasons: mortgage or rent arrears, an unaffordable rent increase, overcrowding, domestic violence, family disputes, or the demolition of their homes.

This book examines the strategy of dwelling occupations, examining them as pertaining to the sphere of 'makeshift urbanism' that, in Vasudevan's (2015) conceptualisation, means acts of precarious, informal, experimental, and collective world-making that contribute to alternative political imaginaries. Examining housing exclusions and their contestations gains relevance in the

---

1   All of the names in this book have been pseudonymised to protect the identities of the interviewees and other research participants.

FIGURE 1.1   Rock in Riot demonstration in Lisbon, 24 March 2018
             Note: All of the photographs in this book were taken by the author, unless
             otherwise indicated

current context, in which homelessness is growing and evictions are increasing in numbers, due to neoliberal housing governance. Housing exclusions are quickly becoming an important factor causing poverty (Desmond, 2016). It is crucial to understand how diverse population groups are differentially affected by the processes of neoliberal urban governance, in order to also enable a design of inclusive urban policies. Considering the inability of the states to provide or guarantee adequate housing for all, the variegated improvised tactics through which the urban poor and the 'urban majority' (Simone, 2013, 2018) seek to secure some forms of housing for themselves become increasingly important. Throughout history, both in the 'global South' and the 'global North', land and dwelling occupations have emerged as a central tactic to resist housing exclusions. In the Lisbon Metropolitan Area, many improvised strategies can be identified to access housing, used by groups with less economic resources, predominantly immigrants or racialised groups: 1) self-built construction on occupied land; 2) occupation of vacant social housing dwellings; and 3) room and bed-sharing. My study focuses on the second one of them, the so-called need-based occupation of council housing dwellings.

Occupations of vacant dwellings offer an interesting case for exploring makeshift urbanism because they have the purpose of directly enacting the right to housing, providing one of the few immediate housing solutions, contrasting with the time-consuming processes of social housing provision or housing construction. They bring to the fore the conflict between the valorisation of private property, or the exchange value of the property, and the use value of housing. For Lefebvre (2012 [1968]: 39), the use value of the city should recuperate its primordial statute in relation to the exchange value of the city. The urban reality should, therefore, be intended for its users, not for speculators, capitalist promotors, or plans of the technicians. In this context, occupations – even when they are not collective – can be conceived of as a reappropriation of urban property, transforming it from something to be exchanged for something to be used (Lefebvre, 1968). In this reading, residents thus become makers of the urban, realising their right to the city through a concrete process of city-making, immediately enacting the solution to their housing problem (Agier, 2015). Exploration of occupation offers essential indicators of the performance of housing markets and housing policies in terms of inclusiveness of access to housing, specifying, for instance, why people are in some cases obliged to occupy. It also provides valuable insights into agency.

To analyse occupations, I zoomed into the agency and subjectivities of three groups of actors involved with social housing occupations and evictions: women who occupy, municipal employees and local politicians working with housing issues, and housing activists and members of local associations. The research was conducted between December 2017 and April 2019 in two municipalities in the Lisbon Metropolitan Area, engaging in multi-sited and activist research, using predominantly methods of engaged ethnography. The research was carried out in close association with the Habita association, through which I obtained initial contact with families that were occupying vacant council homes.

In the Northern urban theory analyses of occupations, the focus has been overwhelmingly on the political claims and collective action of 'politically motivated' occupation movements (Mayer, 2013; SqEK, 2014). 'Need-based' occupations, in other words, occupations that are undertaken to secure housing, have often been kept analytically separate, with the argument that they cannot be part of a transformative movement, as their primary motivation is to 'remedy a desperate situation' (Cattaneo & Martínez, 2014; Mayer, 2013). Yet this dichotomy is increasingly being questioned by an examination of housing struggles from a decolonial and feminist angle, looking 'for "radical housing" within 'everyday practices of dwelling at the margins' (Lancione, 2020: 275). Through this examination, the possibility opens up to consider what 'resistance' or 'political' can look like, paying increasing attention to political contestation that takes place in the margins, by subjects other than young white men (Gonick, 2016). Hence 'need-based' occupations have recently been conceptualised as *recuperación* – acts of recuperating that challenge regimes of property ownership – (Gonick, 2016), as an essential contribution to claiming Henri

Lefebvre's (1968) 'right to the city' (Aguilera & Bouillon, 2013; Grazioli, 2017), indicating paths through which practices of 'quiet encroachment' can become politicised (Pradel-Miquel, 2017), and even as 'urban commoning' (Martínez, 2020c). Yet this literature tends to exclude the occupation cases that are not a part of an organised movement. These are often presented as a practice that the most socioeconomically marginalised are almost obliged to engage in, due to the lack of choice, ignoring the potential that these practices might have in terms of making and remaking the city (Lancione, 2020). In the last years, a few studies on 'need-based' and 'individualistic' occupations have been published in the 'Global North', focussing on analysing needs-based occupations of empty apartments or buildings (Esposito, 2022; Esposito & Chiodelli, 2023; Herbert, 2018b).

'Need-based' occupations have received much more attention in the literature of land occupations in the 'global South'. Much can be learned by engaging with this field, and lately works that initiate this dialogue have begun to emerge (Amin & Lancione, 2022; Burgum & Vasudevan, 2023; Chiodelli et al., 2021; Gonick, 2016; Lancione & Simone, 2021; Vasudevan, 2015). Many of the questions that have predominated in Euro-American urbanisms in recent decades, such as discussions about 'marginality', 'informality', and 'housing exclusions', have long been at the heart of the study of urban poverty in Latin America (Auyero, 2011; Roy, 2009a). Similarly, the popular challenge to neoliberalism was clearly articulated in Latin America in the 1990s and then in South Africa, India, the Middle East and in much of East and Southeast Asia (S. C. Motta & Nilsen, 2011). Last but not least, there are very insightful analyses on how the everyday practices of the urban poor can be, or become, collective and politicised (Bayat, 2015; Caldeira, 2017; Holston, 2008), and on the conditionalities that the poor face in trying to engage in politics and in political mobilisation (Bayat, 2015; Caldeira, 2015; Chatterjee, 2004; Das, 2011; Nygren, 2016; Saaristo, 2015; Simone, 2015a).

Accordingly, this research has benefitted immensely from the theoretical dialogue with the literature of land occupations in the 'global South', but also with the significant contributions on land occupations in Portugal (Ascensão, 2011; Beja Horta, 2006; R. Á. Cachado, 2012; Castela, 2011; T. C. Pinto, 1998; Salgueiro, 1972), another geographical periphery in terms of urban theory-making. The importance of this dialogue becomes particularly evident when considering the strong parallels, notwithstanding the obvious differences, between the occupations of dwellings in social housing estates and land occupations in the Lisbon Metropolitan Area:

1. They are not a collective movement with a politicised discourse, but an autonomous practice undertaken to secure housing needs.

2. Both kinds of occupations are framed as illegal and informal, and suffer from insecurity of tenure, resulting in a constant risk of eviction.

3. Both seek to engage in negotiations with the state, with the aim of regulating the existing occupation, or securing an alternative housing solution.

4. In both cases, there are often complex interactions with social movement actors, and tensions mount between movements initiated by the inhabitants themselves, and movements initiated from outside.

5. In both kinds of occupations, there is strong representation by Afro-descendant and Roma populations.

To analyse the subtle dynamics of 'makeshift urbanism', I will draw from some of the literature on urbanisms in different countries of the 'global South',[2] which has produced extensive analysis of the subjectivities, subject formation, possibilities, and constraints of agency in these contexts. This literature offers valuable insight into how the everyday practices of the urban poor and the urban majority contribute to the making of the city. Thus, I accept the challenge put forward by Robinson (2003) and Roy (2009) to dislocate urban theory production, building upon contributions from the South to theorise the North. Yet the objective is not to produce a grand theory of 'subaltern urbanism', nor liken the occupation practices to a 'subaltern identity' (Roy, 2011; Spivak, 2005), but to explore occupation practices as relationally produced by specific contexts of housing precarity, discriminations, and by diverse actors involved, such as housing managers and urban dwellers in different council estates. It is thus important to try to understand how residents in different urban contexts try to create themselves spaces of operation with the means they have available and how these spaces are shaped and constrained by forces outside their immediate control (Simone, 2016).

Moreover, in this book, I propose to analyse council housing occupations in the Lisbon Metropolitan Area as a case of 'feminised resistances' (S. C. Motta & Seppälä, 2016), presenting them as a transgressive strategy used predominantly by racialised women in their struggle against homelessness. As Motta and Seppälä (2016: 6) note, in the prevailing representations of politics and resistance, racialised, feminised, marginalised, and oppressed groups are frequently presented as helpless victims, or at most, subjects that promote 'identity politics', without relevance to broader theory-making on political agency. In this way, the forms through which racialised and socioeconomically marginalised women make and experiment with new political subjectivities and re-imagine emancipatory solutions are excluded from analyses (Motta & Seppälä, 2016: 7).

---

2 Definitions of the 'global South' and the 'global North' vary. For more, see Mahler (2017).

These gaps have to be recognised, as has been eloquently argued by Michele Lancione: 'Why are the efforts of millions of women fighting to live within their homes relegated to the rubric of "empowerment" and "capabilities", or registered only within the remit of feminist debates, rather than being seen as part of a quintessential fight to liberate housing from its patriarchal, masculine, violent ethos?' (Lancione, 2020: 277). To create a richer understanding of agency and resistance, we must find room to incorporate these struggles, while recognising all the inherent tensions and ambivalence, escaping the tendency of victimisation, but also recognising oppressions. Veronica Gago (2017: 6, 7), describing popular economies in Argentina, conceptualises this tension as 'vital strategies' through which 'feminized figures (the unemployed, women, youth, migrants) who go out to explore and occupy the street as a space of survival' transform cities, bringing about new politization and new political subjectivities.

The question of framing occupations is central to this book, and hence, the choice of key concepts to analyse and discuss occupations needs thorough consideration. When focusing on occupied buildings and apartments, the English literature tends to use the term 'squatting'. Authors who do not use the concept mainly refer to 'occupations' (Earle, 2012; Hoover, 2015; Roy, 2017; Wilhelm-Solomon, 2020), while Roy (2017: A3) also refers to 'urban homesteading'. Occupation is also the concept that works written in Spanish or Portuguese tend to use: *ocupaciones* (or *okupas*) and *ocupações*, respectively. However, as pointed out in the book *La Vivienda no es delito* (2017), dealing with occupations in Madrid, the disadvantage of this concept is that it is quite ambiguous: 'occupation' can refer to many kinds of phenomena, ranging from 'occupying the streets' to 'occupying a bank' (La Coordinadora de Vivienda de Madrid, 2017). In addition, 'occupying a home' can refer to a standard procedure of moving in after buying or renting an apartment.

In the book *Vivienda no es delito*, some interesting problematisations of the terminology used can be found (La Coordinadora de Vivienda de Madrid, 2017). The terminology in Spanish bears a close resemblance to the concepts that I became familiar with in the Lisbon Metropolitan Area. *Ocupar*, to occupy, was the term most frequently used by the Lisbon-related media, municipal employees, politicians, social movement actors, and the families themselves. However, the politicians and municipal employees, as well as legal and policy documents often added an adjective to this term: *ocupações abusivas* (abusive) / *ilegais* (illegal), / *indevidas* (unjustified) / *não autorizadas* (unauthorised). *Habitações ocupadas ilegalmente* (illegally occupied dwellings) is the concept used by Statistics Portugal (INE, 2015b); Lisbon City Council uses *ocupações abusivas* and *ocupações não autorizadas*; and the National Housing Framework Law (Law no. 83/2019) mentions '*ocupações ilegais*'.

The main purpose of the addition of these adjectives seems to be to emphasise the illegality of the actions, without considering other perspectives that might legitimise, or legalise, the occupations, such as legislation on the right to housing, or unequal distribution of resources. The families who occupy also frequently used the verb *arrombar*, to break in, to describe the act of occupying an apartment. Among the social movement activists, the verb *habitar*, to inhabit, was used, both in meetings with the families and in protests, with the intention of reframing and legitimising the occupations.

In this book, while acknowledging the concept's shortcomings, 'occupations' and 'to occupy' are used to refer to the act of inhabiting apartments or buildings without the permission of their owners. Hence, the definition used is in line with a commonly used definition of 'squatting': 'Urban squatting is living in – or otherwise using – a dwelling without the consent of the owner' (Pruijt, 2013). In this book, the concept 'occupation' is however preferred over 'squatting', to maintain the connotation the term has in the Portuguese language. It also enables me to salute the literature that associates land struggles and occupations with the unequal distribution of land that has its origin in colonialism, followed by the usurpation of land by industrial and urban capitalists (Oliveira, 2001).

This study provides accounts of the efforts of single-mother households and other families struggling for decent housing and survival, of the endeavours by collectives to mobilise urban dwellers and to contest discrimination and exclusion, and of the actions taken by state officials to provide housing and to urge low-income residents to settle based on the solutions they offer. These accounts, at times characterised by struggles for social transformation and at other times by the maintenance of the status quo, unfold in a complex web of relations in which the post-colonial power relations, the current urban redevelopment efforts, the neoliberal housing policies and the financialisation of housing play important roles. In what follows, I will provide a brief contextualisation of these dynamics.

2   Hands Off Our Homes!

On 22 September 2018, hundreds of people marched through the streets in Lisbon, shouting *Habitação, sim! Despejos, não!* (Yes to Housing! No to Evictions!), and *Sai, sai, sai, sai da minha rua; vai, vai, vai, e leva a tua grua!* (Go,

FIGURE 1.2   Demonstration for the Right to Housing, 22 September 2018

go, go, go away from my street; go, go, go, and take your crane with you)! The protest called for dignified housing solutions for all. It marked a collective effort by nearly 30 associations and collectives, which, many other differences notwithstanding, shared an impression of the increasing difficulties people were facing in accessing housing in Lisbon, Oporto and their Metropolitan Areas. In the last 40 years, the housing sector in Portugal has witnessed an extraordinary transformation from the context of a severe housing shortage to the current situation whereby there is a surplus in terms of existing buildings, although they are not accessible to the population in need (A. C. Santos et al., 2014). Some essential dynamics are highlighted here to contextualise this research.

2.1   Long-Standing Housing Crises: Migration and Postcolonial Housing Exclusions

After the economic and financial crisis of 2008, housing deprivations and exclusions began to spread to new groups of the population in Portugal, increasingly becoming a problem also for the middle classes. This is not to say that housing crises were a new phenomenon in Portugal. The large-scale urbanisation in the country began after WWII, being closely related to the process of industrialisation (Costa, 1993). However, the most significant mobility period was between 1960 and 1981. The rural-to-urban migration increased from the 1960s onwards, and after the independence of former colonies in 1974/1975, large numbers of *retornados* (Portuguese settlers in the former colonies who came back to Portugal) and nationals of the ex-colonies moved to Portuguese urban centres, mainly to Lisbon, Porto and their environs (Beja Horta, 2006; Costa, 1993; Guerra, 2010).

The fact that a part of this immigrant population could not find affordable housing provoked a noteworthy phenomenon of clandestine home construction, especially in the Lisbon region. This had two main dimensions: the zoning of agricultural land for housing without permission, which is referred to today as *AUGIs* (*Áreas Urbanas de Génese Ilegal*, Urban Areas of Illegal Genesis), and the use of private or public land without permission for the same purposes, a process that gave rise to what are commonly referred to as *bairros de barracas* ('shack neighbourhoods').[3] It is estimated that in the 1970s, around 40% of housing construction in Portugal was not licensed, and that at the end of the 1980s, around 150,000 people lived in *bairros de barracas* in the Lisbon and Porto areas (Guerra, 2011). In addition, approximately 300,000 people, around 12.5% of the population, lived in unlicensed housing (Guerra, 2010).[4]

When it came to these processes, immigrants from former colonies in Africa – with the exception of the *retornados* – were often in a disadvantageous position: they had difficulties in accessing rental accommodation due to discrimination by white landlords, and they often had less knowledge about what was possible to build where (Ascensão, 2011). Social class was also a key factor in the future development of neighbourhoods: the less educated people were and the lower their class, the less capable they were of negotiating with political parties and the administration for improvements in the neighbourhoods, and the more unaware they were about the legal implications of the land occupation, which often got them into trouble later on. The convergence of all of these particularities contributed to the fact that although white people of Portuguese origin also lived in *bairros de barracas*, the migrant population from former colonies were disproportionately represented (Ascensão, 2011).

In the second half of the 20th century, these neighbourhoods started to be addressed through various rehousing and demolition initiatives, both by the central government and the Lisbon municipality (Antunes, 2018). These culminated in the PIMP (*Programa de Intervenção a Médio Prazo*) and PER (*Programa Especial de Realojamento*) programmes, which focussed on the resettlement of residents in social housing estates. The first programme targeted only the

---

3 For more on the typologies of clandestine home construction, see Ascensão, 2011; Beja Horta, 2006; R. d'Ávila Cachado, 2011; I. Raposo & Valente, 2010.

4 It is important to note that despite the derogatory name, *bairros de barracas*, most of the homes in these neighbourhood have evolved over time and are built in brick.

FIGURE 1.3   Half-demolished neighbourhood of 6 de Maio, Amadora, October 2018. The majority of the residents are of Cape Verdean origin

municipality of Lisbon and was implemented from 1987 to the end of the 1990s, while the second targeted Lisbon and the Porto Metropolitan Areas from 1993 onwards (Antunes, 2018; R. Á. Cachado, 2012). Slum upgrading initiatives were given much less emphasis despite the landmark SAAL (*Serviço de Apoio Ambulatório Local*) programme that was implemented in 1974–1976 (coinciding with the Portuguese revolutionary period PREC, *Processo Revolucionário em Curso*) and received considerable international attention (Ascensão, 2013, 2016; Bandeirinha, 2011; Nunes & Serra, 2003).

The PER programme resettled tens of thousands of families but was never concluded in some municipalities, allegedly due to a lack of funding (Agência Lusa, 2017), with some 3,000 families left out (R. Á. Cachado, 2013; Morais et al., 2018) in municipalities such as Amadora. Tragically, the rehousing programme has since become an instrument of forced eviction because it has continued to rely on surveys on resettlement needs that were undertaken from 1993 to 1995 (Alves, 2016; R. Á. Cachado, 2013; Farha, 2017; Morais et al., 2018). For instance, in its report on the PER implementation, the Amadora municipality classifies the families it has evicted without an alternative housing solution simply as 'exclusions', amounting to 2,425 cases out of 6,046 'solved' cases of slum eradication (Câmara Municipal de Amadora, 2017).

Due to the resettlement background of many social housing estates, their population composition reflects that in the previous 'informal' neighbourhoods, with a clear over-representation of PALP (*Países Africanos de Língua Portuguesa*, Portuguese-speaking African Countries) residents (J. M. Malheiros

& Vala, 2004). These neighbourhoods face various forms of territorial stigma (Wacquant, 2008; Wacquant et al., 2014). For example, the suburban parishes that mainly include social housing estates have more young people than other parishes; there are serious problems of a lack of success at school, higher indices of unemployment, and the public spaces and buildings are of inferior quality (J. Malheiros et al., 2007). There are significant constraints on the integration of the social housing estates, such as their location far away from the urban centres and their disconnectedness from the rest of the urban fabric (Carreiras, 2018), as well as their reduced number, which means that social housing is offered only to the practically 'insolvent' households (Carreiras, 2018). The projects and programmes that have sought to promote integration have had limited success (Carreiras, 2018). These social housing estates are often perceived as 'no-go areas': chaotic, dangerous and degraded, and frequently framed in the media as 'racialised and illegal spaces at the margins of society' (Alves, 2016). Their residents are also recurrently depicted as criminals (O. Raposo et al., 2019).

Racism and the colonial past have been heatedly debated in Portugal in recent years. Lusotropicalism – the myth that Portuguese colonialism would have been better and more benign than other colonialisms – was first invented by Brazilian sociologist Gilberto Freyre (1933) and adopted by Portuguese dictator António Salazar from the 1950s onwards (Castelo, 2011). To the present day, the idea enjoys strong adherence in Portugal (Ba, 2017; Vale de Almeida, 2000), with a related belief that Portugal is a country of *brandos costumes* ('mild manners') where no racism exists (Abrantes & Roldão, 2019; Gorjão Henriques, 2018). Signs of adherence to these ideas are visible, for example, in the celebration of the 'discoveries' in museums and theme parks, sometimes played out in ways that completely ignore the violence of colonialism and conquest (Pöysä, 2018), and in schoolbooks that naturalise colonialism, slavery and racism (Araújo & Maeso, 2012).

Racism and violence by the police against Afro-descendants and the Roma have been one of the most extreme manifestations of this heritage, denounced by numerous activists and organisations, including the European Committee for the Prevention of Torture, which expressed serious concerns about the failure of the Inspectorate General of Home Affairs to investigate and prosecute cases of alleged ill-treatment (Council of Europe, 2018); and the UN Committee on the Elimination of Racial Discrimination (CERD), which highlighted reports of 'abusive acts against ethnic minorities, notably Roma and Africans/people of African descent, by the police, and the insufficient measures to redress them' (CERD, 2017). In this light, the decision by the Court of Sintra in 2019 to convict eight police officers for assaulting and kidnapping six black youngsters of Cova

FIGURE 1.4   Bairro da Jamaika, Seixal, March 2018

da Moura, Amadora, was considered ground-breaking (Gorjão Henriques, 2019a), even though nine other police officers who had been involved were acquitted and that *Ministério Público*, the Public Prosecution Service in the Country, had already dropped the accusations of torture and racism earlier (O. Raposo et al., 2019). It has been argued that neighbourhoods inhabited predominantly by Afro-descendants face multiple discriminations due to their ethnicity but also the segregation and bad public image of their neighbourhoods (Almada, 2020; O. Raposo et al., 2019).

The institutional, structural and daily violence is being contested by various associations and collectives of activists such as Plataforma Gueto, Afrolis, Djass, and Nu Sta Djunto (Gorjão Henriques, 2018; Rodrigues, Anabela Fernandes et al., 2017). Up to today, it has been difficult to grasp the scale of the racism in Portugal, as the censuses do not collect racial or ethnic information, despite the recommendation by CERD (2017). There was a long process to change this for the national Census of 2021, but eventually, Statistics Portugal decided to veto the issue despite the recommendations of the advisory group, because of the 'complexity of the question' (Gorjão Henriques, 2019b).

Despite the lack of statistical data, there is evidence that discrimination in terms of access to housing is also widespread in Portugal. It has been documented by CERD (2017) and by the UN Special Rapporteur to Housing, who notes that 'some communities in Portugal live in particularly inadequate housing conditions, such as the Roma and people of African descent' (Farha, 2017). In a Eurostat survey, 21% of respondents of African descent in Portugal stated that they suffered from one or more of four housing deprivations: the lack of a bath and toilet, a dwelling that is too dark, rot in the walls or windows, or a leaking roof, compared to 5% of the rest of the population (FRA, 2018). Similarly, 48% of Afro-descendants stated that they lived in overcrowded conditions, compared with 10% of the general population (FRA, 2018: 61), and only 23% lived in accommodation they owned, compared with 75% of the general population (FRA, 2018: 58). Furthermore, Afro-descendants have presented evidence on discrimination towards them in the private rental market (Gorjão Henriques, 2017).

2.2   *Residual Social Housing*

The municipality of Lisbon is the largest social housing owner in Portugal, with 26,592 council homes, while the municipality of Loures has only 2,503 council apartments (INE, 2015c). A comparison with the population size in 2015 (Lisbon 504,471 inhabitants, Loures 205,807 inhabitants (INE, 2015d)) and total residential housing stock (323,477 dwellings in Lisbon, and 100,021 dwellings in Loures (INE, 2015a)) shows that the proportion of social housing is more significant in Lisbon (representing 8% of the housing stock) than in Loures, where it represents only 2.5% of the total housing stock, making it thus more in line with the average situation in Portugal: around 2% of social housing of the total housing stock.

The social housing estates present their particular dynamics of eviction, which are also the focus of this investigation. Due to the low percentage of social housing available, only 2% of the residential housing stock nationwide (INE, 2015b; T. C. Pinto & Guerra, 2013), it is very difficult to access social housing. The queues are enormous: in the Lisbon Metropolitan Area, the municipalities report having 22,812 families on the waiting list, while having only 152 vacant apartments (Moleiro, 2019). The city of Lisbon tops the list for accessing council apartments, with 3,484 families on the waiting list (Moleiro, 2019). This contradicts to the latest statistical data, according to which there are 3,000 empty social housing dwellings, representing 5.6% of the total social housing stock, while illegally occupied dwellings represent 0.6% of the total (INE, 2015b). In the Lisbon Metropolitan Area, there are 52,141 dwellings for social housing altogether, out of which 48,070 are rented out, 3,471 stand vacant, and 600 are illegally occupied (INE, 2015b). On the level of the municipalities, according to INE (2015c), there would be 2,637 vacant and 305 illegally occupied council homes in Lisbon, and 12 vacant and 49 illegally occupied in Loures.

When questioned about this, the Lisbon City Council states that the vacant apartments need major refurbishment before they can be handed over to the residents (author's fieldnotes 2018, public meeting of the Lisbon City Council, 26/4/2018). However, this does not explain the significant difference between the number of vacant apartments reported by the municipalities, on the one hand, and by Statistics Portugal, on the other. Residents and associations allege that this difference is due to problems in social housing management in that many apartments stand vacant without the municipalities knowing. Sometimes these empty apartments are then occupied without authorisation, for accommodation, and sometimes for other activities, such as drug trafficking (Cristino, 2018). Periodically, the city councils evict the occupiers, while some residents manage to stay for years and even legalise their occupation.

The law that governs social housing in Portugal is *Lei do Arrendamento Apoiado* (LAA, the Law for Subsidized Renting no. 32/2016, 24 August 2016), with the last changes in 2016. It also regulates the rents for social housing. In 2014, the law was changed in relation to the calculation of the rents, which in some cases resulted in extreme changes. Some families had been paying the same amount of rent since the 1970s, for example, 5 euros monthly, so the proposed updated rents in 2015 amounted, in some cases, to 60 times more (Lusa, 2017). In 2015, the average monthly rent was 56 euros, whereas for the new contracts established in 2015, the average rent was 113 euros (INE, 2016).

Many families have not been able to pay these updated rents, resulting in rent arrears and, in some cases, eviction letters due to unpaid rents. The law was updated in August 2016, stipulating that the rent cannot be over 23% of the net income of the family; that is, it must be proportionate to the family in terms of size and possible disabilities, and families cannot be evicted without the identification of alternative housing for them (Lusa, 2016). The LAA is combined with a regulation on access to social housing,[5] the conditions of access of which stipulate that anyone can apply as long as they have a residence permit in Portugal, do not have the 'economic-financial conditions' to access housing, do not have a house of their own, and are not receiving housing subsidies (Articles 5 and 6).

In addition, the municipality of Lisbon uses the regulation on access to the municipal housing regime, RRAHM. Article 5 of the regulation determines the conditions for access to social housing:

a)   The household members do not own a dwelling in the LMA nor receive public financial support for housing purposes.

b)   They are residents of the Municipality of Lisbon.

---

5   Regulamento de Acesso e Atribuição de Habitações do IHRU, I. P., em Regime de Arrendamento Apoiado, n.º 84/2018.

c)   They or their spouse or partner are not a holder of a municipal dwelling in Lisbon.

d)   None of the household members has, by choice, received an indemnity instead of a municipal dwelling in case of resettlement.

e)   The household has an income (RMC, *rendimento mensal corrigido*) of less than three IAS (indexante dos apoios sociais[6]), or less than five RMC in the case that the applicant is 65 or older.

f)   If the household has more than three members (or five in the case that the applicant is 65 or older), and they have an RMC per capita equal or inferior to one IAS (Câmara Municipal de Lisboa, 2009).

2.3   *New Housing Crises: Financialisation of Housing and Real-Estate Speculation*

In addition to the challenges highlighted earlier, there is a widely held perception that much has changed in the past ten years. According to Ana Cordeiro Santos, the 'housing question' – referring to Friedrich Engels' classic (Engels, 1873) – in Portugal today fundamentally differs from that in the 1990s, or before that (A. C. Santos, 2019b). Many recent publications in Portugal have focussed on the new dynamics related to housing, such as the financialisation of housing, such as the book *A nova questão de habitação*, coordinated by Ana Cordeiro Santos (2019b), which argues that housing provision in Portugal cannot be understood without considering its increasing articulation with the financial sector (A. C. Santos, 2019c).

Some studies contend that the neoliberal turn in housing policies in Portugal is a relatively recent phenomenon (Mendes, 2018). However, other authors highlight a more extended continuum of neoliberal urban policy-making in the country (Barata Salgueiro, 1994; Tulumello, 2016). According to Serra (2019), housing has always been *a parente pobre*, the poor relative in the family of social policies. The newly democratised Portugal in 1974 was an impoverished country. In the process of developing its social sector, priority was given to the establishment of public education and public health systems. In the housing sector, the chosen approach was a continuation of the housing policies that had been practised under the authoritarian regime until 1974, meaning an approach that attended to the most severe situations of housing deprivation, including ambiguous, indirect housing provision mechanisms that were based on incentives for private promotion (Serra, 2019). Still, between the end of the

---

6   428.90 euros in 2018. More information can be found at: https://www.economias.pt/valor-indexante-dos-apoios-sociais/. Last accessed 06/06/2018.

military dictatorship in 1974 and 1985, Portugal witnessed a period of significant state investment in public housing development, with a maximum of 17% of public housing promotion reached in 1984 (Paulo, 2017).

These developments were compromised in an agreement negotiated between the government of Mário Soares and the International Monetary Fund in 1984, after which the Portuguese government decided to cut public and cooperative housing provision (A. F. Ferreira, 1988). From 1985 onwards, more robust and effective housing credit regimes were established, including home loan interest-rate subsidies, the subsidised home loan regime for young people, and other special credit and saving regimes (Serra, 2019). From 1985 to 1995, the governments of Prime Minister Cavaco Silva opened the real-estate sector to financial groups (Paulo, 2017). Public housing promotion consequently decreased to around 4% of total construction in the 1990s (Serra, 2019). In Portugal, public financing for housing peaked in 2002 and 2003, with around 650 million euros spent on housing in both years. After those years, financing for housing started steadily declining, reaching a low of 173 million euros in 2011 (IHRU, 2015a). Since then, the figures have not increased significantly: Portuguese expenditure on 'housing and community amenities' represented 0.4% to 0.5% of PIB from 2011 to 2018 (Eurostat, 2020a). In 2019, the total budget for housing was 156 million euros (L. Pinto, 2018).

In 2004, many laws favouring private endeavour over public one, public-private partnerships and competitivity in the housing sector were approved, and societies for urban rehabilitation were created (Mendes, 2017). Significantly, from 1987 to 2011, despite the PER programme, Portugal's central housing policy comprised home loan interest-rate subsidies, which received 74% of the housing budget (IHRU, 2015a). The total implemented housing budget grew from 184 million euros in 1991 to 631 million euros in 2000, after which it decreased dipping to a low of 174 million euros in 2011 (IHRU, 2015a). In all these years, the interest-rate subsidies received more than half of the budget, representing between 63% and 95% of the total budget (IHRU, 2015a).

These subsidies favoured the banking sector providing loans for home acquisition (Paulo, 2017) and contributed to the increased indebtedness of Portuguese families (A. C. Santos, 2019c). These policies are reflected in the statistics on the type of family dwelling occupancy: renting, which in the 1970 census represented almost 46% of the forms of dwelling occupancy, fell to around 21% in 2011 (INE, 2011). On the other hand, there was an increase in privately owned permanent dwellings, rising from 55% in 1970 to almost 79% in 2011 (INE 2011; see also (Guerra, 2011; IHRU, 2015b). The policies are also reflected in the construction boom: from an average of 39,000 dwellings per year between 1981 and 1985, via an average of 63,000 dwellings per year in 1991–1995, to an extreme 97,000 dwellings per year in 2001–2005 (Serra, 2019).

In 2011, after the worldwide economic crisis, the European Central Bank, the European Commission, and the International Monetary Fund made the granting of loans to Portugal subject to certain conditions. Among these conditions was an amendment to the rental law that gave rise to the New Urban Rental Regime (NRAU, *Novo Regime do Arrendamento Urbano*, Law no. 31/2012) of 2012, which, through its actualisation of rents, permitted their increase to levels that a good part of the population could not afford. In addition, it facilitated evictions through the creation of an extrajudicial agency, the National Rental Desk (BNA, *Balcão Nacional de Arrendamento*) (A. C. Santos, 2019c).

According to various authors, NRAU was just another part of Portugal's more general neoliberal turn in urban politics (Mendes, 2017; Morais et al., 2018). NRAU coincided with the promotion of investment initiatives that stimulated the real-estate sector in Portugal and contributed significantly to real-estate speculation and the financialisation and commodification of housing. These initiatives include Golden Residence Permits[7] for those investing in, for example, real estate in Portugal (approved in 2009) and tax exemptions or benefits for wealthy foreigners who wish to buy property in the country (Decree-Law no. 249/2009); as well as tax exemptions for international investment funds[8] (approved in 2015) and corporations that operate in the real-estate market (Decree-Law no. 7/2015). Moreover, recent legislation has created even more favourable conditions for investors, such as a decree-law on urban rehabilitation that simplified the procedure for creating urban rehabilitation zones (Decree-Law no. 53/2014), and on tourist accommodation in private homes (Decree-Law no. 128/2014). Due to the current legal framework and policies, it has been argued that housing has lost its status as a right, and has gained the statute of a commodity in the context of the financialisation of real estate (Mendes, 2017).

In parallel, or as a consequence of these policies, Lisbon became a very popular tourist destination with short-term rentals popping up, pushing residents out of their neighbourhoods and further out of the city. Evictions due to 'Airbnbisation' have become an increasingly common phenomenon. A groundbreaking study by Ana Gago (2018) demonstrates how this process has

---

7   See http://portugalglobal.pt/EN/General/Pages/GoldenResidencePermitProgramme.aspx. Last accessed 30/11/2019.

8   See https://www.pwc.pt/en/pwcinforfisco/tax-guide/2016/cit/investment-funds.html. Last accessed 30/11/2019.

unfolded in one of the most affected neighbourhoods in Lisbon, Alfama. The study focussed on an area around Rua dos Remédios, where, according to the residents, the first apartment for tourist accommodation appeared in 2011. By 2015, 16 apartments were available for tourist accommodation, and in 2016, 235 of the existing apartments, representing 25% of the total number, were used for this purpose (A. Gago, 2018; A. Gago & Cocola-Gant, 2019). During my fieldwork in 2018 and 2019, Lisbon became known as the European city with the most Airbnb apartments compared to the population size (Sapo, 2019).

As a result, rental and real-estate prices have skyrocketed in the Lisbon Metropolitan Area. In the municipalities of Loures and Lisbon, the two areas this study focuses on, real-estate prices per m^2 went up by 21% in Loures and 49% in Lisbon from 2011 to 2018 (J. P. Ferreira et al., 2019). Within some parishes of Lisbon, especially the historical neighbourhoods of the city centre, the rise has been even more drastic, with the parish of Santo Antonio leading with a rise of 92% between 2011 and 2018 (Ferreira, Silva, & Costa, 2019: 182–183). Rental prices have gone up along the same lines, increasing by 71% from 2013 to 2018 in Lisbon(Idealista, 2018b), averaging 8.1 euros/m^2 in the Lisbon Metropolitan Area, but exceeding 13.5 €/m^2 in some parishes in the city for new rental contracts (INE, 2019).

Salaries in Portugal have not kept pace with this rise, creating a considerable gap and leading to the impoverishment of many. One only has to compare the Portuguese minimum salary (600 euros per month in 2019 (PORDATA, 2021a)) and average salary (922.60 for women and 1,073.80 for men in 2019 (PORDATA, 2021b)) with rental market prices. A large part of the population, 22%, earns the minimum salary in Portugal (PORDATA, 2018), meaning significant parts of the population struggle with gaining access to housing. Single-parent households seem to be under particular strain. In 2019 (PORDATA, 2019b), 25.5% of single-parent families were considered to be at risk of poverty after social transfers. In comparison, the at-risk-of-poverty rate after social transfers for all households with dependent children was 17%, while for the general population, it was 16.2% (PORDATA, 2019b).

The expenditure of Portuguese families on housing has consequently increased significantly since the 1980s, when it represented 12% of the family budget, to 32% of the budget in 2015–2016 (FEANTSA & Foundation Abbé Pierre, 2018). The number of families overburdened[9] by housing costs in

---

9   Eurostat defines the housing overburden rate as the 'percentage of the population living in a
    household where total housing costs (net of housing allowances) represent more than 40%
    of the total disposable household income (net of housing allowances)' (Eurostat 2020).

Portugal has increased by 80% (FEANTSA & Foundation Abbé Pierre, 2018). The situation is worse for poor households: in 2016, about 7.5% of the general population and 29.1% of poor households were overburdened by housing costs (FEANTSA & Foundation Abbé Pierre, 2018). In 2018, the IHRU (*Instituto da Habitação e da Reabilitação Urbana*, the National Institute for Housing and Urban Renewal) conducted a survey on housing needs across the country and identified over 25,000 families in 'clearly unsatisfactory housing conditions' and in need of resettlement, out of which 50% were living in the Lisbon Metropolitan Area (IHRU, 2018). However, many claim that these official figures are vastly underestimated.

These dynamics provoke both direct displacement (Marcuse, 1985) and indirect displacement, when the residents leave 'voluntarily', selling their apartments or renting them out to tourists. These displacements can be conceptualised as processes of transnational tourism gentrification, in which the tourism-related mobility of the middle classes drives out the residents of peripheral economies, which tends to happen in cities where tourism represents a central factor for development and growth (Cocola-Gant, 2018). Here, the lack of official data presents a significant challenge to attempts to understand the scale of the problem. The *Balcão Nacional de Arrendamento* (BNA), which was created with the NRAU to facilitate evictions, publishes data on the eviction cases it handles. These cases doubled from 2013 to 2016, with 5.5 cases being processed per day in the country (Mendes et al., 2019). In 2017, around 1,000 evictions went through the BNA up to September (DN/Lusa, 2017).

However, the BNA only registers the processes it undertakes, related to private rental accommodation, and not the cases that go to court or that are resolved through agreements of some sort, or those cases where residents are evicted simply for not renewing their rental contracts, which seems to be the most common form of displacement. Some additional data exist through the parishes. For example, according to the data of the parish of Santa Maria Maior in the historical centre, 2,000 families were evicted in four years, so that the number of families in the parish decreased from 12,000 to 10,000 between 2013 and 2017 (Fernandes & Pinto, 2018).

2.4   *The New Urban Housing Policies*

The difficulty in accessing housing in Portugal might not be a new phenomenon, but it undoubtedly gained more visibility when it started to affect new population groups, especially the Portuguese white middle classes. The increasing cost of housing started to attract more criticism, and housing became an important theme in the municipal elections of 2017, gaining in emphasis as

FIGURE 1.5   Campaign by the Portuguese Communist Party for the right to
housing and against real-estate speculation, June 2018

the legislative elections of 2019 approached. There are many new social movements that defend housing rights, notably Movimento Morar em Lisboa and Stop Despejos, along with the Habita Association, which has formally existed since 2012, although it started its work back in 2005 as a working group of the *Solidariedade Imigrante* Association. As this study will show, these movements have played a fundamental role in putting housing on the political agenda.

Prime Minister Antonio Costa's surprise government after the 2015 elections created a new state department for housing, under the Ministry of Environment in July 2017. The architect Ana Pinho was chosen as the Secretary of State for Housing and tasked with the challenging job of coming up with the 'New Generation of Housing Policies' (NGPH, *Nova Geração de Políticas da Habitação*). A primary objective of the NGPH came to be 'guaranteeing the access of all to adequate housing, understood in the wide sense of dwelling and oriented towards the people' (Secretaria de Estado da Habitação, 2017). Related legislation has been approved since then, such as the new social housing and resettlement programme *1 ° Direito* (First Right, Decree-Law no. 37/2018) that is 'intended to create conditions for adequate housing for people who live in degrading housing situations and who do not have the financial capacity to find a housing solution through the market', and *Programa de Arrendamento Acessível* (Programme for Affordable Renting, Decree-Law no. 68/2019), 'to promote a wider selection of housing for rental at lower prices' (Government of Portugal, 2018).

However, the NGHP has been criticised for simply being one more instrument in the commodification and financialisation of housing. Its main logic is based on fiscal stimulation and financial solutions to stimulate private and public entities, favouring the real-estate sector, and it is considered unlikely that it will achieve its objectives in the promotion of housing for people on a low or middle-income (A. C. Santos, 2019a). It will not address the core causes of the housing crisis, and most importantly, it will not try to regulate the housing and real estate market. Being dependent on attracting foreign investment, these new policies will not touch the measures that promote it, such as Golden visas or the fiscal benefits for non-residents (Santos 2019: 314). Rather than offering new solutions, the NGPH might deepen the perception of housing as a commodity and financial product rather than as something that should have a social function (Mendes, 2019). In the words of Rita Silva, 'the New Generation of Housing Politics is not new, and does not defend housing' (R. Silva, 2019b).

Ahead of the legislative elections of 2019, the new policies and legislation addressing housing, including the design of the national housing framework law, were constantly in the news. In 2019, the Ministry of Infrastructure and Housing was created, with the new Minister, Pedro Nuno Santos, sworn in in

February. It can thus be asked whether housing became a political concern only when the housing crisis started reaching the middle classes. Still, the most socioeconomically marginalised populations continue to be the most affected. These include low-income families (those who receive the minimum wage), women, single-parent households, immigrants and ethnic minorities, especially the Roma and the Black population, the elderly on low pensions, and persons with disabilities (R. Silva, 2019a). Funding for the new programmes has also been scarce: for instance, the budget for the 1 ° Direito programme in 2020 was 40 million euros, while a survey estimated that at least 1,700 million euros would be needed to resettle the 25,762 families it had identified as being in a unsatisfactory housing situation (IHRU, 2018).

2.5   *The Global Context: Forced Evictions and Rising Housing Costs*

These dynamics are not at play only in the Lisbon Metropolitan Area and in Portugal. However, the effects can be more substantial in a country like Portugal, where access to housing depends heavily on the private sector. Globally, there has been a U-turn in the main housing and urban policy agendas in recent decades, with policies based on the withdrawal of states from direct housing production, the creation of stronger and larger market-based housing finance models, and the commodification of housing, including the use of housing as an investment asset within a globalised financial market (Rolnik, 2013a).

The results have been visible, with a profound impact on the right to housing (Rolnik, 2013a). Forced evictions have increased dramatically in frequency, number and level of violence, affecting low-income workers across both public and private rental housing throughout the world (AGFE & UN-HABITAT, 2007, 2011; Soederberg, 2018; UN-HABITAT & OHCHR, 2014b). The right to housing is inscribed in Article 11.1 of the International Covenant on Economic, Social and Cultural Rights (ICESCR, 1967), in which the state parties to the covenant recognise the right to adequate housing and agree to take 'appropriate steps to ensure the realisation of this right'. In a general comment to the ICESCR, the UN Office of the High Commissioner for Human Rights (OHCHR) defines forced evictions as the 'permanent or temporary removal against their will of individuals, families and/or communities from the homes and/or land which they occupy, without the provision of, and access to, appropriate forms of legal or other protection' (OHCHR, 1997). The OHCHR also emphasises that 'evictions should not result in individuals being rendered homeless or vulnerable to the violation of other human rights' (OHCHR, 1997, Art. 16).

This means that while not all forced evictions are prohibited, they should be carried out in accordance with the law and in conformity with the provisions of the International Covenants on Human Rights (OHCHR, 1997, Art. 3). Therefore, the eviction process should include the genuine participation of the affected communities and never result in homelessness or deterioration of housing and living conditions. This is a far cry from actual practice around the world. Today, forced evictions are a lived and embodied matter defining the experience of home for millions of urbanites worldwide (Brickell, 2014; Brickell et al., 2017).

The OHCHR identifies two principal kinds of evictions: those 'associated with violence', such as international armed conflicts, and those that 'occur in the name of development' (OHCHR, 1997). This aptly illustrates how many of the evictions are related to the idea of progress and capitalist development in multiple ways, directly and indirectly. These ideals of 'development' are often used to justify evictions and demolitions in 'informal' neighbourhoods in order to make way for large-scale urban or rural development projects or mega-events (Auyero & Swistun, 2009; Bogado, 2017; Doshi, 2013; Lamb et al., 2017; Lund, 2018; Sassen, 2018; Sennett et al., 2018; Seppälä, 2016; Suzuki et al., 2018; Wayessa & Nygren, 2016; Zhang, 2017). The same trend applies to gentrification, which has sometimes been celebrated for supposedly balancing the demography of neighbourhoods and for bringing economic upgrading and political benefits (Slater, 2006). In this way, evictions are often seen as the 'price of becoming a global city' (Cabannes, 2010).

In the European Union, housing rights are also enshrined in the European Convention on Human Rights and Fundamental Freedoms (ECHR). The Article 8 states that '(1) Everyone has the right to respect for his private and family life, his home and his correspondence; (2) There shall be no interference by a public authority with the exercise of this right except such as is in accordance with the law and is necessary in a democratic society in the interests of national security, public safety or the economic well-being of the country, for the prevention of disorder or crime, for the protection of health or morals, or for the protection of the rights and freedoms of others.' Throughout Europe, a substantial and constant increase in housing costs can be observed (Eurostat, 2020b). At the same time, investments in social infrastructure have decreased by 20% since 2009 in countries belonging to the European Union; with an investment gap in affordable housing that amounts to around 57 billion euro per year (Fransen et al., 2018). In most of the EU member states, housing costs rise faster than incomes, and housing cost overburden has become a significant challenge, affecting 10.1% of Europeans in 2019 (Eurostat, 2020d) and 33.8% of Europeans in the first income quintile (Eurostat, 2020c). In general, social housing has had an important role in providing housing in Europe; however, since the 1980s, as public expenditure pressures have grown, liberalisation and privatisation have become the prevailing policies (Scanlon et al., 2015). Homelessness has increased steadily in almost all EU countries (FEANTSA & Foundation Abbé Pierre, 2018), apart from Finland, where it has been tackled through an integrated policy since 2008 (Pleace et al., 2015).

Globally, many social movements fighting for access to decent and affordable housing and against evictions (Cabannes et al., 2010). The actions of these movements have been well documented, for example in Brazil (Bogado, 2017; Caldeira, 2015; Earle, 2007, 2012; Holston, 2008), South Africa (Gibson, 2012; Miraftab, 2006; L. Podlashuc, 2011; Selmeczi, 2014), Ghana (Farouk & Owusu, 2012), India (Das, 2011; Doshi, 2013; Patel et al., 2016), and Argentina (Muñoz, 2017). Many EU countries also have strong movements demanding more affordable, public, and social housing. Some of them are networking Europewide, as in the case of the European Action Coalition for the Right to Housing and to the City,[10] also engaging in research (e.g. European Action Coalition for the Right to Housing and to the City, 2019) and launching Europewide petitions and campaigns, such as #HandsOffOurHomes[11] or the European Citizens' Initiative 'Housing for all'.[12]

3   A Researcher in Solidarity? Methodological Reflections

3.1   *Antecedents*

Epistemologically, the research presented in this book is rooted in a reflexive model of science: a model of science that focuses on engagement as a path to knowledge, starting from the dialogue between the researcher and the research participants (Burawoy, 1998) – or, as in the case of this study, between the researcher-participant, other researchers, and participants. In this study, the reflexive model is understood as a constant interplay between theory and the research findings, in which research design initially springs from theory. However, the theoretical assumptions are constantly being questioned and verified during the research process. In this process of engagement, theory informs the research findings, and the research findings the theory construction.

Before going into more detail on the methodology adopted for the study, it is necessary to consider the context that the research sprang from and the role of the researcher in the process. Following Haraway's conceptualisation of situated knowledge – in other words, recognising that all knowledge is produced from a limited location (Haraway, 1988) – it is fundamental to reflect on the limits of the research posed by the researcher. As a white woman born into a middle-class family with a rural background in Helsinki in the 1980s, I consider that, in addition to my parents' efforts, I owe much of my academic and personal development to the social policies of the Finnish state, given that free, high-quality basic, secondary and university education and other social policies, such as study and maternity allowances, have played fundamental roles in different phases of my life. For me, this background has given rise to a firm belief in the ideal of social justice, leading to an urge to fight against different inequalities.

Yet, after childhood and adolescence, I have lived abroad for most of my life in very different contexts, in Bolivia, Brazil, Mozambique, Tanzania, Portugal, Germany, Cape Verde, and currently Angola. In all of these countries, I have sought engagement with different kinds of groups, associations and collectives that seek to affirm social, political or civic rights for broader groups of the population: for the Indigenous, the rural population, women, minorities, and dwellers in housing that the state considers illegal. This engagement has marked my academic trajectory as well. I understand that my position, as a white, European-born feminist with access to some social, cultural and economic capital, engaging with different social movements, can be described as that of a 'researcher in solidarity' (S. C. Motta, 2011). This means solidarity and accountability to communities on the frontiers of housing precarity, aiming to design emancipatory research methodologies that foster housing justice (Roy & Rolnik, 2020).

This also involves acknowledging that knowledge is produced collectively and within the political action, the researcher being a 'node within a network of emancipatory praxis' (S. C. Motta, 2011). Throughout the study, this has been my aim, along with the objective of uncovering exclusions and discriminations.

Previously, from July 2007 to June 2008, I lived in the neighbourhood of Babilônia in Rio de Janeiro, participating in the activities of the AMABABI residents' association and of the neighbouring community's A.A.C.M association, carrying out a study on the dynamics and structures of the oppression and marginalisation of favela residents in Rio de Janeiro, Brazil, as well as on their modalities of agency. During those years, I learned a great deal about the stigmatisation of residents of low-income, informalised neighbourhoods.

I also realised how most of these residents had, through their everyday practices, contributed to the enhancement of the living conditions in these neighbourhoods, participating in construction, and setting up nurseries, schools and health centres; how some of the residents had, through their insurgence, questioned and contested those marginalisations; and also how some of them had, through their more conformist practices, contributed to the maintenance of the status quo in a hierarchical, segregated city and society (Saaristo, 2015, 2019).

In 2015, I moved to Lisbon with my Portuguese partner and my son and started my doctoral studies in 2016. The aim was to return to Brazil and to continue the research on the struggle for housing in Rio de Janeiro. Yet life often surprises us: I became pregnant and moving to Brazil started to seem economically unviable. At the same time, while getting to know Lisbon better, I began to liaise with a group of activists who combat housing exclusion in Portugal and came to recognise dynamics of marginalisation and stigmatisation similar to those I had known in Rio de Janeiro. In the case of the Lisbon Metropolitan Area, stigmatisation was present in relation to both the residents of self-built neighbourhoods and the residents of social housing estates. I started to engage with collectives that fight for the right to housing, notably with the Habita association and the Stop Despejos collective and became a member of Habita. In many meetings and discussions with other members, I decided that aligning the research with Habita's struggle made sense, including reflection upon the association's practices.

In addition, a researcher's characteristics and life experiences have different repercussions when encountering research participants. Within the social movements and the public institutions working with housing issues, most actors were women, both younger, the same age, and older than myself. Within the collectives, there were many other researchers too, some focusing on urban issues and housing, some on other fields. The people at risk of eviction, although representing all genders and age groups, were mostly low-wage earners; the majority were women, and quite a few of them were immigrants or Portuguese whose parents had been born abroad.

3.2   *Research 'Sites'*

In the first stage of the fieldwork, I mapped key people, activities, events and neighbourhoods about evictions within the Lisbon Metropolitan Area (LMA) and compiled the results of the mapping in a field report. The mapping also included the social movements that work for the right to housing in the LMA.

I interviewed members and participated in the meetings of the following associations and collectives: Habita, Associação dos Inquilinos Lisbonenses (AIL), Associação do Património e População de Alfama (APPA), Associação Renovar a Mouraria, Vizinhos de Areeiro, SOS Racismo, Rede de Solidariedade, Stop Despejos, Morar em Lisboa, and Assembleia de Moradores dos Bairros. In the process, I realised that many of the collectives focus primarily on the city's central areas and on the housing problems faced by white Portuguese, often middle-class families. I noticed that housing challenges faced by the Roma and Afro-descendent populations are much less visible in the media and they do not get to dominate the public discourse. These population groups tend to have strong representation in the social housing neighbourhoods and neighbourhoods of informal origin.

Considering the objectives of this research, I found it most relevant to focus on associations and collectives that work with the most socially marginalised residents and their struggle for the right to housing. Habita is the most active collective working in both 'informal', self-built neighbourhoods andas well as social housing estates, and thus, I became drawn to their work. The Habita Association is a collective that fights for the Right to Housing and to the City. It emerged in 2005 when a group advocating the right to housing was founded within the *Solidariedade Imigrante* association, focussing on the housing rights of the immigrant population. In 2012, the Habita collective was founded and formally constituted as an association two years later. Initially Habita focused, above all, on fighting against the demolitions of self-built neighbourhoods in the Lisbon Metropolitan Area.

Another collective I was involved with was *Stop Despejos* (Stop Evictions), which had its first meeting in December 2017. It emerged as an effort by different collectives to fight against evictions and to build up a platform to mobilise people to stop evictions. It has focused more on direct public protests through street demonstrations and performances, as well as working through social media and mobilising the more traditional media (Bogado & Saaristo, 2021).

Habita and Stop Despejos thus became – in a sense – the 'research sites' of this research project. Despite having a significant focus on ethnographic methods, my research is not a traditional ethnographic case study that focuses on one selected geographical area. Instead, it concerns some specific neighbourhoods but also draws inspiration from the idea of multi-sited research (Marcus, 1995), based on the notion that the social phenomenon under study is not confined to a single place, recognising that space is socially constructed, and that 'contemporary societies are invariable, inevitable, and self-evidently located

FIGURE 1.6   View of Condado, April 2018

within larger wholes' (Falzon, 2009). This study does not go so far as to trace a 'cultural formation across and within multiple sites of activity' (Marcus, 1995) but aligns with the core idea of multi-sited research, which is to follow people, connections, associations, and relationships across space (Falzon, 2009). The study thus adopts a notably different conceptualisation of what constitutes a case compared to the notion of a case as a bounded system (Harrison et al., 2017). The multi-sited research process led me to many different social housing estates where occupations took place. Of these, I ended up spending the most time in Condado, Lisbon, and in Quinta de Fonte, Loures.

In Lisbon, applications to access council homes are made via Lisbon City Council, but a specific municipal company, Gebalis, is in charge of the management of council estates. In Loures, the applications for council housing as well as the management of council estates are the responsibility of the City Council.

The neighbourhood of Condado, better known by its previous name – Zona J – in the parish of Marvila, council of Lisbon, was built with funding from a Council programme from 1965 to 1985. It includes 1,440 council house dwellings and 316 previous council dwellings that have since been sold to tenants. Its total population is approximately 5,000. Quinta da Fonte in Loures was built from 1995 to 2000 through the PER programme. It consists of 54 council housing buildings with around 2,700 residents.

FIGURE 1.7   View inside Condado, showing some of its varied architecture: an apartment block, and smaller, two-storey houses, June 2018

Some of the interviewees in the study also lived in neighbourhoods surrounding Condado:

- Bairro das Flamengas, which was built from 1981 to 1996, firstly through a Council programme and then with financing from the PIMP programme, with 999 council housing apartments, 444 apartments that have been sold to tenants and a population of 4,000.
- Bairro do Armador, built in the 1990s through PIMP, with 1,044 council housing apartments, 292 apartments that have been sold to the lessees, and a population of 3,700.

My involvement with Quinta da Fonte was not as intense as in Condado, for two reasons. First, Quinta da Fonte was much further away from my home in Lisbon, making it more difficult to just 'pop by', resulting in fewer ad-hoc visits. Second, it took me significantly longer to gain access to the City Council of Loures than to the Lisbon City Council. This resulted in different kinds of research data. I, therefore, do not aim to draw strict comparisons between these two councils, but rather to illustrate differences and similarities.

3.3   *Critical Ethnography and Activist Research*

The research methods for this study can be defined as belonging to the field of critical ethnography and activist research, defined as a 'method through which we affirm a political alignment with an organized group of people in

FIGURE 1.8   View of Quinta da Fonte towards the surrounding hills, October 2018

struggle and allow dialogue with them to shape each phase of the process, from conception of the research topic to data collection to verification and dissemination of results' (Hale, 2006). In all phases of the research, I worked closely together with the Associação Habita, participating in the activities with the aim of engaging in 'movement relevant research' (S. C. Motta, 2011), and promoting learning (Lira & March, 2021) within the movements. Techniques including participant observation, interviews (informal and semi-structured), and policy analysis were used in the research, resulting in a total of 1.5 years of fieldwork. The study found inspiration in the extended case method, in which the research and theorising are situated 'historically, socio-politically and as experienced subjectively' (Burawoy, 1998). I thus considered it essential to combine participant observation with methods that respond to these needs. Policy and document analysis, as well as analysis of relevant literature, allowed for contextualising the research historically and socio-politically.

The research sought to understand and analyse the power relations involved in housing occupations and evictions, using an approach that reaches 'up, down and sideways' (Stryker & González, 2014) and aiming for a balanced group (from both 'up' and 'down', as defined by Nader (1972) of research participants that would allow for an insightful analysis in the context of such

FIGURE 1.9 View inside Quinta da Fonte. The murals, resulting from an art project promoted by the Loures City Council, were later removed due to renovation work on the buildings, October 2018

occupations and evictions. The research participants can be roughly divided into the following groups:

– Residents who were occupying council housing dwellings without authorisation and some residents who were living in neighbourhoods at risk of eviction. This group of research participants was considered the most knowledgeable in relation to the current practices in these neighbourhoods. In open-ended life-history interviews, they were posed questions about their background, aiming at a brief 'housing biography': How did they end up in their current situation? Where did they live before? What has their life trajectory been like in general? We also discussed their interaction with state and social movement agents.

– Local politicians and municipal employees responsible for social housing policies or for managing social housing. These research participants shed light on the dynamics of implementing social housing policies and managing social housing. We also discussed the formulation of social housing policies: Why certain approaches were adopted and what presumptions had led to these approaches.

– Social movement activists and staff from non-governmental organisations
  (NGOs) that work with questions related to housing and the right to the
  city. This group of research participants was helpful in better contextualising the research questions, considering the most recent developments in
  the city areas, and supporting the reflection on social mobilisation against
  evictions. The questions posed to them aimed to inquire about the most
  pressing issues from the point of view of these organisations, find out about
  their strategies, and potentially reveal some differences in their approaches.
All of the interviews were recorded and transcribed. After giving the matter
considerable thought, a decision was taken not to reveal any of the actual
names of the interviewees in this research. This is a decision that I considered problematic, especially as many of the interviewees (occupiers, activists,
and municipal employees alike) specifically stated that they would be happy
to forego anonymity. It also contributed to the long-standing practice in social
science of making research participants invisible, putting only the researcher
in the spotlight. Yet the EU General Data Protection Regulation 2016/679
(GDPR) does not recommend revealing the identities of research participants.
Therefore, pseudonyms were used for the residents of council housing neighbourhoods, while the interviews with activists and municipal employees were
numbered (see Appendix A).

Urban Governance and City-Making

1 Introduction

This research examines housing occupations and evictions, and the associated dynamics of social contestation and transformation. It explores the notion of occupations and evictions as practices of city-making, inquiring whether and how occupations could potentially (re)produce new forms of urban citizenship and give rise to new democratic practices that can challenge the dominant capitalist and neoliberal forms of production of urban space. To contextualise the research approach, it is important to consider contributions that explore the causes of globally increasing housing exclusion and growing numbers of evictions. The literature on the production of urban space, including the examination of urban (re)development processes, which analyses the production of space under neoliberalism, points towards the financialisation and commodification of housing and the change in the state's role in the housing sector as the main promotors of these housing exclusions, along with other practices associated with accumulation by dispossession and advanced capitalism (Harvey, 2003; Rolnik, 2013a; Sassen, 2014). In these processes, the state has often been a significant facilitator of the advancement of capital and expulsions of the poor, aligning with the logic of the maximisation of the value of urban space (Brenner et al., 2010a; Rolnik, 2013a; Soederberg, 2021).

Consequently, housing exclusion and homelessness are evidently phenomena that affect different population groups in dissimilar ways and, therefore, should be conceived of as a classed, racialised and gendered phenomenon. However, housing exclusions cannot be perceived simply as by-products of capitalism, racism, or patriarchy. Urban dwellers – and here I also include state actors – shape urban processes, transforming them into 'sites of intense struggles between disparate interests and multiple stakeholders, whose ideas, influences and actions together ultimately shape today's urban realities' (Bayat & Biekart, 2009). The state actors, as well as urban residents, extend and remake the boundaries of the state, seeking to secure survival or justice in the everyday (Das & Poole, 2004), or producing further injustices, marginalisations and vulnerabilities through differentiated forms of governance (Nygren & Wayessa, 2018). This study explores the subjectivities that are being formed and remade in these processes and analyses the diverse everyday practices of marginalised urban dwellers, together with the policies and everyday practices pursued by state actors that unfold both in the context of neoliberalism 'from above' as well as 'from below' (V. Gago, 2017).

2 Urban Neoliberalisms

2.1 *Neoliberalism as a Capitalist Project*

Much has been written about urban neoliberalism. The diversity and even incompatibility of different uses and definitions of neoliberalism have been highlighted by numerous authors (Fine & Saad-Filho, 2017; Foucault, 2008; Peck & Tickell, 2002; Wacquant, 2009). Following Keil (2016), approaches to urban neoliberalism can be grouped into two broad modes of explanation. The first conceives neoliberalism as a capitalist project 'from above' that bases itself on as well as promotes the further neoliberalisation of cities and communities. In contrast, the second line of thought is a Foucauldian approach in which neoliberalism is seen as a form of governmentality, in which it also becomes 'anchored in territories' and 'strengthened in popular subjectivities' (Gago, 2017: 11).

Numerous authors have highlighted the conceptual confusion that the diverse readings of neoliberalism have caused, maintaining that, therefore, 'neoliberalism' or 'neoliberalisation' manages to confuse more than it explains (Barnett, 2005). In a more sympathetic position, Keil (2016) notes that, at the very least, we should beware of the tendency to see 'everything in the city' in the light of neoliberalism. An end to neoliberalism has also been frequently declared, especially after the economic and financial crisis of 2008 (Brenner et al., 2010a). Yet in this study, conceptualisations of neoliberalism and neoliberalisations, as presented in this chapter, have been found helpful in conceptualising both general tendencies in urban governance, as well as the practices and forms of governmentalities encountered in the governance of occupations and evictions from social housing dwellings. Other studies have found the combination of neo-Marxist and post-Foucauldian conceptualisations of urban governance useful, such as the analysis by Schipper (2014) of the financial crisis and urban governance in Frankfurt and the investigation by Pozzi (2019) into 'expulsionscapes' and 'economies of eviction' in Italy.

In the first group, the Marxist and neo-Marxist literature on the connections of capitalism with urbanisation and urban development, initiated by Henri Lefebvre (1974) and David Harvey (1978), conceives of the built environment as a critical outlet for both creating and storing surplus value, acting as an important 'spatio-temporal fix' (Harvey, 2003), so that surpluses of capital are absorbed in the built environment. Moreover, urbanisation depends on the mobilisation of surplus, which ends up establishing a crucial connection between urbanisation and capitalism. This connection also turns urbanisation into a class phenomenon, as the surpluses must be extracted from somewhere and from somebody (Harvey, 2008). Considering that capitalism always has a need to expand, in order to increase the surplus, it has a tendency to drive market mechanisms into more and more aspects of social life (Luxemburg, 1951).

This is arguably what has happened, with increasing speed, in the last forty years of neoliberalism, with many of the processes of primitive accumulation (Marx, 1976) – or 'accumulation by dispossession' as Harvey (2003) reframed the concept, emphasising forced appropriation in the capitalist system – accelerating significantly, like the commodification and privatisation of land, expulsions of peasant populations, privatisation of natural resources such as water, and financialisation. Property capital has a central role in steering these processes of production of value, which tend to lead to the expulsion of the poor or working class from potentially profitable areas (N. Smith, 2002). According to Harvey (2008), storing of urban surplus by urban transformation amounts to 'creative destruction' because the poor, the underprivileged and the marginalised tend to suffer most in this urban restructuring, which often involves the displacement of these populations. Interests of urban capital formations often have the capacity to steer and tweak regulatory frameworks to their benefit, overriding or cancelling more socially progressive orientations or participatory policies (Ascensão, 2016).

The fiscal and economic base of many cities has eroded within advanced capitalism, leading many cities to seek alternative strategies to promote local development and economic growth. Harvey (1989) has argued that 'urban entrepreneurialism' – the search for new ways to promote local development and employment growth, instead of focusing on the provision of services and benefits to local populations – has emerged as one of the key strategies to address these challenges, promoting competition between cities. Swyngedouw et al. (2002) refer to the dominant forms of neoliberal urbanism as the 'New Urban Policy'. This agenda has at its core the precedence of property rights (as opposed to social and political rights) and the conceptualisation of housing as exchange value, as capital or as a financial asset (Haila, 1988; Rolnik, 2013a; Sassen, 2014), being generally complicit with placing planning in the service of private interests (Borja & Carrión, 2017).

The ascendance of finance, in particular, has been highlighted as a key characteristic of today's form of primitive accumulation, a key structural transformation of advanced economies since the 1970s, achieved through 'complex operations and much-specialised innovation', including outsourcing and algorithms of finance (Sassen, 2014). Fernandez & Aalbers (2016) define financialisation as 'the increasing dominance of financial actors, markets, practices, measurements and narratives, at various scales, resulting in a structural transformation of economies, firms (including financial institutions), states and households.' Housing and other forms of real estate are important objects of financialisation because they are considered to have a secure fixed value, but also because they offer other important advantages, including scale in mortgage debt and rental housing income (Aalbers, 2017).

After the financial crisis of 2008, the housing sector was severely hit in many countries, having itself become a 'fictitious commodity' taken over by finance. This has resulted in the reinforced conceptualisation of housing as a means to wealth: its 'value is the possibility of creating more value', depending on the speed and number of transactions capable of generating value appreciation (Rolnik, 2013a). According to Aalbers et al. (2020), 'capital has increasingly morphed into real estate (...) With finance and real estate becoming increasingly interdependent, we can thus think of a "real estate – finance nexus" to denote the intensified connections between both sectors.' The massive acquisition of urban property by corporations also promotes the de-urbanisation of the city by reserving large parts of space and buildings as a 'storage space for capital' (Sassen, 2018).

In this context, Brenner et al. (2010a) characterise neoliberalisation as a tendency for regulatory change that has begun to take place across the global capitalist system since the 1970s, whose principal characteristics are the prioritisation of 'market-based, market-oriented, or market-disciplinary' regulatory responses, a push to 'intensify commodification in all realms of social life'; and the mobilisation of speculative financial instruments to expand capitalist profit-making. In this field of literature, 'neoliberalism' is often distinguished from 'neoliberalisation', emphasising its conceptualisation as a process that is variegated and relational, involving diverse forms of subject-making and regulatory restructuring (England & Ward, 2016). While urban neoliberalism has often been understood as a retreat by the state from the realm of housing promotion and other forms of urban development – which Peck & Tickell (2002) argue was the case in the early phases of neoliberalism, in what they call its 'roll-back' phase – current analysis tends to emphasise that the state should instead be perceived as a facilitator of the process of neoliberalisation (Keil, 2016; Schipper, 2014). This 'roll-out' phase of neoliberalism is instead characterised by new forms of institution-building, governmental intervention, and policy-making (Peck & Tickell, 2002). Moreover, neoliberalisation tends to reinforce, normalise and extend the logic of urban entrepreneurialism in several ways, promoting a 'growth-first' approach to urban development, privileging lean governments, privatisation and deregulation, putting pressure on alternative solutions like those based on social redistribution, and encouraging a competitive posture among cities (Peck & Tickell, 2002).

Brenner et al. (2010b) also maintain that neoliberalisation is variegated: it should be understood as an incomplete process that is 'experimental and ultimately polymorphic', yet also path-dependent in each consecutive tendency for regulatory restructuring. Of particular importance for this study is their argument that marketisation and commodification under capitalism are mediated through the state institutions in diverse policy arenas – including labour, housing, land and social protection. Following this line of thought, neoliberalisation can be regarded as one of these mediating processes: as a form of regulatory reorganisation that modifies and recreates forms of governance, promoting and consolidating marketised and commodified forms of social life. Consequently, neoliberalisation should not be understood as a totality that encompasses all aspects of regulatory changes in any context (Brenner et al., 2010a). Rather, neoliberalisation can be conceived of as an analytical category that is opposed to regulatory processes that seek to counter marketisation and commodification, or to those that further entirely different agendas (Brenner et al., 2010a).

In the literature, evictions have been theorised as 'an expulsion from today's core social and economic opportunities' (Sassen, 2014), resulting both from the fundamental dynamics and characteristics of capitalism's linkage with urbanisation (Harvey, 2008; Lefebvre, 1970; N. Smith, 2002), as well as from the state's active promotion of maximisation of the value of the urban space (Brenner et al., 2010a; Rolnik, 2013b; Soederberg, 2019). Evictions are one of the key elements of 'creative destruction' (Harvey, 2008) of capitalist accumulation, by which the urban poor tend to be particularly affected (Doshi, 2013; Harvey, 2008). For example, evictions for increasing profit on land tend to happen where people do not have land titles and where the security of tenure is weak (Cabannes, 2010). Soederberg (2018) analyses urban accumulation by building on Harvey (2006), arguing that evictions should be seen in the light of broader processes and practices of exploitation through which the working poor are socially reproduced: and that the monetised, individualised and privatised housing regime plays an important role in this reproduction process.

Debt can be seen as directly connecting urban governance, housing and poverty: rental arrears can be considered one of the most complicated forms of debt, as they can often lead to eviction and homelessness (Soederberg, 2017). This likewise applies to foreclosures, whereby people's lives remain subject to debt servicing practices, sometimes even after the bank repossessed their mortgaged home (García-Lamarca & Kaika, 2016). Similarly, Sassen (2014) conceptualises evictions as a form of expulsion from today's core social and economic opportunities, be they due to foreclosures that result from predatory lending schemes, or displacement of local villagers from land acquired for large-scale agriculture projects. Just as the inability to pay rent causes evictions, evictions and displacements have been identified as key factors causing poverty and dispossession (Desmond, 2016; Sassen, 2014). In addition to being a direct violation of the right to adequate housing, evictions very often result in other severe human rights violations, such as the human right to food, water, health, work, property, security of the home and person, and freedom from cruel, inhumane and degrading treatment (UN-HABITAT & OHCHR, 2014a, 2014b).

The role of the state, and on another level, of the international organisations, such as the European Union, are arguably crucial in these displacements, as they have promoted regulatory changes that have stimulated financialisation and commodification by facilitating speculation, driving up the prices of land and property (Çelik, 2021; Haila, 2016; Soederberg, 2018, 2021). For instance, the EU has in its legislation prioritised economic competitiveness, growth and stability over social and labour market policies (classified as 'soft' areas), and hence, it can be argued that by empowering capitalists over labour interests, it has had a significant role in shaping urban displacements (Soederberg, 2021, p. 66, 71). The state can also directly intervene in the market as a 'market maker', for example by using land expropriation to generate conditions for housing financialisation, or as a 'direct developer', treating the land as a financial asset, for example, the state housing agency acting as a regulator and developer, enclosing and privatising public land, and expelling residents of 'informal' settlements, using the expropriated land for more value creation (Çelik, 2021).

In the aftermath of the 2008 financial crisis, these processes have only intensified; according to Peck (2012), there has been a shift to 'austerity urbanism', which can be described as an extension and intensification of neoliberalisation, characterised specifically by destruction in all types of welfare programmes and collective services, deficit policies, and devolving the risk and responsibility to local authorities, without the allocation of adequate resources. While unlocking land value, those who cannot afford to live in areas where prices continually increase are pushed into inadequate housing, overcrowding, or further away from their sources of livelihood. This promotion of housing as a commodity or financial asset (Rolnik, 2019) can be challenged by the conceptualisation of housing as a social right that gives shape to living conditions, largely defining the conditions of social life (Stavrides & Travlou, 2022: 2). Thus, for all, a stable home is central for the achievement of a degree of power and agency both inside and outside the home.

2.2 *Displaced Survival – Gender, Labour and Housing Precarity*

Yet these processes are often not simply class-based dispossessions, but rather negotiated through political processes that involve differentiation between and negotiation with urban dwellers. Doshi (2013) calls this 'accumulation by differentiated displacement' whereby residents are differentiated 'in relation to regimes of redevelopmental rule' through workings of market-based policies and institutionalised forms of participation. This links to the more general tendency of differential access to rights, based on social, economic, ethnic or gender criteria, for example (Fanon, 1963; Holston, 2008; Mbembe, 2019; B. de S. Santos, 2014). Santos (2014) describes this separation in terms of an 'abyssal line', existent in dominant forms of 'abyssal thinking', which draws a line between different human and nonhuman realities, and invisibilises the realities that exist on the other side of that line by constructing them as illegal, false, or even subhuman. Santos (2017) applies the notion of the abyssal line to access to human rights as well, noting that on one side of the line are the people who can realistically claim rights. In contrast, on the other side, the social exclusion is abyssal or radical. In this context, the question arises: 'Who can count as the subject who can claim home and land?' (Roy, 2017: A10).

Diverse marginalised groups face many specific challenges and discriminatory practices to have access to housing. The distinct challenges that racialised, non-binary, and transgender people might face in accessing housing have attracted considerable attention in the academic literature (Alves, 2022; Fields & Raymond, 2021; Roy, 2017), also highlighting the impact of racial capitalism (Fields & Raymond, 2021). An even broader focus has been attempted, recognising that experiences of housing insecurity and discrimination are shaped by multiple intersecting factors, with the aim of fostering wide-ranging housing justice (Roy et al., 2019). Yet, few researchers have addressed the question of how housing exclusions relate to other essential commodities, such as labour power (tenants, debtors) and money (wages, rents, welfare payments), which can contribute to masking the class, gender, and racial relations that are inherent to the production of urban displacements (Soederberg, 2021). Many women, especially racialised women, struggling against displacements and housing precarity work in the precarious low-wage service sector (Sassen, 2009; Soederberg, 2021), notably in the care sector (Farris, 2013; Ferguson & McNally, 2015; Tronto, 2013), not earning a sufficient salary to cover living costs.

Soederberg (2021, p. 50) conceptualises these processes as 'displaced survival', describing the cycles of displacements, such as overindebtedness, evictions, and homelessness, that low-wage tenants face, being displaced by their places of survival (rental homes). She maintains that it is important to juxtapose housing to other essential commodities, such as labour power (tenants, debtors) and money (wages, credit, rents, welfare payments, debt), considering that many people struggling against displacements and housing precarity work in the precarious low-wage service sector (Soederberg, 2021). She argues that the state actively produces rental housing insecurity through exploitation (rent and consumer credit), evictions, and invisibilising people experiencing homelessness (Soederberg, 2017).

Soederberg's model focuses on the role of rental housing in producing disposable workers. These often racialised and gendered workers, although indispensable to maintaining cities and societies functional within global capitalism (Ferguson & McNally, 2015), are treated as disposable in the sense that they do not earn sufficient wages to survive (Bhattacharyya, 2018; Marx, 1976). Care work continues to be a profoundly gendered, classed, and racialised sector, with women, racialised people, and lower classes made responsible for care work, of which a significant part occurs in informal and unpaid sectors, making the workers less well protected and receiving fewer benefits (Ferguson & McNally, 2015; Fraser, 2013).

In addition to being exploited in wage labour, women are also made responsible for unpaid reproductive labour (Federici, 2004; Fraser, 2013; Gilligan, 1993), for which women continue to bear more responsibilities than men (UN DESA Statistics Division, 2023). Nancy Fraser interprets today's 'crisis of care' as arising from the way our regime of financialised capitalism ignores and undermines the tasks related to social reproduction, treating them as external to the functioning of our economies, although no society, as she points out, could work without this affective and material labour: 'without it there could be no culture, no economy, no political organization' (Fraser, 2016: 99). Federici assigns this tendency to Marx's theory of capitalist accumulation, highlighting how women's unpaid labour is not integrated to the theorisation (Federici, 2021). The care responsibilities directly affect the financial situation of women – and consequently, their possibilities to rent or buy a home: salaries paid for work care work tend to be low, while unpaid care responsibilities affect the availability of women for waged labour. This feminisation of poverty is related to the 'feminisation of housing deficit' (Lages, 2022), with women disproportionately affected by housing precarity.

The question of gender also becomes central when homelessness is conceptualised. As many authors (Kern & Mullings, 2013; Pleace, 2015) point out, women's homelessness tends to differ from men's, while research and policy responses focus on types of homelessness that tend to characterise the homelessness of single adult men (Bretherton, 2017). In comparison to men's homelessness, women's homelessness constitutes a more hidden phenomenon.

First, many homeless women do not sleep rough or occupy public space (Kern & Mullings, 2013), mainly because women and children sleeping on the streets are even more prone to violence and abuse than men. In particular, mothers with small children avoid the street for fear of their children being taken away from them (Smolen & Harrison, 2013), relying on informal support, depending on their friends, acquaintances, or relatives to keep them accommodated, and approaching homeless services only if these other forms of support are exhausted (Bretherton, 2017). Second, the causes of women's homelessness also tend to differ from men's homelessness, with domestic violence, unstable family background and economic marginalisation being the leading causes of women's homelessness (Blunt & Dowling, 2006; Bullock et al., 2020; Busch-Geertsema et al., 2010; Lewinson et al., 2014; Smolen & Harrison, 2013). Homelessness can be thus understood as a highly gendered phenomenon that has been recorded as disproportionally affecting young single women with children in Europe (Pleace et al., 2008).

However, definitions of homelessness used to map homelessness or design policy responses tend to be too restrictive. They focus on the most visible group of the homeless: the ones who are sleeping rough – who are predominantly men – and excluding other forms of homelessness (Bretherton, 2017; Pleace, 2015). FEANTSA, the European Federation of National Organisations Working with the Homeless, has argued for the need to use an inclusive typology, called ETHOS, the European Typology of Homelessness and Housing Exclusion, which captures various categories of homelessness:
- rooflessness (sleeping rough or in an overnight shelter);
- houselessness (with a place to sleep, but in a temporary institutions or shelter);
- living in insecure housing (temporarily with family or friends, or living under the threat of eviction due to non-authorised occupation, no legal (sub)tenancy, or domestic violence);
- living in inadequate housing (in caravans on illegal campsites, in unfit housing, in extreme overcrowding) (FEANTSA, 2017).

Yet, in many countries, only the first two categories – rooflessness and houselessness – are considered. This approach entails the fundamental problem of ignoring the fact that forms of homelessness are gendered. By ignoring gendered forms and causes of homelessness, focusing only on 'rooflessness' and 'houselessness', official homeless statistics, responses and policies in Europe, as well as research on homelessness, tend to approach homelessness through the particular case of adult single men who live rough and in emergency accommodation, excluding homeless women of statistics and policy responses for the people without housing (Bretherton, 2017). It is important

to note that in general, women's lack of housing contributes to the perpetuation of inequalities for the whole family because the traditionally gendered
nature of home and childcare means they take the primary responsibility for
children, even when being homeless or evicted (COHRE, 2008), and mitigating
daily housing-related challenges and struggles (Muñoz, 2017).

2.3   *Neoliberalism as a Mode of Government*

In addition to the broader political and economic dynamics that produce
housing exclusions, institutional mechanisms and multifaceted forms of governance can have a significant role in the production, reproduction and transformation of the possible positions of the urban poor, shaping the life options
that are made available to them and their opportunities to act in the face of
neoliberal governance (Wacquant, 2016). Displacements and dispossessions
are moulded by interconnections between forms of governance, mechanisms
of marginalisation and experiences of injustice (Amin, 2014; Lancione, 2017;
Nygren & Wayessa, 2018; Wacquant, 2008).

Another prominent reading of neoliberalism dwells upon this theme,
understanding neoliberalism as a mode or modality of government, a form of
'governmentality', which Foucault, in his lectures of 1978, described as encom-
passing the 'ensemble' that institutions, procedures and tactics form to allow
for the exercise of political power 'that has the population as its target, political
economy as its major form of knowledge, and apparatuses of security as its
essential technical instrument' (Foucault, 2007). According to Larner (2000),
a principal characteristic of governmentality relates to the making of political
subjects, who increasingly perceive themselves as 'individualized and active
subjects responsible for enhancing their own well-being', which enables 'governing at a distance': direct state intervention is not necessarily needed, as
people regulate themselves instead. Foucault (2008: 131) argued in his lectures
of 1979 that the defining characteristic of neoliberalism was the logic of competition: applying the principles of a market economy to the exercise of political power, to the 'general art of government'. Here, it should be noted that in
Foucault's conceptualisation of neoliberalism, competition is not conceived
of as in classical liberalism – a natural process that should not be disturbed.
Rather, it is something that must be actively constructed and promoted by the
state, also extending to the lives of individuals who are encouraged to interio-
rise the norm of competition and act as entrepreneurs (Dardot & Laval, 2018).
However, it is important to note that the resulting neoliberal logic cannot be
conceived as totalising and homogeneous in its effects (Gago, 2017).

'Entrepreneurial governmentality' is one of the instruments for pursuing
the widening of neoliberal governmentalities. It illustrates how values such

as commodification, competition and commercialism have become dominant in neoliberalist societies, affecting modalities of governance, organisations, and the building of individual subjectivities (Dardot & Laval 2013: 303). 'Self-responsibilisation', often reframed as 'participation', is one of the other common features of neoliberal governmentalities, shifting the responsibility from the state to poor urban residents in particular (Nygren, 2016). Many authors observe how the meaning of participation has often been twisted to suit various needs and interests, often becoming only a buzzword to legitimise state politics (Neveu, 2011) or a new criterion of conditionality in order to receive subsidies or loans (B. de S. Santos, 2003). Literature on urban planning has called attention to the importance of transgressive, insurgent practices through which marginalised groups contest state-directed planning practices and urban space (Ghertner, 2011; Sandercock, 1998), breaking with inertial institutional planning procedures as well as contesting the disjunction between formal and substantive inclusion (Miraftab, 2009).

Accordingly, scholars have argued for the need to break with the idea of an ordered and planned city, switching to planning for a more open, disordered city (Sendra & Sennett, 2020). The 'inclusive city' is seen less as a 'matter of policy' and instead as a result of enabling residents to gain 'access to diverse spaces of operation' where they can interact and engage ((Simone, 2008). Consequently, scholars have argued for the need to enable transgressive participation: 'invented spaces of citizenship' (Miraftab, 2004), in contrast to 'invited' forms of participation. The latter are seen as spaces legitimated by the state – or by the donors – and that focus on mitigating the effects of structural injustices (Miraftab, 2009). On the contrary, in 'invented' participation, collective actions 'directly confront the authorities and challenge the status quo' (Miraftab, 2009: 39).

It is also important to note how neoliberal urban policies can influence neoliberal governmentalities. Struggling with decreasing housing budgets, the state agents begin to act guided by the 'moral economy' (Palomera & Vetta, 2016; Thompson, 1971) of housing resources being scarce and thus adopt the role of a gatekeeper, necessitating an intense evaluation of each case to make sure there is no gaming of the system (Wilde, 2020). This means that despite the intentions of social workers to provide 'caring spaces', such as psychosocial and material support (including housing) for people experiencing homelessness the lack of social housing (due to neoliberal urban policies) leads social workers to adopt other approaches. Therefore, they might recommend 'in the meanwhile' solutions to people facing housing precarity, such as shelters or other temporary accommodations, even when they do not consider them suitable (Clarke & Parsell, 2020). Moreover, the need to manage this tension often prompts the housing officers to apply more punitive practices towards the homeless (Clarke & Parsell, 2020).

In addition, neoliberal governmentalities can often intersect with other more authoritarian or disciplinary modes of governing (Coates & Nygren, 2020). For example, Auyero (2010) identifies three basic ways of subordinating the poor and regulating poverty: 'visible fists' of the state, meaning open repression of protest or forced evictions, 'clandestine kicks', such as the state's use of 'para-police', but also 'invisible elbows' – a term coined by Tilly (1997) – which comprises a less evident form of domination: the way the urban poor are forced to wait to have access to their rights. These subordinating tactics are used to put people 'in their place', making urban dwellers more insecure when they are already in highly uncertain situations, creating further precarity, confusion and marginalisation (Auyero, 2010; Muñoz, 2017).

The neoliberal and disciplinary governmentalities generally have intimate connections to social biases; towards the poor but also towards single mothers (Murphy, 2020; Wardhaugh, 1999), black and indigenous mothers (S. Motta, 2016), homeless mothers (Bullock et al., 2020), or residents of 'informal' housing (Bhan, 2014). The biases promote the pathologisation of the individual, who is depicted as the 'deviant' by the State. Hence, instead of considering a candidate for social housing as simply someone who needs state support in accessing housing, the candidate is rather framed as someone needs more discipline, necessitating 'moral reformation', and teaching of 'correct values'.

Informality is another concept that needs to be introduced in this section, as it serves as a key concept in this study to analyse the practices of both state actors and urban dwellers. Considering that informality is a concept that has been defined in various ways (Acuto et al., 2019; Bhan, 2013; Castela, 2011; McFarlane, 2019), it is important to clarify that in this study, informality is defined principally based on Roy's (2003, 2009) conceptualisation of the term. Perlman (1979) argued that the marginality of the urban poor, consisting of informal or extra-legal practices, is not a feature that belongs outside of the margins of the state or society, but is rather tightly tied to it, albeit through forms that are unfavourable to the interests of the urban poor. Roy (2003: 140) builds upon this idea, borrowing the concept of an extra-legal system from de Soto (1986), and defines informality as 'a realm of regulation where ownership and user rights are established, maintained, and overturned through elaborate extra-legal systems.' Yet contrary to de Soto's notion of extra-legal systems as an 'invisible hand' (Smith, 2007 [1776]), Roy (2003) conceptualises these systems as techniques of discipline and power which involve constant negotiation and reproduction of social hierarchies.

Therefore, informality does not necessarily coincide with poverty, but it is also associated with wealth and power. Informality also operates inside the state: the state actors themselves often function in informal ways, the difference being that the elite informalities are valorised and legalised, while subaltern informalities are criminalised (Bhan, 2013; Ghertner, 2011; Holston, 2008; Roy, 2009b, 2015). In this way, informality can also be considered a modality of governance and mode of production of space (Roy, 2015), in which political institutions simultaneously deploy legal and extra-legal mechanisms of control and discipline.

3   Urban Contestations

3.1   *Examining Occupations*

After reviewing literature focusing on the political, economic and social dynamics related to the *causes* of housing exclusions and precarity, I will take up Bayat & Biekart's (2009) call to examine how diverse groups of urban dwellers interact with these dynamics. Consequently, a theoretical framework that has a capacity to analyse how autonomous and fragmented acts contribute to remaking and challenging the existing urban power relations is needed. To analyse the subtle dynamics of occupation practices it is necessary to build a theoretical framework that can discern the nuances of subalternised agency and subjectivities. To what extent can occupations effectively promote alternative urbanisms and urban realities? Vasudevan (2015) examines occupations as 'makeshift urbanism', arguing that they can be thought of as acts of collective world-making that can contest housing exclusions and contribute to alternative political imaginaries. Similarly, Butler (2011) argues that occupations should be seen as acts that are undertaken with the desire to receive a response, demanding the right to stay and remain in the place by enacting the demand directly (Mitchell, 2012). In the process, urban dwellers become makers of the urban, realising the right to the city through a concrete process of city-making (Agier, 2015). The act of occupation alone, the refusal to succumb to the existing conditions, is an act of delegitimation of the state (Butler, 2011; Stevens, 2019).

In the context of Europe, studies on the political content of 'deprivation-based,' in contrast with 'politically motivated' occupations (Martínez, 2020b; Pruijt, 2013), are an emerging line of research, slowly bridging with the vocabulary that has previously been undertaken mainly in the context of Southern urban practice (Bhan, 2019; Lancione, 2020; Simone, 2019b). In contrast, if housing struggles were examined from a decolonial and feminist angle, looking 'for "radical housing" within everyday practices of dwelling at the margins' (Lancione, 2020: 275). Through this examination, the possibility opens up to consider what 'resistance' or 'political' can look like, paying increasing attention to political contestation that takes place in the margins, by subjects other than young white men (Gonick, 2016).

Recent investigations have analysed occupations as recuperating housing through challenging regimes of property ownership (García-Lamarca, 2017; Gonick, 2016), transitional commoning (Ferreri, 2023) or a particular form of commoning (Dadusc et al., 2019), and as an important part of claiming the 'right to the city' (Aguilera & Bouillon, 2013; Grazioli, 2017). However, most of this research focuses on occupations that are coordinated or promoted by activists or other collectives, instead of examining occupations as a sheltering strategy for individuals in need of housing.

Researchers have elaborated on diverse ways of classifying occupations. One of the most referred-to is Pruijt's (2013) taxonomy, categorising occupations into five distinct types, including 'deprivation-based squatting' and 'squatting as an alternative housing strategy'. These categories vary in focus, ranging from addressing immediate housing needs to broader political objectives such as cityscape preservation or anti-systemic activism. Martínez's (2020: 141) refinement of the classification into tactical and strategic squatting further complicates the discourse based on whether the occupation is seen as a tactic among other political objectives or an end in itself, respectively. While these frameworks provide valuable insights into housing activism, they may reflect underlying paternalistic attitudes, particularly in failing to account for cases where marginalised groups autonomously engage in occupation without external support. By 'autonomous', I mean that external social movement organisations do not directly promote the occupation.

Esposito and Chiodelli (2023) and Herbert (2018b, 2018a, 2021) conduct in-depth analyses of autonomously promoted need-based occupations, focusing on the characteristics that define such practices. Esposito and Chiodelli examine the occupation of empty public buildings and flats in Naples, Italy, conceptualising it as 'individualistic need-based squatting', while Herbert studies 'survival squatting', the occupation of vacant homes without owners' permission in Detroit, United States. From their research, several key insights emerge. Firstly, in both cases, occupations are driven by housing precarity, stemming from homelessness, precarious housing, and difficulties accessing social housing. This precarity is rooted in broader issues such as ineffective policies, housing commodification, financialisation, as well as personal characteristics of the occupiers, such as labour or legal situation, gender, and race (Dotsey & Chiodelli, 2021).

Secondly, the availability of empty homes is a precondition for these occupations. In Naples, empty public apartments and buildings designed initially for commerce or public services are targeted, while in Detroit – a 'shrinking city' – abandoned private housing stock is occupied due to severe population decline and an abundance of vacant properties.

Thirdly, in the two cases, the context of abandonment has led to some degree of legitimacy of occupiers' practices in the eyes of their neighbours as they are seen as caring for vacant homes and properties (Esposito & Chiodelli, 2023; Herbert, 2018a). Both Naples and Detroit demonstrate a tolerant public approach to occupations. While occupations are criminalised in Italy, regularisations of occupations are frequent due to authorities' lack of capacity to manage public housing estates or evict illegal occupants. Similarly, in Detroit, 'good occupations' that contribute positively to the community are often tolerated by local authorities as they 'demonstrate care and concern for the property and the neighbourhood' (Herbert, 2018a: 246).

Fourthly, occupations in both cities exhibit what Esposito & Chiodelli (2023) call the 'camouflaging agency' and Herbert (2018b) 'under-the-radar' nature of occupation. Occupiers blend in with other residents rather than standing out, strategically avoiding eviction by authorities. A fifth important aspect is the embeddedness in local networks. In Naples, occupiers rely on neighbourhood connections to identify vacant apartments, while in Detroit, embeddedness in the neighbourhood is established through an 'ethos of care', where residents assess occupations based on their contribution to community and neighbourhood well-being. However, while Naples occupiers may see occupation as a strategic choice for accessing better housing conditions (Esposito, 2022), Detroit occupants are depicted as being in 'survival mode', driven by urgent housing needs (Herbert, 2018). Overall, these insights shed light on the complex dynamics and motivations underlying autonomously promoted need-based occupations, offering valuable insights into the lived experiences of occupiers in different urban contexts.

It is to this emerging line of research that this book also wishes to contribute to deepen the analysis of the forms of agency involved, asking how these modalities of agency can be conceptualised and understood. Neither the theories of resistance nor those of everyday practices seem adequate for this context, as examining these processes through the vocabulary of resistance seems counterproductive because occupations for housing purposes do not necessarily involve a politicised use of the language of resistance. Conversely, the language of everyday practices ignores the active – and often well-thought-of – decision to occupy, which does not easily lend itself to examination from the perspective of ordinary, mundane activity. Instead of engaging in debates on whether occupations are a form of resistance – be they 'everyday resistance' or other forms of resistance (Bayat, 2013; Scott, 1985). I am interested in theory building that advocates for a more nuanced approach that recognises the diverse and often subtle ways in which urban residents assert agency and contest oppressive power structures (Das & Walton, 2015). To think about this question, I propose it is helpful to draw from two fields of literature that focus on agency from the perspective of those in a subaltern position: 1) Feminist literature on agency and 2) subaltern urbanisms.

3.2 *Insights from the Feminist Literature of Agency*

Feminist literature has presented the dilemma of agency as here expressed by Nancy Fraser: 'On the one hand, feminists have sought to establish the seriousness of our struggle by establishing the pervasiveness and systematicity of male dominance. Accordingly, we have often opted for theories emphasising the constraining power of gender structures and norms while downplaying the resisting capacities of individuals and groups. On the other hand, feminists have also sought to inspire women's activism by recovering lost or socially invisible traditions of resistance in the past and present. Under the sway of this imperative, we have often supposed quasi-voluntarist models of change. The net result of these conflicting tendencies is the following dilemma: *either* we limn the structural constraints of gender so well that we deny women any agency *or* we portray women's agency so glowingly that the power of subordination evaporates.' (Fraser, 1992: 16–17.)

Poststructuralist feminist theorists (e.g. Benhabib, 1992; Young, 1990) have approached this dilemma by decentring agency from the idea of the rational and sovereign agent, proposing instead that agency should rather be conceived as an 'emergent outcome of relational and negotiated processes within conditions of unequal access to essential livelihood resources and claims-making instruments' (Alves de Matos, 2023: 4). In this line of research, I find Saba Mahmood's (2005, 2006) work very insightful because she departs from the idea that agency is to be identified only in subversive actions that resist norms. Drawing from the analysis of the women's mosque movement in Egypt, she suggests that 'we think of agency not as a synonym for resistance to relations of domination but as a capacity for action that historically specific relations of subordination enable and create' (Mahmood, 2006: 33).

Consequently, agency can be located not only in acts that resist norm but also in the variegated ways that norms can be 'lived and inhabited, aspired to, reached for, and consummated' (Mahmood, 2006: 28). This enables an analysis that escapes the binary terms of resistance and subordination, which Mahmood considers insufficient to capture the multiple motivations, aspirations and objectives people have for their specific acts or forms of agency.

This analysis acquires a capability of discerning forms of agency even in a subordinating context where alternatives appear quite limited; not in a sense of establishing a universal moral rule that would guide women's agency, but more in line with Foucault's conceptualisation of ethics, a cautious examination of one's activities to live in harmony with one's aspirations and ethical norms (Mahmood, 2005: 187). As Alves de Matos (2023: 10) argues in her study on women's care practices in Portugal during the austerity period, her research participants did not just 'passively accept their feminised destiny'; instead, their responses to the oppressive conditions were critical to enable the survival of their families. Grounding her observations on the notion that 'the personal is political' (Hanisch, 1970), her work contributes to our understanding of how women's agency and political engagement remain contested terrains, 'torn between the constraining power of gender structures and women's embodied capabilities of subversion and transgression' (Alves De Matos, 2021: 1004).

Hence it is fundamental to analyse the forms and practices through which women 'experience, survive, challenge and resist' instead of focussing only on 'transformatory' perspectives or stakes on agency (Hume & Wilding, 2020). These practices do not draw from the principles of rationality, autonomy and independence advocated by orthodox economics and liberal philosophy; rather, they 'constitute a form of agency produced by, and productive of, embedded interdependent caring practices, relationships and investments across space and time to define, fulfil and negotiate the inescapable existence of fundamental needs.' (Alves de Matos, 2023: 11). Various authors (V. Gago, 2017; S. C. Motta & Seppälä, 2016; Sassen, 2000) have conceptualised these forms of agency as feminised resistances or circuits of survival, grounded in the multiple oppressions faced by workers, the unemployed, migrants and women, but highlighting at the same time the strength of these feminised figures which 'transforms cities and redefines the metropolitan space, the family and women's space' (Gago, 2017: 7). The constraints and conditions that shape women's action should not be seen as constant; instead, they are negotiated and politicised in multiple ways, and 'shaped by locally specific configurations of political and cultural institutions, agents and social practices' (Hume & Wilding, 2020).

3.3   *Insights from Subaltern Urbanisms*

Providing a strong parallelism with the feminist literature on agency, the literature of subaltern urbanisms has explored how urban dwellers in marginalised positions have acted to create conditions of living for themselves. The concept of the subaltern has been advanced most famously by the Subaltern Studies collective in India, which built upon and expanded Gramsci's (1978) idea of the subaltern[1] to question the elitist writing of historiography. In Guha's (1988) writing, the subaltern equalled the 'people' that shared a general subordination in South Asian societies, be it 'in terms of class, caste, age, gender, office or any other way'. Spivak (1988) developed the idea further, theorising about the possibilities and limitations of subaltern agency, locating the agency of change in the insurgent or the 'subaltern'. Das (1989) builds upon these notions, arguing that the subaltern is not a category, but rather a perspective, and that this subaltern perspective employed by researchers is not engaged in understanding a particular social group or social organisation per se, but that the 'object of the study is the 'contract' which such groups have been compelled to establish with forms of domination belonging to the structures of modernity' (Das, 1989). In her later work, Spivak (2005) seems to have refashioned her theorisation along similar lines to Das, arguing that 'subalternity' is not an identity, but 'a position without identity'. Here, the subaltern duly emerges as a perspective as well as a relation, a position within the wider society as a result of a collective social negotiation (Spivak, 2005). In extensive work that builds upon the notion of the subaltern, these different nuances have often not been retained. The term subaltern is often used without any definition, taking the dominance of a certain group of people and the subaltern status of another group somewhat for granted. This dilutes the fact that at any given time, there would probably normally be different groups in relatively dominant positions disputing control over a particular resource or over a certain group of people (Baiocchi & Corrado, 2010).

As the feminist literature on agency, the literature on subaltern urbanisms has struggled to create a balanced depiction of agency: there is a fine line between romanticising the possibilities of the agency of the subaltern, on the one hand, and completely depriving them of agency, on the other. In many analyses, the poor and the subalternised are represented as being essentially defined by their capitalist, class, or colonial oppression, depicting the systems

---

1   Due to Gramsci's imprisonment, he was unable to present conclusive remarks on the notion of the subaltern but left behind only scattered notes on the concept. See Green (2002) and Spivak (2005).

of oppression as so pervasive that there is no way of escaping them. These representations have longstanding academic roots, considering that in academic literature, the poor and the subaltern have often been constituted incapable of engaging in politics through different kinds of reasonings. Some political philosophers, like Arendt (1963), have argued that because the poor are driven by the immediacy of need, they are incapable of the kind of collective action that constitutes the realm of politics (see also Das & Walton, 2015).

In contrasting views, the accounts of political agency 'from below' are sometimes utterly romanticised, conflating the possibilities of insurgency while the empirical evidence of political efficiency is lacking. Ananya Roy (2011) has noted how subalternity thus became more than the 'general attribute of subordination'; it also became a theory of agency, that of the 'politics of the people.' Important conceptualisations that arise from this field are the notions of 'insurgent citizenship' (Holston, 1998, 2008) and 'political society' (Chatterjee, 2004), which are both based on the idea that substantial parts of the population, predominantly the poor, are excluded from accessing citizens' rights and democratic processes, and that in order to challenge this status quo, they use tactics of insurgent citizenship or the 'politics of the poor' (Chatterjee, 2004). Yet oftentimes, these concepts tend to create an imaginary community of groups of urban dwellers, granting a distinctive form of political agency to a mass of urban subalterns (Roy, 2011), and erasing any signs of power struggles within poor communities (Das & Walton, 2015). They also often ignore the co-production of these forms of agency, involving, for instance, middle-class activists, militants, lawyers, politicians, engaged scholars, and students in addition to poor urban communities (Forment, 2015).

Therefore, instead of essentialising the urban poor or 'the subaltern', there is a need to consider not only the experiences of poverty and precarity that shape their lives, but also how these experiences are aligned with other conditions of life, such as the possibility of democratic participation, access to housing, social markers such gender or race, or policy and political conditions, such as development projects and infrastructure that might rapidly change the living conditions of these urban dwellers (Das & Randeria, 2015). Drawing on Das (1989) and Spivak (2005), I contend that the term 'subalternisation' can be applied to analyse these questions, using the ideas of the 'subaltern' as a perspective and a relative position. Consequently, instead of using the word 'subaltern', I refer to the *processes of subalternisation* to highlight the idea that the subaltern is not a category or an identity, but a fluid, relational process. I propose that the agency of the subalternised can be analysed precisely from that perspective: the focus has to be both on the limitations of participation and on doing politics, as well as on the ways that 'all the people try to reassert their place in the society' (Muñoz, 2018).

The analysis of the agency of urban marginalised dwellers thus necessarily has to depart from the notion of a situated and relational agency. It does not begin with assigning a distinctive political agency to a mass of urban poor, but rather with the conditions and constraints that shape their struggle; through 'the series of operations in and through which people weave their existence in incoherence, uncertainty, instability and discontinuity' (Mbembe & Roitman, 1995: 325). It is thus important to understand how residents in different urban contexts try to create spaces of operation for themselves with the means they have available, and how these spaces are shaped and constrained by forces outside their immediate control (Simone, 2016).

The literature on southern and subaltern urbanisms contributes significantly to this debate by providing detailed analyses of urban practices and subjectivities in contexts of urban precarity, analysing how occupiers seek to remake the city, but on the other hand, bearing in mind the precarious conditions and the fragility of these practices (Scheba & Millington, 2023; Wilhelm-Solomon, 2020). Nevertheless, precarity can also represent more than material and social insecurity: it can also be an opportunity for translating the experience of temporary housing and infrastructure beyond conventional formulations of politics (Simone, 2010; Vasudevan, 2015).

Bayat's (2013) concept of 'quiet encroachment' highlights the persistent and often clandestine efforts of dispersed urban residents to carve out spaces of autonomy and resistance within the constraints of oppressive urban regimes. Simone's (2019b) notion of 'improvised lives' sheds light on the everyday practices of a large number of fragmented people and the ways they operate in the world, making, remaking and unmaking relations. Caldeira's (2017) work on 'peripheral urbanisation' underscores the agency of urban residents in shaping their built environment through long-term processes that produce spaces that are always in the making. Caldeira (2007) highlights the residents' role in building the infrastructure (autoconstruction); the transversal engagements with official logics; the new types of political subjectivities created in the process; and the heterogeneity of spaces created through these processes. Bhan (2019) emphasises 'squatting', repairing and consolidating as characterising 'Southern' urban practices. Vasudevan's (2015) concept of 'makeshift urbanism' is also closely related to peripheral urbanisation, improvised lives and quiet encroachment: it is conceived of as an act of collective world-making through which the sense of the city is continuously remade. In this way, occupations are seen 'not just in its tensions with formal logics of law and planning, nor merely in the material forms of housing, but as a mode of practice that embraces uncertainty, measures itself against limited temporalities, and operates to move forward incrementally in any way it can' (Bhan, 2019: 645). All of these authors draw attention to improvisation in creating the tactics and practices of everyday city life, arguing that instability and precarity result in the need to invent tactics with the means available. Creativity acquires particular importance: What matters most is not necessarily what one has (social capital, networks) but how urban dwellers manage to mobilise, in order to put into use what they have at the right moment (Schilling et al., 2019). Another key characteristic is the capacity for adaptation while coming up with long-term strategies of resistance becomes increasingly difficult.

The focus in these theories is on long-term processes that gradually produce spaces that are always in the making, continuously remaking the city.

The materiality of practices also characterises forms of makeshift urbanism as in occupied spaces, different materials are used and adapted in the context of everyday survival, as well as a specific political imaginary that intends to develop alternative urbanisms basing itself directly upon on the realities of creative destruction and accumulation by dispossession (Vasudevan, 2015). This literature thus pays attention to the contexts of instability and precarity faced by many urban dwellers, grounded in gendered, classed and racialised forms of exploitation and dispossession.

3.4 *Coalescence into Collective Action*

Sometimes, the dispersed struggles of fragmented groups of urban dwellers may become part of broader political struggles, coalescing into social movements. This study examines these kinds of interactions by analysing what kinds of contradictions arise within them, what kinds of opportunities they afford, as well as the kind of urban movement strategies that can be identified to support urban dwellers in the struggle against housing exclusions. While I have opted to use terminology like 'affected people/people at risk of eviction' and 'social movement activists', these categories are by no means clear-cut. It also needs to be observed that the boundary between collective and 'individual' action is extremely fluid. The occupiers' movements complicate this category, given that the same actions might have more broadly collective aims (changing legislation, politics, policies, political practices), aims at the community level (stopping an eviction from a particular neighbourhood, regularising a neighbourhood, or improving the living conditions there), and aims at the individual/family level (stopping the eviction of a particular family, improving the home of a particular family). Social movements are defined in this research following (Tilly, 2004), being characterised by collective claim-making target-ing authorities, diverse 'claim-making performances', and 'WUNC': displays of the cause's Worthiness, Unity, Numbers and Commitment.

The social movement literature has long investigated what prompts peo-ple to participate in social movements, and why and under what conditions they emerge. Various reasons have been suggested to explain participation in collective action, and my objective here is not to establish an exhaustive list but to give some indication of the variety of explanations. The research has affirmed that people participate in collective action because they face griev-ances (Smelser, 1962), or because social movement actors were able to mobilise resources for their action and, consequently, collective action emerged as a result of rational calculations (McCarthy & Zald, 1977). The construction of cultural frames that give moral legitimation to the action have been singled out as essential for movement construction (Snow et al., 1986; Snow, 2004), as well as the emergence of a political opportunity or threat (Tilly, 1978).

The 'political process' approach, first theorised by (McAdam, 1999), also emphasises political opportunities and constraints, but pays more attention to the political and institutional contexts of social movements. However, the approach has come in for persistent criticism, such as the problem of defin-ing the relevant dimensions for the concept of political opportunities, its lack of attention to the cultural context or the structural origins of protest (della Porta & Diani, 2006). In fact, even some proponents of the political process approach consider that it is better viewed as a framework to be combined with other insights from social movement theory (Tarrow, 2011). (Rutland, 2013) crit-icises the political process approach, as well as studies on urban movements in general, for having paid scant attention to the process of subject forma-tion, perceiving the activist political subject as rather universal and invari-able. Yet some of the social movement literature has analysed at least parts of the process of making activist subjects. These include the idea of 'mobi-lising structures', highlighting the importance of groups and social networks in constructing collective action (Diani & McAdam, 2003). Furthermore, the notion of collective action frames, which are used to construct a shared idea and understanding to validate and stimulate collective action (McAdam et al., 2001), can also be considered essential in the making of political subjects.

From the fields of subaltern studies and urban theory, some additional insights into the formation of collective subjects emerge. Bayat (2015) seems to incline towards the political opportunity theory when claiming that coa-lescence into collective action can occur when the gains are threatened or when an opportunity for collective resistance and mobilisation becomes avail-able: for instance, when the police control softens, the state slips into crisis, or some large, contentious movements come to fruition. The importance of construction frames for grievances is also highlighted, as it is affirmed that the articulation of demands in terms of rights promotes collective action (Bayat, 2015; Holston, 2008). One of the preconditions for expansion into collective action seems to be that urban dwellers are able to see the threat, such as an eviction, as collective, calling for action on behalf of a wider group of people (Das & Walton, 2015). There is a need to be able to set differences aside to construct a collective identity. This can be done by drawing on the identity that can be used to form a collectivity (leaving other identities in the background) (Simone, 2013; Spivak, 2005), or by subsuming various identities in the overarching framework of common residence (Simone, 2013).

Another fundamental aspect in the building of collective mobilisation is challenging the feeling and narratives of guilt and personal failure – the idea that the person in question is responsible for being homeless or at risk of eviction, the 'neoliberal model of personal responsibilisation' (Di Feliciantonio, 2017). It is fundamental to break the political subjectification of a homeless person as an 'outcast' (García-Lamarca, 2017). This can occur through a process whereby people are empowered to challenge the 'socialisation of guilt', replacing it with the 'socialisation of activism for housing rights' (Casellas & Sala, 2017).

However, it is not easy to form collective identities nor to promote the 'socialisation of activism'– they are not easily established or maintained. Many authors contend that the neoliberal restructuring of the city has weakened the capacity for urban movements. Blokland et al. (2015) note that in Berlin and Tel Aviv, for example, the shift towards entrepreneurial urban politics co-occurred with diversification of urban populations, resulting in the splintering of citizenship claims into specific agendas, into 'situational city-zenship' in these cities, as well as in many other 'Western' democracies (Blokland et al., 2015: 656, 664). They argue that this often renders the processes of claim-making, voicing, and striving for recognition fragmented. The tendency of neoliberal urban regimes to co-opt activists as 'community partners', suffocating in this way more oppositional forms of politics, has also been affirmed in the literature (Pruijt, 2003; Rutland, 2013).

Research has likewise demonstrated that promoting collective action across groups with different social backgrounds can be challenging (Bayat, 2015; Florea et al., 2018; Simone, 2013). In recent literature, there have been attempts to analyse the challenge of forming a coherent collective identity and maintaining participation in the movement, contending that the capacity to retain key activists is fundamental to passing on knowledge (Wilde, 2019). Caciagli (2019) focuses on housing occupations, analysing them as 'educational sites of resistance' that support and further the formation of collective political subjectivities. She highlights spatiality in shaping political subjects: the occupiers in collectively occupied buildings engage in concrete spatial practices to make a home out of an abandoned building. These practices support the building of the spatial identity of the occupation and 'forge the attitude of resistance' in the occupiers (Caciagli, 2019). Like Wilde (2019), she emphasises the role of the more experienced activists in transmitting the knowledge and triggering collaboration. Yet, passing on knowledge might not be enough when confronting oppressive situations. (Ismail, 2019) argues that popular education work promoting critical consciousness, as conceived by Freire (1990), can have 'powerful effects' in terms of challenging oppressive situations, yet these potentials are strongly dependent on the political context, including on how responsive the State is to the efforts of the marginalised.

In research on social movements for the right to housing, as well as in broader research on social movements and non-governmental organisations, the movements formed by the 'affected people' – the homeless or those at risk of eviction – are often contrasted, and even opposed, with the movements formed by 'outside' actors. Many authors have pointed out that non-governmental organisations (NGOs), and social movements that are not formed by affected people themselves, might not understand the local economic and political realities and how they condition the struggle that the local residents engage in (Ismail, 2019; Kuttab, 2014; Muñoz, 2017; Stahler-Sholk, 2010). Establishing one's 'own' independent organisation is highlighted as a crucial step on the path from 'dependence to independence' (Ismail, 2019; L. Podlashuc, 2011). In a similar vein, NGOs' or wider social movements' involvement might subvert the objectives of the actual struggles of the residents (Miraftab, 2009; Osuoka, 2018; L. Podlashuc, 2011), engendering more harm than benefits for the struggle engaged in by marginalised urban dwellers (Ismail, 2019; Simone, 2019b). Some authors also emphasise the difference between NGOs and social movement actors (Souza, 2010), stating that they often have two key issues of divergence: who speaks for whom and how the struggle is seen – as a process or as a project (Cabannes, 2013). NGOs are seen as too constrained by the political and policy stances of their donors to engage in revolutionary action (Harvey, 2010). In contrast, social movements are seen as more autonomous (Souza, 2010).

In addition, even when the collective action arises 'from the grassroots', it is important to ask whose city is being claimed while struggling for the Right to the City. Most of the studies stay silent on the internal divisions within the movements of urban dwellers from marginalised neighbourhoods, ignoring the role that gender, race and class divisions play in political participation (Baiocchi & Corrado, 2010; Doshi, 2013; Nygren & Wayessa, 2018; Simone,

2015b). Within social movements fighting against evictions, the hierarchies tend to mirror those of the society at large, reproducing gender and other inequalities and, therefore, failing to address the rights of women or ethnic minorities (Miraftab, 2006; Seppälä, 2016).

While drawing attention to the power relations among actors is extremely pertinent and important, I also argue for the need to conceptualise cooperation among actors. In many cases, collective action might be coproduced between diverse groups of people, rather than being initiated solely by 'affected' people or 'from below' (Forment, 2015). These diverse groups might play important roles in linking local struggles to activists, researchers, and other actors, as well as in facilitating contacts and information (Bayat, 2013; Das & Randeria, 2015; Florea et al., 2018). Building solidarities has been highlighted as essential in promoting transformative action (Karaliotas & Kapsali, 2021; Wilde, 2020). Activists might also contribute to building up politics of scale that are understood here as a collective perspective that implies a common experience, even if it retains its barriers of exclusivity as well as inclusion (Graddy, 2010), duly coming close to the process of collective identity-building described by Spivak (2005). Transnational exchanges are also seen as relevant for many urban and housing movements, such as Slum Dwellers International (L. N. Podlashuc, 2007), South Africa's Abahlali baseMjondolo, and parts of the Argentinian Piquetero Movement, and the Brazilian Sem Teto (Souza, 2010).

The transnational exchanges entail many challenges, such as the easier participation of the 'North' due to their economic privileges, the risk of participation occurring only at the top of the social ladder in each country, and the 'North' advocating unworkable solutions for the 'South' (Carty & Mohanty, 2015). Yet they can also have many strengths, sharing values and solidarity across differences, developing a common discourse through dialogue and action, and changing the structural inequalities and the deepening impact of globalisation on gender, class, race and ethnic relations (Baksh & Harcourt, 2015). Nonetheless, the current key international networks that are active against forced evictions often appear fragmented, with very limited coordination capacity, and each one of them appears to be related to a particular group (Cabannes, 2010).

3.5   *Movement Strategies*

In analyses of social movements and resistance related to forced evictions, collective mobilisation has been identified as the single most effective strategy to counter evictions (AGFE & UN-HABITAT, 2007, 2011). However, the works documenting actual practices and strategies against evictions are somewhat limited, although a wide variety of organisations and coalitions are fighting against evictions worldwide. In analyses of social movements related to the Global North, there is a deficit of systematic analysis that would focus on the strategies of social movements in general (Meyer & Staggenborg, 2012), while in the social movement literature related to Latin America, they have received more attention (Krausova, 2020). Yet recent literature has highlighted to the importance of strategy in housing struggles. Collective occupation has undoubtedly been the most scrutinised strategy, with extensive literature focussing on diverse occupation movements, analysing both occupation movements in general (V. Lima, 2021; Martínez, 2020b; Pruijt, 2013; SqEK, 2014) as well as occupation as a strategy more specifically (Caciagli, 2019; García-Lamarca, 2017; Grazioli, 2017; V. Lima, 2021; Martínez, 2020b; Stevens, 2019). It has been claimed that *okupa* movements can be conceived as alternatives to capitalism (SqEK, 2014), and in certain cases even as anti-capitalist urban commons (Martínez, 2020c). In a similar vein, it is contended that occupation movements "represent alternative forms of social reproduction in post-welfare neoliberal cities" (Grazioli, 2017; Grazioli & Caciagli, 2018), and consequently have the potential to update and specify Lefebvre's notion of the Right to the City (Grazioli, 2017; Martínez, 2020a). There are also insightful analyses of the strategies and tactics of housing movements directed towards influencing policy (V. Lima, 2021), especially through negotiations and engagements with the state (Cahen et al., 2019).

In most of the literature, what is meant by a 'strategy' is not quite explicitly stated. 'Strategy' is often used as a synonym for 'tactic', a form of action, or both terms are applied interchangeably. 'Repertoire of contention', defined by Tilly (1995) as 'the ways that people act together in pursuit of shared interests', is a related concept, referring to the collection of tactics or forms of action that social movements engage in. The notion of the 'repertoire of contention' intends to draw attention to the culturally and socially specific ways of collective action (Tilly, 1978, 2005). Meyer & Staggenborg (2012) propose a framework for defining the concept of strategy, identifying four essential elements in its formulation: 'the *demands* or claims made by collective actors; the *arenas* or venues of collective action; and the *tactics* or forms of collective action', complemented by the selection of the *targets* of collective action. This framework has the advantage of providing a clear conception of what a social movement strategy means. While the framework itself does not directly consider the context in which the strategy decisions are taken, Meyer and Staggenborg (2012: 5) do refer to Tilly (1978) in recognising that various constraints, such as the political and cultural environment, the community influences, and the internal organisation of the movement limit strategies.

The strategies can be categorised in terms of how much they challenge the status quo and existing spaces of participation. McAdam et al. (2001)

divide 'contentious politics' into two subcategories: 'contained contention' and 'transgressive contention'. As they both pertain to 'contentious politics', they concern episodic, public politics that involves interaction between the claim-makers and others, and includes the government as a mediator, target, or claimant (McAdam et al., 2001). The difference between 'contained contention' and 'transgressive contention' relates to the parties in the process and the innovativeness of the action: in 'transgressive contention', at least some parties are 'newly self-identified political actors' and at least some employ 'innovative collective action' (McAdam et al., 2001). However, these categories do not consider the extent to which the strategies challenge entrenched practices and the status quo. Miraftab (2004: 1) in her analysis of 'invited' and 'invented spaces of citizenship' focuses precisely on that distinction: the first are defined as the spaces 'legitimised by donors and government interventions', while 'invented spaces of citizenship' are those 'directly confronting the authorities and the status quo'. These categories can also be usefully applied to the analysis of strategies, considering whether they are 'invented' or 'invited', according to the degree to which they transgress official norms and policies and disrupt the status quo. In this study, I will call the first group 'transgressive' strategies, strategies with a high 'degree of transgression', while the second is characterised by a low 'degree of transgression'. However, it needs to be considered that in practice many strategies fall between these two extremes, which are neither completely legitimised nor totally confrontational. I therefore consider it useful to add the category of 'in-between' strategies, which contains a moderate 'degree of transgression.'

Some authors argue that transgressive strategies are particularly needed to bring about change: transgressive political agency is required to disrupt oppressive relationships perpetuated by neoliberal governance (Earle, 2012; Miraftab, 2009). García-Lamarca (2017) draws on Rancière's (1999) notion of outcasts – defined as those who have no part in the dominant system – to argue that the more insurgent practices – she refers mainly to the recovery of empty bank-owned housing with and for evicted families in Spain – have high emancipatory potential as they both demand equality for the 'outcasts' as well as question the capitalist and neoliberal logics of the production of space and accumulation by dispossession. Likewise, in the context of the Philippines, Dizon (2019) describes a victorious strategy of 'arouse, organise, mobilise', which led to the occupation of thousands of social housing units, contending that it was precisely by taking the offensive against the state actors that the results were achieved.

According to other views, progress towards alternative urbanisms can be gradual. Urban dwellers employ tactics like partial appropriation of state norms to create new urban standards and challenge power relations; for example, Mack (2013) and Nielsen (2011) suggest that grassroots actions can lead to significant changes in urban structures and policies. Bayat (2013) emphasizes the transformative potential of everyday politics, attributing significant urban transformations to atomised individuals' aggregate actions. Simone (2019b) takes a middle way in a sense, advocating for an exploration of everyday practices without preconceived notions of their transformative potential. Despite criticisms for being vague (Watts, 2005), Simone suggests that everyday practices can lead to renegotiations of power relations and questions about societal values, challenging dominant framings of informality and illegality and ultimately contributing to more politicised action. For example, Cahen et al. (2019), describing housing struggles in New York and Chicago, locate the most successful strategies in the middle, in the 'in-between' strategies category. They refer to 'invited inventions and invented invitation' to argue that movements achieved their greatest success when they were able to combine negotiation with occupation: they had to invent housing by identifying abandoned properties, and create new invited spaces to negotiate with the authorities to formalise their claims (Cahen et al., 2019). Similarly, V. Lima (2021) argues that a combination of strategies, including direct action, building a strong narrative, and mobilising allies, was needed to open up a new discursive political space on government housing policy in Dublin.

However, it must be noted that the relative success of the strategy will not depend solely on the 'degree of transgression' nor the tactics adopted. As highlighted by the 'contentious politics' approach (McAdam et al., 2001), it is necessary to have a relational approach to the analysis of social movements, considering the interaction of diverse actors involved as well as to the political and social context. Scale can also matter, as some authors argue that the scale of the neighbourhood has more potential for building access to housing rights than the actions at the city level (Bastia & Montero Bressán, 2018).

In this chapter, I have intended to complicate several theoretical dichotomies in the academic literature concerning resistance to evictions, occupations, social movements, and subaltern subjectivities. The binary between the needs-based and political occupations does not reflect the wide variety of examples that highlight the different shades of practices and forms of agency, ranging from everyday improvisations and infra-politics to occasional collective action, insurgent practices, and activism promoted by collectives and associations. When seen through processes of makeshift urbanism, peripheral urbanisation, quiet encroachment or improvised lives, it can be understood that fragmented practices also have political implications, which does not mean they should necessarily be classified as 'resistance'. These practices might be conceived as transformative in a variety of senses: at the level of individual families, in the sense of securing access to housing, or in the sense of promoting the building of political subjectivities; or at the level of influencing policies, management practices, and legislation, by promoting access to affordable and adequate housing for wider groups of the population, and also by questioning the broader dynamics of urban accumulation by dispossession. I will engage with these arguments throughout the book, using them as lenses to examine council housing occupations.

Gendered, Classed and Racialised Forms of Housing Precarity

[T]he home is described as a place of both fear and desire, and as a place to escape from and to escape to.
BLUNT & DOWLING, 2006: 130

∴

1   Why Occupations?

In this chapter, I will focus on the question of *why* the people I interviewed resorted to occupation. I use the lens of displaced survival to examine homelessness and displacements in contemporary Lisbon. In doing that, my objective is to mobilise this conceptual framework to bring light to the complex web of relations that promote the housing exclusion of low-wage single mothers. I show how these families, expelled from housing programmes and unable to afford housing in the private rental sector, are left to suffer from a cycle of displacements, leading to accentuated poverty and dispossession, which also leads to over-generational perpetuation of poverty. I argue that their housing precarity is profoundly affected by their positions as 'disposable' workers within the low-wage service sector, mainly the care-domestic sector; by their general position as women and mothers, responsible for social reproduction; and by their omission of the policy responses to homelessness.

Drawing on Das (1989) and Spivak (2005), I contend that the term 'subalternisation' can be applied to analyse these questions, using the conceptualisation of the 'subaltern' as a perspective and a relative position. I propose that the collective social negotiation to establish this 'contract' (Das, 1989) of the subaltern with the neoliberal capitalist society is created through a multifaceted process of subjectification that encompasses two meanings of the word subject: 'subject to someone else by control and dependence and tied to his own identity by a conscience or self-knowledge. Both meanings suggest a form of power which subjugates and makes subject to' (Foucault, 1982). Consequently, instead of using the word 'subaltern' to describe my research participants who face housing exclusion, I refer to *subalternisation* to highlight the idea that the subaltern is not a category or an identity, but a fluid, relational process.

The focus in this chapter will be on *gendered* forms of housing exclusion, concentrating especially on the case of single mothers who occupy council homes without permission. This focus is justified by the reality that their role and presence were so significant in the actions of the Habita association, of which I was actively a part during my fieldwork. Single parents are statistically a relatively large population group in Portugal, and single parents in Portugal tend to be women: in 2019, there were 459,000 single-parent households in Portugal (11% of all households), and in 85% of the cases, the household was headed by a woman (PORDATA, 2019a). In other words, there were more than 390,000 families with a child or children being raised by a single mother. The single-parent households also have a particularly high rate of poverty risk: in 2019, after social transfers, 25.5% of single parents' families were considered at risk of poverty (PORDATA, 2019b). In comparison, the risk-of poverty rate after social transfers for all households with dependent children was 17%, while for the general population, it was 16.2% (PORDATA, 2019b). This means that there is a large number of families headed by a single mother that are at risk of poverty. The austerity period (2010 to 2015) also left women particularly strained, as they were largely held responsible for the well-being of the family in the crisis situation (Alves de Matos, 2021; A. P. de Lima, 2023).

These aspects were reflected in the data gathered during Habita's open-door sessions, comprising 276 cases of housing problems between January 2018 and December 2019 (Table A.2). Of these cases, 219 were raised by women, compared with 46 raised by men and 11 by couples. This reflects how housing is often perceived as women's domain, with the domicile forming the traditional 'female' sphere. Many people, 43% of the cases, came to seek Habita's support because of problems faced in private rental apartments, including eviction, non-renewal of a contract, lack of building maintenance, and an inability to pay the rent because of health issues or unemployment. Altogether, 12% came because of problems with council housing, making complaints, above all, about overcrowding, family conflicts, or lack of maintenance. A further 5% were completely homeless. The category "other" comprises a range of housing problems, such as house fire, problems with a rental room, and having only a van for accommodation.

What surprised me the most, however, was the high percentage – 36% – of people coming because they had occupied a council apartment without authorisation. Frequently, these families, mostly headed by single mothers, affirmed that they had occupied because of extreme overcrowding and/or family conflicts in their previous housing arrangements. Almost all had a long history of trying to apply for council housing, sometimes for years, without success. Many had also tried to rent an apartment through the private market, which they were then unable to pay for. Consequently, I started to ponder the reasons for their predicament: Why do these women not have access to housing through legal means?

TABLE 1   Habita's open-door sessions in 2018 and 2019[a]

Year	2018	2019	Total
All cases total	192	84	276
Women	155	64	219
Couples	8	3	11
Men	29	17	46
Housing problem			
Occupation in public housing	76	22	98
Problems with public housing	27	5	32
Problems with private rental housing	75	45	120
Demolition of home	4	2	6
Sleeping rough	9	4	13
Mortgage default		2	2
Other	4	3	7
National origin			
Portugal	93	65	158
Angola	4	1	5
Brazil	3	4	7
São Tomé	1	1	2
Cape Verde	3	4	7
Other EU countries	3	4	7
Guinea-Bissau	7	2	9
Syria	0	1	1

a   The significant reduction in the number of cases from 2018 to 2019 is because in addition to the open-door sessions, Habita opted to organise "Resistance Assemblies", in which cases are discussed collectively with the participation of Habita members and people affected. While this has increased the participation of people affected, it has made it more challenging to gather data on each specific case

TABLE 1   Habita's open-door sessions in 2018 and 2019 (*cont.*)

Year	2018	2019	Total
Ethnicity			
Afro-descendant	28	15	43
Roma	17	6	23
Migrant	10	4	14
White	68	55	123
Employment Status			
Employed	59	36	95
Unemployed	43	30	73
Informal job	14	8	22
Retired	3	8	11

In exploring these dynamics, life histories allowed the specificities in the women's life conditions to be conveyed more fully, resulting in 'housing biographies.' I chose three life-history interviews in particular because these three women conveyed many central issues observed during the fieldwork, by myself as well as by the other activists at Habita. In this chapter, I present long excerpts from these interviews to be able to convey the details of their stories, as well as to do justice to their ways of storytelling. At the time of the fieldwork, the three women were living and raising their children alone, occupying a council apartment. They had all spent a significant part of their lives on the council estate of Condado, or Zona J, as they called it.

Their stories demonstrate the extreme challenges that the women face due to housing exclusion, although none of them would be considered a 'homeless person' according to the current definitions in Portugal. Through these testimonies, I do not intend to present these women as 'victims' or 'heroines' (Varley, 2013). In contrast, I argue that their conditions of precarity, being marginalised and subalternised by institutions and the neoliberal capitalist labour conditions, present the framework from which the analysis of their forms of agency can stem.

Cátia is from Mozambique, but her father is Portuguese. She is in her forties and has a ten-year-old son. She moved to Portugal with her mother and siblings when she was eight years old. She has worked as an assistant in an old

FIGURE 3.1 View of Condado, including some of its emblematic pink buildings, January 2019

people's home in Santa Casa for over 13 years. I met Cátia at the family assembly organised by Habita in 2018 and we used to talk a lot. In 2018, she was actively involved in many of Habita's actions and meetings. In June 2018, we walked together around the neighbourhood of Condado and started to count the vacant council apartments that had been closed with a steel plate. We counted 80 apartments in 24 buildings in just a few hours (Figure 3.2). After summer, Cátia gradually attended fewer of Habita's meetings, saying that she had been too tired and stressed out. In April 2019, we recorded an interview at her home. She had worked a nightshift the night before and was quite exhausted, also because she felt disillusioned and depressed with her life and future prospects.

Ema was born in São Tomé. She came to Portugal when she was six years old. In 2019, she was 29 with three children: a two-year-old son, a daughter of eight, and another son, twelve. Before meeting her, many people had spoken to me about her. For many in the neighbourhood, she seemed to embody the 'mother – fighter – occupier' spirit. The interview was recorded the second day we met, after a brief meeting the day before, when Cátia and I ran into her, and Cátia introduced us. We sat in the park, and Ema told me about her life.

Sara, in her thirties, is a mother of two: a ten-year-old daughter and a toddler son who is about to turn two. She has worked in clothes shops and also does gel manicures. She is white Portuguese, with Portuguese parents. I met Sara at Habita's meetings near Condado, and she agreed to an interview at her home in Marvila. We ended up talking for three hours about her life, politics in Portugal, and the difficulties in securing housing, while her son was playing nearby.

FIGURE 3.2   Council homes in Condado, some closed with a steel plate, April 2018

2   Housing Histories: Cycles of Displacement and Dispossession

2.1   *Immigrating to Portugal and Resettlements*

In the following excerpts from the interviews, Cátia, Sara and Ema speak about their childhood, adolescence, and their housing conditions during those times. Cátia and Ema also recall the process of arriving in Portugal. In this subchapter, I examine the processes that brought them to the situations in which they now find themselves.

> At that time [when I arrived in Portugal with my mother and siblings in 1978], we went to live in a pension because my father, when he came [from Mozambique to Portugal], was assigned a Red Cross apartment. It was just that my father came first, and he found another woman here, while we were waiting to come. When my mother arrived, he had to put us in a pension, and after that, we went to live with my father's godmother in São Sebastião, and we stayed there. From there, we went to the Algarve, then we returned. When my mother returned from the Algarve, she started seeing and hearing things about him and didn't want to be with my dad anymore. That was when the problems started.
>
> We stayed at a pension, and she started working. But then, many people came from Africa to Lisbon, and many had no money to pay. And what happened was that the pension caught fire. [...] So, we left and the

Civil Protection Department put us in another pension and paid for it for one month. Then the money ran out and, we had to go on the street, so we went to a park. We stayed next to Cais do Sodré square. There were lots of families living in the park. That was around 1978 or 1979. [...] Then it was the city council that got us out of there. You know Forno de Tijolo, above Intendente? Behind the square, there are steps. Behind a gate, there was a string of sheds, like partition walls, so they made a room for each family. We spent around two to three years there. Until they gave us this [council] house here. I came with my mother and four siblings. We got an apartment with three bedrooms, a bathroom, a living room, and a kitchen. I was 12 or 13 or more.

CÁTIA, 2019

Cátia, being slightly older than the other interviewees, is able to recall the events related to the 1970s, which marked the independence of the previous Portuguese colonies. Her narrative also brings up the case of children born out of colonial encounters. Cátia was thus part of a significantly large group of immigrants in and after 1974/1975 that moved to Portugal, mainly to Lisbon, Porto and their surroundings, arriving in a context of an acute housing crisis (Bandeirinha, 2011) and provoking a considerable increase in self-built informal settlements. Most of these families were resettled, especially during the 1990s and early 2000s. Cátia's family was resettled in Zona J in the early years of the council estate.

I came here [to Portugal] with my mother when I was six. We went to live in another neighbourhood, in Charneca. The house belonged to my stepfather, but the land belonged to the city council. It was a huge house, a two-storey villa. I had a good life at the time. But the city council needed the land to build a motorway, and I think my stepfather was given a sum of money and allocated a council apartment. In the meantime, he and my mother separated, and my mother, because she had small children, was given another council apartment here in Zona J. I think it was 2001 when we came here, to this neighbourhood.

EMA, 2019

Ema came to Portugal in the early 1990s. Portugal was investing heavily in infrastructure at that time (Pereira & Pereira, 2016), including in motorways, such as the *Eixo Norte-Sul*, which crossed the neighbourhood where her stepfather lived, and the construction of social housing estates through the PER programme. Ema's family too, was resettled, as was Sara's around the same time.

2.2 *Displacement Caused by Violence at Home*

Sara and Ema's housing precarity is intimately connected to the instability in their families and the different forms of violence that resulted in the impossibility of staying in their previous homes.

> My story is very complicated. My mother moved in with my stepfather when I was 12. My sister, my brother and I stayed with our grandparents. My father was in prison, but when I was 16, he was released. My maternal grandmother died, and I went to live with my paternal grandmother, my sister and my father. But we were overcrowded there, and in the meantime, my grandmother managed to get us a council apartment. That was when they were getting rid of the shacks, so they [the city council] gave us a house here at the foot of Rock-in-Rio in Bela Vista. We got a T2. I was 16, and my sister 17. But because of my father's drug addiction problem, we couldn't have anything at home. My father didn't buy school supplies, he didn't buy the bus pass so that I could go to school. I reached 11th grade and dropped out of school. But I loved school; I always liked to study. I started to work, and my sister started to work as well. But what happened at the end of the month, when we made basic purchases like shampoo, washing powder, and hygiene products? We came home to find the bedroom door broken down, and we had nothing. In other words, it became absolutely unsustainable to live with such a person.
>
> When I turned 18 and met my daughter's father, that was a way to leave the house. At first, it went quite well, but from time to time I got annoyed with him and went to my father's house, and then came back because I couldn't be there either. I had always dreamt of becoming a mother – of being that person for someone because I never had that – and I got pregnant. So that's when things got complicated. I think he kind of thought, "Now I really have you on my hands. You were already going to your father's house, but you came back because you couldn't stay there. And now you're pregnant." That's when domestic violence started. It was mostly psychological, but also grabbing, shaking, shouting, slapping every now and then. But when my daughter was born, in 2009, it was unthinkable to go back to my father's house to live with a drug addict.
>
> There was one day when I got really beaten up, when my daughter was six months old. She was in her room sleeping in the cot, but I thought, "What if she was already walking? And already speaking? What if she already understood things?" She would have seen her mother getting beaten up. And that would be the worst thing. So it was at that moment that I really decided it would be the last time.

Meanwhile, I used to go to these meetings. It was the APF, the Apoio aos Pais e às Familias (Support for Parents and Families). So there were groups of mothers, with their children, who had been young mothers, and each had their own story. I met a girl there, and we rented the house. That's when my eviction adventure began.

SARA, 2019

Sara's early childhood was also tied to resettlement programmes, although she herself had already spent her childhood in council housing. However, for Sara and her sister, the new apartment did not provide the children with the experience of a safe home. Sara and her sister were not 'houseless' but experienced 'insecure housing' (FEANTSA, 2017), an 'unhomely home' (Blunt & Dowling, 2006) that was produced by domestic violence. This also contributed to children's homelessness, both in the case of Sara's daughter as well as of herself and her sister.

In 2006, I had the baby, and my mother thought that I had no right to be in her house. Because we Africans are a little bit complicated, too. My mother didn't like the fact that he was Guinean, and that we made this mixture. Guineans and São Toméans don't get along.

My mother told me to leave the house. At that time, I made my first application [for council housing], but as I was still 16, they didn't accept it right away. I left my mother's house and found an empty storage room in one of the building blocks. I spent the entire pregnancy sleeping in a storage room. And then there was this friend of mine, who told me, "Look, Ema, there's that apartment over there. It's vacant. Maybe they won't bother you."

EMA, 2019

Quite suddenly, Ema found herself living in grossly 'inadequate housing' (FEANTSA, 2017). While her story differs significantly from Sara's, they both began their displacement cycles when they began their reproductive labour: their pregnancies triggered violence at home, which also contributed to children's homelessness. They share the experience of suddenly being pregnant without a safe space to live in – a situation in which their unstable family backgrounds played a significant role, which is a factor that has been highlighted as central in contributing to women's housing exclusion (Smolen & Harrison, 2013). This made Ema 'roofless', while Sara was experiencing 'insecure' housing, an 'unhomely home' (Blunt & Dowling, 2006), resulting in displacement

FIGURE 3.3   View of Condado, April 2019. Self-built homes previously occupied these hills.

produced by domestic violence, a common cause of women's homelessness (Blunt & Dowling, 2006; Brickell, 2012; Lewinson et al., 2014). Globally, domestic violence makes the home the most dangerous place for women (and children) (UNODC, 2018). Yet readings of home are often based on understandings of family as white, nuclear and heterosexual, ignoring cases in which the home cannot be considered a safe space (Hume & Wilding, 2020). This lack of safe space has been theorised by Wardhaugh (1999), who refers to the possibility of being 'homeless at home', in the sense of having a home that lacks a sense of home, and 'home as a prison', when a woman's or a girl's life sphere is so controlled that she can hardly make her own choices.

2.3   *Housing Exclusions Due to Inaccessible Social Housing*

Cátia'a, Ema's and Sara's narratives also provide some answers as to why it is not easy for them to access any supported form of housing. In Portugal, as in many other countries, Sara, Ema and Cátia are not considered homeless and cannot thus access the support provided for homeless populations. The 'National Strategy for the Integration of the Homelessness People' (ENIPSSA 2017–2023) in Portugal defines homelessness as including only two groups of people: those sleeping rough and in emergency accommodation; and those that are in temporary shelters designated for the homeless (Government of Portugal, 2017: 3925). The municipal strategy for the homeless in Lisbon also uses the same definition (Câmara Municipal de Lisboa, 2019a). Getting access to council housing was thus their main objective. They tried to access housing in many legal ways, and sought help through different municipal institutions and services, but they were not considered eligible for support.

> I stayed [with my mother] until I was 19, then I emigrated. I went to Spain. I came back when I was 26. It wasn't working out anymore. There were already so many foreigners working there. I was also tired of being abroad, without my family. I regret having quit studying. Then I returned to my mother's house and I met my son's father and went to live with him. After I got pregnant, we quarrelled a lot and I left. I went back to my mother's place. When I went back the second time, they were already doing "desdobramentos".[1] Two of my siblings were living in my mother's house but they never did any desdobramentos. At that time, applying for council housing was a matter of luck. We were already grown up, each with our own children. In our parents' house, with the children, with the husbands, right? Then the city council took the initiative and said that it was going to do desdobramento when there were a lot of people living in a house. Some were done, others were not. They did what they wanted.
>
> CÁTIA, 2019

Cátia, Ema and Sara were all resettled when they were children. Yet, after the turn of the millennium, little new public housing has been built and funds for managing and maintaining of the public housing estates have been scarce (Carreiras, 2018). This has resulted in overcrowding being a significant problem in many of the council homes in Lisbon and Loures (Guerra, 2010; R. Silva, 2019a), as faced by Cátia, although the quantitative data on the problem tends to be largely inaccurate. The *desdobramentos*, 'splits', that Cátia refers to were part of Lisbon's housing policy until 2009, when they were suspended. In a *desdobramento*, a part of a household was allocated a new apartment due to family overcrowding. Prior to 2010, *desdobramentos* were available for some families, but in a sporadic way. Cátia's narrative shows how the criteria for *desdobramentos* have been unclear; her sense is that she has been forced to apply, but no justification has been given by the city council for the rejection of the application.

> I have been applying [for council housing] for many years, but I was never lucky. I've been to the city council services at Entrecampos. I went

---

1 A "split" of the household, in which the adult children who are living with their parents in council housing are allocated new council apartments.

there, and talked to the social assistant, but it's always the same story: it's because of the points system. But I don't see what that system is – I mean, I don't understand. How do people live if they don't work? If they have an income, they cannot have council housing. But if they don't have an income, they don't get one either. I don't know how they allocate the houses now. Here, the apartment next door was free. They only give homes to gypsies now. And the rest, what happens to them? And in the prize draw, there are too few houses.

CÁTIA, 2019

Cátia's account describes the diverse housing options available in Lisbon, but her case fails to qualify for any of these schemes. She raises an issue that has become very polemic when discussing access to council housing: the points system. In Lisbon, there were previously no clear criteria for accessing social housing.[2] The criteria for the allocation of social housing were established in 2009 through *Regulamento do Regime de Acesso à Habitação Municipal* (RRAHM, Regulation of Access to Municipal Housing Regime (Câmara Municipal de Lisboa, 2009), which includes a classification matrix for assessing the applications. This continues to be the case in Loures, where the application procedure consists of writing a letter to the mayor/city council asking for a council apartment (Interview ME9, April 2019). The applications are given points according to income, family composition, type of current housing, and disabilities that the family members might have, among other criteria. Nonetheless, the points system gives the most weight to income, resulting in a situation in which households with no income tend to receive a higher score. Single parents with jobs often complained about the lack of options for those who receive the minimum wage or slightly more. Their applications for council housing tend not to receive a high enough score because they earn 'too much'.

When Ema's first child was one year old, the city council found her in the occupied council home and gave her an eviction order.

In 2007, they found me. A Gebalis social worker came to my place: "Oh, you can't stay here occupying the house, this and that ...". I said, "Look, the

---

2   The scandal dubbed "Lisboagate" in 2008 might have triggered the process of establishing a score matrix. In "Lisboagate", it was found that some local politicians serving on the Lisbon City Council had been allocating apartments to relatives and friends in a discretionary manner since the beginning of the democratic period. This mainly concerned apartments that belonged to the "dispersed patrimony" of the municipality, scattered around the city rather than situated on the council estates (Â. Silva & Lima, 2008).

social assistant at Gebalis knew that I had been kicked out of my home, and was in a precarious situation, but nobody ever bothered to come and see if I was all right." At the time I had no papers. I always had my passport in order, but I didn't have a residence permit. So the social assistant gave me an eviction order and sent the police there. The police came and broke the door down. The baby was crying. They filed a criminal case against me, for trespassing on city council property, and the police gave me a notification saying that I had to leave the house. And I said: 'I won't leave because I have nowhere to go. If I leave, I'll be on the street. You'll have to take me by force because it isn't right to throw me out onto the street.' They said I had to go and live with my mother. How can I live with my mother if I didn't even have access to the house? It's a bit complicated. After a while, the journalists came, which is what they [the city council] fear the most: journalists. They don't want those things on television. And so I gave the interview one day, and the next day they [Gebalis] called me to cancel the eviction. They called me to visit their office, and when I went in, I saw them with my file. My first housing file. They gave me a letter saying that I should wait for a transfer to another house. They said they would resolve my situation. I made an application, I brought all the documents they asked me for, I handed in my passport, as I was waiting for the residence permit, and I handed in my son's papers. Then I went back to the occupied apartment.

       EMA, 2019

Ema's struggle for housing was further complicated by not having Portuguese nationality. This might have excluded her from some alternatives available to the Portuguese, as she suggests when mentioning her first application process. Later in the interview, Ema referred to the year 2009, when the first municipal regulation on access to council housing (RRAHM) in Lisbon was published. At that time, the city council decided that 2009 was to be considered 'year zero' in the sense that those families occupying council homes at the time would all be interviewed and subject to the points system to determine whether they could stay. All but four families were considered eligible to stay, and these four were not evicted because they were all older than 65 (interview ME4, November 2018).

Consequently, had Ema not agreed to leave, and if she had stayed in the council home she was occupying instead, she would almost certainly have been entitled to remain. Not only was she forced to leave, but she also faced criminal charges due to the occupation, a clear example of the state using its 'visible fists' (Auyero, 2010). In addition, according to the current regulation, occupiers are ineligible to apply for council housing for two years after being evicted (Câmara Municipal de Lisboa, 2013). As a result, Ema considered that the City Council and Gebalis had betrayed her, as they pressured her to leave the apartment along with false promises about receiving a council home later on. These kinds of stories were commonplace among many occupying women who sought Habita's support.

When Ema left the first occupied council home, she rented an apartment with support from Santa Casa. The Santa Casa da Misericórdia can be approached for rental assistance.[3] Lisbon's Santa Casa da Misericórdia is an institute of Catholic origin, which has the status of a public institution in the city. In the municipality of Lisbon, Santa Casa participates in the provision of many social services, including emergency shelters and housing. Yet many families considered the option of Santa Casa highly arbitrary, depending on the particular social worker and their discretion as to whether the institution could offer support to a particular resident of the municipality (Jorge et al., 2020). This was also reflected in a response I received from an assistant at the city councillor's office for housing, who told me that she had no idea under what conditions and for how long Santa Casa could provide rental assistance. The city council assistant had received the response that Santa Casa assesses cases individually, considering the specificities of each case (fieldnotes, February 2019). This vagueness concerning the available support can be interpreted as a tactic used by the institutions to put the urban poor 'in their place' (Muñoz, 2017). Yet even with Santa Casa's support, paying a marked rental prise quickly became unaffordable for Ema and she had to leave, this time for an institution for single mothers run by nuns.

> I was there for almost a year. I couldn't adapt to that. There were a lot of people. I put my children to bed at six in the evening. The children were no longer well, and my son, who had never wet the bed before, started to do that.

The living conditions at the institution did not give the possibility to have privacy and tranquillity for the children, so Ema decided to occupy again.

---

3   I tried to approach Santa Casa on various occasions for an interview, but never managed to secure a response.

2.4 *Displacement Due to Unaffordability of Private Rental Sector*

In the following section, Cátia, Sara and Ema describe the challenges they faced when trying to contest their housing exclusion and make it on their own in the private rental market.

> So, we rented a house in Camarate. The owner had gone to Oporto to live with a brother. By coincidence, she was also an African and rented the house to me. But then I was the only person who worked at home, and it was not possible to pay the rent alone. I got tired and left to stay at my mother's house. But it wasn't possible to stay there either – I also wanted to be independent.
>
> CÁTIA, 2019

> I left [the occupied apartment], and my life from then on became hell. I went to rent a house, but I couldn't keep the house, and when I say house, it's not only the house, but also the electricity, water, and food.
>
> EMA, 2019

Ema and Cátia, employed as assistants in older people's homes, illustrate workers treated as disposable but who are indispensable for the working of our societies (Bhattacharyya, 2018; Tronto, 2013). While generally considered a profession of importance, these professions are usually pushed on women, racialised, immigrant and lower-class workers, with low remuneration that does not cover living costs (Ferguson & McNally, 2015; Sassen, 2009; Tronto, 2013). These professions are both valued and devalued at present in Europe: while considered a profession of extreme importance, its valorisation does not translate into a decent salary for those undertaking the work. Their income simply does not cover all of their expenses, including housing, school, electricity, water, gas, clothes, school fees and materials, and so on.

> So, with my friend, we rented a house near Lóios. At first it went well, but then my housemate stopped paying her share. I had two jobs at the time, to pay a rent of 500 euros. I was counting the pennies so that I could pay the rent. I held on, until the time came when I couldn't pay one month, nor the next, and the following month I had to leave. I went to Cacém, to a house owned by my mother's friend, who was abroad at the time. [...] Later I found a place in Moscavide. I stayed in that house until I could no longer afford to pay. Because it was 350 euros, plus gas, water, electricity, food, transport, school. So, once again, I knew that I had to leave.
>
> SARA, 2019

Sara does not work in the care sector, but as with Ema and Cátia, her case illustrates the challenges of single mothers in a society in which care is considered a female obligation (Gilligan, 1993; A. P. de Lima, 2023). The care responsibilities make it considerably more challenging to access some better-paid jobs that demand more flexibility in terms of working hours. In addition to being exploited in wage labour, these mothers are also responsible for unpaid care labour at home, while the fathers of their children get 'passes' as (Tronto, 2013) describes the situation, meaning that social and political institutions make some to bear the care responsibilities while others are allowed to escape from them. In Portugal, 'the obligation of care and the responsibility to ensure the wellbeing of children remains a central gender marker in symbolic practices and representations in Portugal.' (Lima, 2023: 10). These gendered obligations tend to reinforce themselves in times of crisis, like under austerity when women's role as the primary welfare provider and carer inside the household re-emerged (Alves de Matos, 2021). As noted by Sara, 'Since my pregnancy until today, everything that my kids have has come from me. I had to be the mother and father because the father just says "Hello" on the street, and gives his child a kiss. "Is everything okay? All right, bye then."'

With an average rent for a 50 m^2 apartment of more than 400 euros in the Lisbon Metropolitan Area, but exceeding 13.5€/m^2 in some parishes in the city for new rental contracts (INE, 2019), paying them clearly falls out of reach of families that earn a national minimum of wage, which was 600 euros in 2019 (PORDATA, 2019c). Such forms of housing exclusion can be interpreted as examples of the reproduction of urban poverty and the exploitation of low-wage women workers (Cho, 2003; Mohanty, 1991). To secure a living for themselves and their children, the women had few options other than to 'carry on', being forced into a constant situation of trying to make ends meet, a situation which Alves de Matos (2021: 1004) portrays as the extraction of women's bodily resources: 'women's bodies became a privileged site with and through which a broader reconfiguration of capital and labour relations was implemented.' As Cátia explains:

> Life is so … one does not have time, one works so, so, so much. I don't know when we'll have time to live. You reach old age, you're already sick, you have no patience for anything. In Portugal, we will work until we're 60 or so, with a miserable paycheck. Then, we're going to retire, with a miserable pension; we're sick … So, what do we do with our lives? Nothing, just work. To eat, to pay bills. Isn't that so? What a miserable life. So much fighting, so much struggling. For what?

Ema talks about the situation in very similar terms:

> It's a daily fight. There comes a point where the person gets overwhelmed.
> You can't be angry. And then people wonder why people commit suicide.
> There comes a time when one gets fed up, even with life. Ah, if it wasn't
> for my children, I don't know. When I look at them, it's like laughing a
> little, because it's always the same thing, it's the misery, and the difficulty.
> It takes a lot of willpower.

It can thus be affirmed that, at least in these women's lives, the end of austerity
politics has not made much difference.

2.5   *Evictions Causing Further Dispossession*

Sara has already faced forced eviction, a 'domicide' – a deliberate destruction
of the home (Porteous & Smith, 2001) – several times. In the first case, after
leaving a private rental apartment due to rent arrears, she had occupied an
apartment in Zona J and had stayed there for two months, and then she and the
baby were evicted by the police. She rented a basement room and stayed there
for a while until she could not afford it anymore. By that time, Sara's father was
off the drugs, and Sara decided to move in with him again in the council home.
But the father did not pay the council rent – and did not tell Sara about it – and
one day, she received a call saying the city council was evicting them.

> It was the most complicated situation at that time because I can say
> that I was truly homeless. I left my daughter at her father's place. All the
> stuff from the house had gone to Gebalis's warehouse, and I said, 'And
> now? Where am I going?'. So, I spent one night at one friend's house, then
> another night at another friend's house, until, you know, It is nice to visit
> for the first two or three days. So, my father was sleeping in the house
> from which we'd been evicted. It was on the ground floor and the win-
> dow had been left open. So, at night, he lifted the blinds and went there
> to sleep, and I started doing the same. We'd been evicted from our house,
> and we started using the house like intruders.

She was houseless, living in an 'inadequate housing', and she decided to occupy
again, this time a ruined council home. She put a floor, windows, and toilets in
the apartment, but one year later, experienced again a domicide: 'Gebalis and
the municipal police went there one year later, and took all my stuff and put
it in the street, and broke the toilets, the windows, everything, in front of the
kids.'

Ema has also occupied and been evicted several times. As she recalls,

FIGURE 3.4 Domicide, after the eviction. November 2018

I occupied an apartment again, you see those over there [pointing], those ruined ones. It had no door, no window, no floor, and there was no toilet. I settled in there little by little. I put a floor in, windows, toilets. The house turned out fine – a place that we could live in. But Gebalis and the municipal police went there one year later and took all my stuff and put it in the street, and broke the toilets, the windows, everything, in front of the kids.

Despite the odds, Cátia, Ema and Sara tried to break the cycle of exclusion and exploitation. They began to question their subalternised condition – the 'contract' (Das, 1989) that their families and society had made with them – subject to the will of others and denied access to their rights, and embarked on a quest for a home of their own by occupation. Contrary to the arguments of the city council, which present the unauthorised occupations as an attentat against the norms and regulations, Sara, Ema and Cátia consider the occupied apartment their last option, the ultimate place of survival, as Sara described:

My only option was to occupy another house because otherwise I really wouldn't have made it. I had already spent many years moving from one place to another. My daughter will soon be ten and I've lived in about nine or ten different houses since she was born. So, this is the only place, my last chance. After this, there is nothing else.

Ema describes her situation in very similar terms:

I think this is not right. I think that any human being has the right to housing. If I didn't have children, I'll be honest, I wouldn't be here occupying city council housing. I wouldn't. I would rather rent an apartment, and have more expenses, of course, but not have this headache. I always go to sleep worrying about them coming here and saying 'Get out'!

Lisbon City Council has not held back from directly causing homelessness and dispossession, evicting mothers and care workers with their small children from their places of survival, causing a domicide. Sara, Ema and Cátia have cared for the council dwellings and renovated and inhabited them, but nevertheless they are put on the street. These evictions are a clear violation of international law that prohibits forced evictions, highlighting that they can be permitted only 'after all feasible alternatives to eviction are explored with the affected person or community' and 'after due process protections are provided to the individual, group or community,' including the provision of adequate alternative housing (AGFE & UN-HABITAT, 2011; UN-HABITAT & OHCHR,

2014b). In fact, after the Habita Association denounced an eviction case to the Committee for Economic, Social and Cultural Rights (CESC), Lisbon City Council received a communication from the CESC requesting it to suspend one of these evictions or alternatively, to provide the family with an alternative housing appropriate to their needs, 'in the framework of genuine and effective consultation' (Habita, 2022).

The evictions result in many cases in the loss of all the material assets owned by the evicted family, including all the investments they had made to create comfortable conditions in their places of survival. Inevitably, an eviction causes irreparable damage to the whole organisation of the family life. Many times, forcing women to skip work – and to face the consequences of this: salary cuts or even being fired, making it impossible for the children to go to school or to kindergarten, not even to mention the destabilisation of all the support networks the women might have had within the neighbourhood. The scarcity of housing resources cannot be a justification for the state to directly cause homelessness (UN-HABITAT & OHCHR, 2014b) as displacement exacerbates the already dire conditions that families face.

Furthermore, not knowing whether they will be able to provide a home for their children causes anxiety and distress, which is in line with previous research identifying the adverse consequences of evictions, not only in material terms but also in terms of mental well-being (Desmond & Kimbro, 2015; Lewinson et al., 2014). Moreover, the fear of losing custody of their children is an additional institutional violence inflicted on these mothers. It is consistent with institutional traditions in many countries that have often sought to responsibilise poor mothers for their conditions and to 'educate' them (Bullock et al., 2020; S. Motta, 2016; Murphy, 2020). It is difficult to estimate how often children are institutionalised because of the homelessness of their parents. In 2016, Portugal was condemned for this by the European Court of Human Rights, which stated that children cannot be taken away from their parents because of the socio-economic situation of the family. Yet, according to Habita and the women I interviewed, this decision has not changed the practices of institutionalisation, and mothers who are occupying or are homeless still risk losing custody of their children. During my fieldwork, I talked to two mothers who had been forced to hand over their children to institutions because of their homelessness. For Ema, this was also a very concrete fear:

> They will say 'Get out', and then you can't afford to rent a house. And then, what are you going to do? I've seen many such situations. Losing the house means the mother is in no condition to be with the children. They end up taking the kids away, and the kids are forced to go to an institution

because you don't have the money to rent a house. This is often the case. It's sad, but it's the reality.

Consequently, these women fear social workers and the police and end up fighting against the institutions that are supposed to support them and their families.

3 To Conclude

In this chapter, I have demonstrated how understanding the conditions that poor urban dwellers live in is fundamental to enabling an analysis of their agency. Labour precarity, inaccessible housing, and the production of housing insecurity through evictions can be conceived of as mechanisms of marginalisation or 'subalternisation', in which the subject is excluded from rights they should be entitled to and is persuaded to accept their exclusion. The subalternisation of these women appears as processes of collective social negotiation (Spivak, 2005) with the wider society, in which the women are persuaded to accept their housing exclusion and to agree to stay on the other side of the 'abyssal line' in terms of access to their rights (B. de S. Santos, 2014).

Building upon Das (1989), Das & Randeria (2015), Soederberg (2021) and Spivak (2005), I have advanced the argument that the production of housing insecurity is one form of subalternisation, through which the urban poor are marginalised, excluded from their rights, and persuaded to accept their exclusion. The forms of subalternisation present in Cátia's, Ema's and Sara's stories are strongly gendered. The displacement cycles that Ema, Sara and Cátia continued to endure were all initiated by having their first babies, which triggered violence at home, rejection by the rest of the family members, or simply pinpointed the lack of adequate space they had for themselves and their children. After that, during the following twenty years, the cycle of displacement has implied various forms of housing exclusion and homelessness, ranging from roofless to houseless, insecure and inadequate housing, always due to reasons typically associated with women's homelessness: domestic violence, poverty, and rent arrears. Facing specific challenges due to being a mother without having a home of their own and being made solely responsible for providing for the needs of their children strongly conditions their room for manoeuvre.

The economic exclusion faced by Cátia, Ema and Sara is tied to their condition as 'disposable but indispensable' workers (Bhattacharyya, 2018) – one that disproportionally affects women, racialised persons, and migrants – in the kind of wage labour that is not secure nor sufficient to earn a salary that would provide for their basic needs. These women exemplify the conditions faced by a care worker, both in paid and unpaid labour, as in addition to – in the cases of Cátia and Ema – providing care in the market, they alone are responsible for the provision of care at their homes, while the father of their children has opted for not getting involved. The fact that these three women were made solely responsible for providing for the needs of their children strongly conditions their room for manoeuvre, as it makes it more challenging to access better-paid jobs that demand more flexibility in terms of working hours. Considering the heavy economic burden they also bear as the sole providers in their families, it can be clearly seen how they are exploited for the reproduction of the displaced low-wage worker (Soederberg, 2021), both as wage labourers as well as for the reproduction of the labour force (Federici, 2004). Similarly, the lack of attention to practices of care and the labour it involves is arguably a political choice resulting from the gendered, classed, and racialised nature of care work. Yet, as Tronto (2013: 97) argues, 'as long as care continues to shape differently the capacities of citizens to be citizens, there can be no genuine equality among citizens in their capacity to exercise political rights.' The income women receive from their waged labour does not permit them to acquire a safe and adequate home for themselves and their children through the private market, in the context in which urban policies consider housing and real estate mainly as means to gain wealth and economic growth, instead of contemplating them as a home and a human right. Not regulating the private rental sector is a political choice that relates to the consideration of the real estate sector as fundamental for the economic growth in Portugal. In this sense, it can be argued that housing precarity is actively produced by the state (Soederberg, 2017) as political decisions have prioritised housing privatisation and commercialisation over the production of social housing, producing homelessness through eviction instead of letting families stay put in their places of survival, as well as invisibilising the phenomenon of homelessness by not collecting data on gendered forms of homelessness.

Their ways of facing housing exclusion are also strongly related to gender and their situation as single mothers. Instead of staying on the streets, they have tried to seek various forms of informal support (Bretherton, 2017). For this reason, for most of their lives, they have been living in either 'insecure' or 'inadequate' housing (FEANTSA, 2017). The women consider that their homelessness has frequently been misrecognised by the institutions, which can essentially be due to the restrictive definitions of homelessness (Bretherton, 2017). The available housing policies failed to address the specific needs of the women and, similarly, the policies for the homeless did not encompass them. This draws attention to the importance of considering the categories of inadequate and insecure housing when analysing homelessness. At a minimum, these mothers should be regarded as persons experiencing homelessness, which would result in higher scores in their applications for social housing and in their inclusion in the policies designated for the homeless.

This chapter also reveals the volatility and unpredictability that pervade the circumstances of the occupying families. It can be argued that housing precarity limits the spheres of possible action, which produces not only informality but also transgressive, albeit fragmented agency, characteristic of this form of makeshift urbanism. In line with this notion, these women have tried to reinvent themselves and continue with their lives. Similarly to many other families, Sara, Ema, and Cátia have not succeeded in gaining access to housing in legal ways and have consequently taken the decision to occupy a council apartment when they identify a vacant one. This is not a decision they take lightly, but only when they do not see any other alternatives on the horizon. For them, the time it takes for the Lisbon city council to 'allocate them a dwelling is simply incompatible with the time it takes for the children to grow up' (Letter to the Lisbon City Council by Habita and a group of women who occupy, 2018). These dynamics will be further explored in Chapter 4, which focuses on the governance of council housing estates.

Governing Access to Housing and Evictions

1 Governing against and through Informality

This chapter will complement the previous one by shifting the attention to the management practices of social housing neighbourhoods. The specific case of the management of occupations and evictions will be a key concern of this chapter, in line with the focus of this study. The experiences of the previous land occupations and their demolitions – resulting in the resettlement of residents of these neighbourhoods – will be compared with the current forms of the management of occupations and evictions. I will duly discuss the kinds of interactions and dynamics that have occurred over the years between the state actors and residents of social housing estates by analysing these processes and pinpointing the continuities in the management approaches.

These questions will be approached by examining the forms of governance and the citizens' participation in these processes. Governance forms significantly contribute to shaping the positions of residents living in socially segregated cities (Nygren, 2016). In the case of the LMA, the analysis of the practices and perceptions of the managers of social housing estates and officials of city council departments in charge of housing reveals central facets of how council estates and evictions within them are managed. Many actors can be involved with the management of social housing and with the execution of evictions, from managers of council housing estates and city council officials to the police, social workers, private landlords, representatives of extra-judicial eviction mechanisms such as *Balcão Nacional do Arrendamento* in Portugal, banks, real estate funds and companies, and paramilitary agents.

Yet few studies focus on the actions, practices, and experiences of the managers of council housing and evictions from such housing. However, their role is crucial in determining who is entitled to housing and how evictions are carried out. The personal biases and the everyday routines of the work of council housing managers and other municipal employees can significantly contribute to further exclusions and alienations (Baker, 2017; Bullock et al., 2020; S. Motta, 2016; Pozzi & Rimoldi, 2017; Wilde, 2020).

Informality, as conceptualised by Ananya Roy (2003, 2009a), emerges as a key concept in this chapter, conceived as a feature that also operates inside the state, with the state itself operating in many instances in informal ways. In this way, informality can also be considered a modality of governance (Roy, 2015). In her later work, Roy (2009b: 84) rejects the association of informality with extra-legality, proposing instead that the formal and the legal are better understood as fictions, as 'moments of fixture' within the urban planning systems, thereby questioning dualisms that are often present when applying the concept (Acuto et al., 2019). Nonetheless, Roy (2009b: 84) continues to argue that it is precisely the convergence of legality and extra-legality in the same process that makes informality so powerful as a modality of governance.

Yet the formal and legal realms continue to be defined in legislation and regulations (AGFE & UN-HABITAT, 2007, 2011; Bhan, 2013; COHRE, 2010). For this reason, and to avoid rendering the conceptualisation of informality hollow, I find it essential to retain the position that informality also implies extra-legal practices, even if the borders between formal and informal are blurred (McFarlane, 2019). Both the urban poor and the state actors challenge and recreate the margins of legality and formality, albeit by different means and by different degrees of power.

This notion is a thought-provoking point of departure that can be applied to analyse both the modalities of governance and the tactics that subalternised urban dwellers engage in. It illustrates how both state actors and occupiers engage in some actions that are characterised by informality, and how both of these groups of actors try to assert the legitimacy and value of their actions and condemn and criminalise the actions that affirm the contrary. It can also be used to examine moral economies with regard to how diverse actors seek to contest the distribution of wealth (Simone, 2019a).

On the other hand, there is a fascinating body of literature that illustrates how the state itself often engages in extra-legal and illegal practices at times of eviction (Auyero, 2010; Desmond, 2016; Soederberg, 2019; Zhang, 2017), including reports by international organisations (AGFE & UN-HABITAT, 2007, 2011; COHRE, 2010) that highlight the brutal impact that this kind of state action inflicts upon families. Here, the state action has been described as 'domicide', the deliberate destruction of homes (Porteous & Smith, 2001).

I will link to this schematisation dominant forms of governance of the urban poor, such as 'invisible elbows' and 'visible fists', as theorised by Auyero (2010), arguing that these forms of governance are used to make the urban poor more docile in acceptance of their subordination. In line with arguments by Auyero (2010), the first form describes the process whereby poor people try to access the state services but end up being obliged to wait, quietly and patiently, for the state to deliver on its promises, while 'visible fists' refers to the state violence during the actual process of eviction.

In this study, I demonstrate how the state agents present a discourse of respecting the law, while their actions are often characterised by illegality. They speak about 'justice' but tend to interpret justice as following the procedures and municipal regulations. I demonstrate how the prevalent governance strategies of occupations and evictions in these housing estates rely primarily on tactics of imputing the responsibility of the housing condition of low-income residents to other state actors, to the residents themselves, as well as to macroeconomic processes. Here, it is interesting to explore how these marginalisations and exclusions are actively produced by different actors (Nygren, 2016, 2018).

Moreover, this chapter focuses on forms of participation in housing governance. To use Faranak Miraftab's (2009: 38–9) classification, the understanding of citizen participation typically encompasses the 'invited spaces of participation' – those legitimated by the government – and excludes 'invented spaces', defined as the collective action by the poor to confront the authorities and the status quo. Following this line of thought, it can be argued that participation in 'invented spaces' is of utmost importance because it enables the participation of groups of populations that would otherwise be excluded from democratic deliberation.

This chapter argues that occupations can be conceived of as an implicit rejection of invited forms of participation and a transgression to participation by invention and invasion, in a context where the urban poor are effectively excluded from these invited spaces. I will argue that the officials of city councils generally cherish participation, but at the same time, prefer that the forms of participation be confined to established, invited initiatives (Miraftab, 2009), showing little understanding towards more transgressive forms of participation. Yet the actual institutionalised forms of participation in Lisbon and Loures offer few possibilities to participate in the governance of housing issues, as I will demonstrate in this chapter. As in the previous chapter, the main focus will be on the parish of Marvila, Lisbon, but experiences from Quinta da Fonte, Loures, will also be presented to shed light on different approaches adopted in different municipalities.

2   Managing Resettlements: Participation in Older Housing Operations

The social housing estates that the study focuses on – Condado and Quinta da Fonte – were built in the LMA from the 1960s to the 1990s to resettle dwellers of informal neighbourhoods through different resettlement programmes. These culminated in the PIMP (*Programa de Intervenção a Médio Prazo*, Middle-Term Intervention Programme) and the PER (*Programa Especial de Realojamento*, Special Resettlement Programme) programmes, which focused on the resettlement of residents of informal settlements into social housing estates. The first programme only targeted the municipality of Lisbon and was implemented from 1987 to the end of the 1990s, while the second targeted the Lisbon and Porto Metropolitan Areas from 1993 onwards (Antunes, 2018; (R. Á. Cachado, 2012). The PIMP was mainly focused on resettling the residents of informal settlements in those urban areas where major infrastructure works were planned, such as the CRIL and *Eixo Norte-Sul* highways (C. Rodrigues, 2012), as well as resettling the residents of provisory homes built from 1937 onwards (ME4, Lisbon, 2018).

The PER, on the other hand, had the explicit aim of eradicating the slums in the metropolitan areas of Lisbon and Oporto, with a total of 48,000 housing units for resettled families foreseen within the programme (Vilaça & Ferreira, 2018). Priority was sometimes given to slum areas for which major infrastructure plans existed, such as the CRIL and Expo '98, and the Lisbon World Exposition (ME9, Loures, 2019).

In Lisbon, the resettlements were mainly implemented in areas of the city considered less central and less 'noble' (Serpa et al., 2018). The resettlement during the PER was conducted at speed, with 3,500 families sometimes resettled in a month, with a total of almost 18,000 families being resettled during the programme in Lisbon (ME2, Lisbon). The eradication of informal settlements was a priority for the then city councillor for housing, and the resettlement of almost 18,000 families over 15 years of the PER programme was hailed as a major success factor by an official of the Lisbon City Council (ME2, 2018). Information sessions were held for those families who were to be resettled, but they were not consulted regarding their views or needs (interview with Miriam, 2018). Rather, a lack of consultation was considered a precondition for concluding the resettlements in order to respect the deadlines:

> The residents were confronted with the need to leave the neighbourhood, and there was no consultation, no participation related to the expectations about the house, the neighbourhood, the localisation. [...] But there was some kind of participation because, before the resettlement, we convened meetings in which the residents learnt of important information about their new rights and obligations as residents of council dwellings. So the municipal services went there to inform people. [...] So real social

intervention was not promoted because the funding and the deadlines demanded a certain rhythm.
ME2, Lisbon, 2018

Some other municipal employees presented more critical views about the way resettlements were conducted, pointing out that the families were not at liberty to choose where they would live (ME6 & ME7, Lisbon, 2018). 'When the slums were eradicated, a series of neighbourhoods were built. When the resettlement was completed, the city was not thought through, and the people were just arranged on shelves. There was no information, no education. Therefore, the cycles of poverty continued' (ME8, Lisbon, 2019).

Similarly, in Loures, the pressure to clear the land sometimes led to resettlement projects being implemented in a hurry:

> Yes, the only thing I can say is that if [resettlement] was difficult for the families, for us [the municipal officials] it was very complicated because of the pressure. Just to give you an idea, on a Saturday we were in the field telling families in one area that X number of residents had to be resettled by the following week. We knew they had to leave, but the families themselves didn't know whether they had to leave from one day to the next. It meant going there and saying: you know, you need to leave tomorrow for your new home.
>
> ME10, Loures, 2019

The need to act quickly made it impossible to prepare the residents of the informal neighbourhoods for resettlement or to consider their life situations. For example, the Quinta da Serra neighbourhood was cleared to make way for the construction of access to the highway and due to time pressure, the municipality of Loures ended up acquiring apartment blocks in Quinta da Fonte that had been built by a housing cooperative previously. This resulted in the resettlement of families from a central area in the LMA, the parish of Prior Velho, to the rural parish of Apelação. This caused the families much distress, forcing them not only to move far away from workplaces and schools but also to leave behind the vegetable gardens that had contributed significantly to their livelihood (ME9, Loures, 2019). A Loures official argued that considerable violence had been inflicted upon the families by just 'dumping' them in a social housing estate without any respect for their social organisation (ME1, Loures, 2018). Only one of the employees expressed strong concern about the low degree of participation and lack of support for the resettled families, even if several employees acknowledged that it contributed to further marginalisation and the perpetuation of socioeconomic inequalities.

Most of the municipal employees referred to the lack of effective participation as something inevitable, justified by the significant interest in having a highway built or by the municipality prioritising the eradication of the informal settlements. These processes had deadlines, and therefore it was considered unviable to involve the families in their design. The process of accumulation by dispossession advanced without due consideration of those displaced. This resulted in spatial segregation and sometimes also in a deepening of social exclusion (Secretaria de Estado da Habitação, 2017), possibly producing 'multiple marginalisations' (Wayessa & Nygren, 2016).

The municipal employees explained how, after the resettlement process, they tried to give the residents of the council estates the support that had not been given during the resettlement itself. The residents of the new council estate could visit the municipal employees in a structure at one end of the neighbourhood to receive advice and information, and to simply chat. In several interviews (ME9, ME10, ME11, Loures, 2019), the municipal employees highlighted how it had been necessary to train the residents to live in council housing. Afterwards, the municipality also started to organise meetings with the residents, electing a resident representative for each building, who then helped the city council to keep track of developments in the building. This work, however, was later discarded due to changes in the internal structure of the municipality that reduced the staff drastically (ME10, Loures, 2019).

The new council estate residents were perceived as in need of training when it came to the skills required to live in an apartment: they had to be 'educated' to take responsibility for their neighbourhood (Wilde, 2020), but their opinion was not considered of interest in the sense of how to organise life on the new council estates. These 'invited' (Miraftab, 2004) forms of participation in place before, during and after can be conceptualised as a validation of council plans rather than substantial participation. The residents of informal settlements who were to be resettled only received information on the processes already been planned and decided upon. Some of the municipal employees recognised the problems inherent in implementing the resettlements. Still, at the same time, many seemed to consider that the results justified the means, arguing that the living conditions of the resettled families improved significantly (ME7, Lisbon, 2018), and paying less attention to the dispossession and marginalisations caused by the displacements, prioritising the urban development objectives.

The municipal employees framed effective participation in governance as an ideal, but the lack of it was justified by an argument that frames this kind of participation as incompatible with the actual management procedures and the speed needed to conclude the resettlements, prioritising the need to promote local development and growth, in line with the ideals of 'urban entrepreneurialism' (Harvey, 2003). This idea constitutes an essential backdrop to current participatory initiatives explored in the following subchapter.

3 Invited Spaces of Participation: Current Co-governance of the Council Estates

Lisbon City Council profiles itself as a municipality that promotes citizen participation, inviting citizens to public meetings to comment on plans and proposals and to submit proposals for the participatory budget (Câmara Municipal de Lisboa, 2020). The city councillor for housing considered it ideal that all of the processes would be participatory, pointing out that this leads to co-responsibility: all of the actors will be bound by the decisions taken together (personal communication, 17 January 2018). In relation to housing issues, Lisbon City Council's participatory model originates from the times when architect and politician Helena Roseta was the city councillor for housing, from 2007 to 2013.

The participatory initiatives were designed as a part of the Local Housing Strategy for Lisbon, approved in 2010. The Local Housing Strategy included the BIP/ZIP (*Bairros e Zonas de Intervenção Prioritária de Lisboa*) initiative, in which 'priority intervention' zones and neighbourhoods were identified (Câmara Municipal de Lisboa, 2010). Some of the priority intervention neighbourhoods have GABIPs, structures for local administration and coordination that have as their objective the development of co-governance processes in those neighbourhoods (Câmara Municipal de Lisboa, 2016). All of the GABIPs work in different ways, depending on their participants and their agenda (personal communication, Lisbon City Council official, 1 February 2018). Yet they are only constituted for specific purposes, after which they cease to exist, meaning that they do not constitute a permanent structure of participation. In addition, the issues to be discussed in the GABIPs are pre-selected by the city council, allowing the residents to decide only 'on minor issues' (personal communication, official of Lisbon City Council, 1 February 2018).

Many council housing estates, which tend to belong to the 'priority intervention neighbourhoods', also have *grupos comunitários*, community groups. They are not a formal structure – they are not mentioned on the website of the city council – and they have different dynamics depending on the neighbourhood (ME6, Lisbon, 2018). Their objective is to 'work together for the community, preferably with the presence of the residents because they have an awareness of the principal problems in the neighbourhoods and can participate in the actions that are planned and developed' (ME7, Lisbon, 2018). However, the principal problem with both the GABIPs and the community groups is that they are managed from the top and, as pointed out by a representative of a neighbourhood project in Marvila (NGO6, 2018), the residents themselves do not tend to participate in the community groups. In the opinion of some residents, information about the upcoming meetings is not shared with adequate notice, which results in poor participation by residents who are not part of an organisation that belongs to the community group.

I participated in three monthly meetings of one of the community groups in Marvila and noted that the meetings were dominated by institutional actors. They were chaired by the representative of Gebalis, and other participants included Santa Casa da Misericórdia, parish council representatives, religious entities (*Centro Paroquial*), *Instituto Apoio à Criança* (Institute of Support for Children), associations/NGOs and residents' associations. It can be assumed that the top-down management structures and population of the groups with institutional representatives restrict, or even eliminate, democratic self-management participation by the residents.

Some of the participatory initiatives that are in place in Lisbon also exist in the municipality of Loures. The residents of the municipality can participate in the public meetings of the city council and make a short intervention via pre-registration. The City Council organises community groups and information sessions on the Loures council estates. Quinta da Fonte also had a community group, but it received criticism from the residents of the council estate similar to that delivered in Lisbon: most of the participating entities were municipal institutions, and the meetings of the group were organised during working hours, which made it difficult for residents to participate (author's field notes, 13 April 2019).

On the other hand, when the residents' association organises a meeting and invites the municipality, the municipality's representatives seldom show up. This is often justified by office hours: while the residents' meetings are organised after working hours or during the weekend, the municipal employees prefer not to participate in meetings outside their office hours (fieldnotes, 13 April 2019).

There were hopes that the funding related to the new government housing strategy NGPH (Secretaria de Estado da Habitação, 2017), which allocated financing for the Strategic Urban Development Plans, would enable the financing of different kinds of social initiatives in Quinta da Fonte (ME11, Loures, 2019). Yet even these processes aroused suspicion from associations working in the neighbourhood, in the sense of being interpreted as only a tentative move to 'legitimate' (Neveu, 2011) the city council initiatives:

> The City Council, together with IHRU,[1] the Social Security Office, Health Centre, Parish Council and Employment Office, are working together to elaborate an integrated plan for the neighbourhood. But they do not involve the associations that work in the neighbourhood. [...] I'm disappointed. I think that [again] the City Council wants to decide everything, and all the projects have to come under its name. They want everything to happen within the community group, but almost all of the entities in the community group are from the City Council.
>
> Personal communication, NGO worker, 23 January 2019

During my fieldwork, interaction with the residents of Quinta da Fonte and the local politicians and municipal employees increased because of the renovation work that was due to begin on the council estate (Câmara Municipal de Loures, 2018). The city council began to organise information sessions for the residents, emphasising that in addition to renovating the buildings, the city council wanted to 'renovate the neighbourhood socially; the economy, social sector and culture, and make the people feel responsibility for their homes' (author's field notes, 4 July 2018).

In addition, the residents of the neighbourhoods were invited to take responsibility for the organisation and cleanliness of the estate:

> We try to work with the people so that they would organise themselves; not just keep things in good shape, but also clean up.[...] we don't have any regulation on that, we just know that people need to collaborate, and they also know that. So, this is where the call for participation starts. However, we don't only want participation, we also want a commitment to building up specific solutions, which we can only do with the people.
>
> ME5, Lisbon, 2018

Rather than 'participation', this view can be characterised as 'self-responsibilisation' (Nygren, 2016; Wilde, 2020): the municipal employees

---

1 Instituto da Habitação e Reabilitação Urbana, the central state institution responsible for housing and urban renovation.

considered that the council estate residents had the responsibility to 'collaborate' in the maintenance of the council estate and, what is more, to be committed to that collaboration. Bullock et al. (2020) categorise this kind of process as 'disciplining', in the sense of transmitting middle-class values and notions of 'proper' behaviour to the council housing residents.

The invited spaces of participation in housing issues, in both Lisbon and Loures, duly fell short of providing spaces of effective participation: in fact, they could be characterised as a legitimisation of council policies, disciplining, or self-responsibilisation instead. In Lisbon, participation structures existed, but the problem was their quality in terms of participation. In Loures, the possibilities to participate could be considered almost non-existent. An additional problem concerned who actually participated in these initiatives: community groups that are dominated by institutional representatives clearly do not promote 'citizen power' (Arnstein, 1969).

4   Managing Council Estates: Invisible Elbows, Competition and Visible Fists

Compared with the mixed views on the management of the resettlements, the municipal employees seem to share a critical view of the actual state of management, in the sense that there is wide recognition of current problems. Nonetheless, the reasons given to explain existing problems tend to vary. One of the enduring challenges has been the management of access to council homes, as well as the issue of keeping records on the current occupancy status of the council homes. Why are there so many vacant council homes in Lisbon? The municipal employees (author's interviews) gave four main explanations for the phenomenon. Their responses, juxtaposed with the interviews of council housing residents, illustrate the array of techniques of governance used in the council neighbourhoods.

4.1   *Invisible Elbows: Faulty Management Intersecting with Social Biases*
Many interviewees indicated management problems as a significant reason for the existence of vacant council dwellings. The managers duly argued that it was difficult to keep all the records updated, and when vacant apartments were identified, the bureaucracy to be able to reallocate them was excessive. The attribution process for vacant apartments is complex and takes plenty of time.

FIGURE 4.1 A council home closed with a steel plate and an alarm, Condado. April 2019

> We can't just look at an apartment and verify that nobody is there, set about changing the lock, and say: now the apartment is back with the city council, and we can allocate it to another family. No! We need to know where the lessee is, where the family members are, what happened. And if there are personal belongings in the apartment, we can't legally just break in.
>
> ME6, Lisbon, 2018

Managers also argued that the council estate residents do not fulfil their reporting obligations. They complained that the municipal tenants do not inform the city council about changes in their family composition or income levels, and do not submit the required documentation (such as information about income tax) on time, although this is a formal requirement of the current legislation on social housing, the LAA (ME5, Lisbon, 2018). They also mentioned a mismatch between available homes and the families that live in them (ME4, Lisbon, 2018). This makes it impossible, they argued, to follow up on which kind of families were living in which apartments.

> This question of failing to update [us] about changes in the family composition is very complicated. For Gebalis and us, [it is important] so that we can know how many apartments are overcrowded and, on the other hand, how many are too big considering the family size. There are cases where the children have already left home, and there is now a couple or a lady living alone in a T4 (an apartment with four bedrooms).
>
> ME8, Lisbon, 2019

Indeed, many of my interviewees spoke about the overcrowding. They mentioned living in a social housing apartment with 10 or more people, and contrarily, larger council housing inhabited only by one person after the decease or moving out of other family members.

Many council estate residents were not convinced by the arguments put forward by council housing managers.

> I think they [the managers] are not doing their job properly, because how is it possible to have an apartment locked for seven, eight years, and say that there are no available apartments? I've been applying for council housing for 15 years and I'm still waiting. This apartment had been empty for two years, and I know of many other apartments that are vacant. How can they not know that the apartments are vacant?
>
> Interview with MARIA, 2018

They argue that if the managers really wanted to update their registers, it should be possible and that the neglectful management resulted in many other problems:

> There are so many people who need housing, but they [the city council] leave the apartments vacant. Then there are problems with domestic violence and the women have nowhere to go. In my apartment block, there are two vacant apartments. One resident passed away, Gebalis put a metal sheet across the door, and left the apartment like that.
>
> Author's fieldnotes, 15/03/2019

Many associations tended to align with what the council estate residents said:

> One member of parliament asked me what I thought about the problems that existed in social housing. I said, OK, they can be summed up in two words: poor management. The problems that occur there stem from bad management. And, of course, they're linked to the political use of this kind of housing for electoral purposes. So, as long as that remains unresolved, it won't work as it should.
>
> Interview NGO1, 2018

Association representatives also argued that the management problems had to do with the attitudes of the municipal employees towards the council housing residents:

> I think there's racism, not only structural but institutional, which manifests itself in the treatment. Have you noticed? They see a black man or a gypsy coming, and they imagine that *já viram o filme todo* [they already know what the person will be like]. They instantly start talking top-down and giving advice.
>
> Interview A5, 2019

Some of the municipal employees themselves shared this critical view towards their colleagues and towards NGO projects, such as this social worker working in Quinta da Fonte:

> [In this project], there's X, who's great, but then there's another employee, Y, who stays in the office, doesn't go to the neighbourhood, just waits. Y belongs to the school project but doesn't go there. Some employees have an attitude: for example, the residents complain about the noise in the

street. The city council says it can't do anything because it happens after working hours, and they aren't working then. But there are certain jobs that you can't do if you always try to respect the working hours. You have to be more flexible.

ME1, Loures, 2018

These comments are significant because they highlight the importance of the municipal employees' attitude towards the residents. Their biases, related to social class, ethnicity or other attributes, can exacerbate the exclusion and alienation of council residents (Bullock et al., 2020; Constance-Huggins, 2011), producing multiple marginalisations and undermining the residents' attempts to question them (Muñoz, 2017; Wayessa & Nygren, 2016). Lack of adequate registers and their updating, combined with the existing social biases, end up promoting 'invisible elbows.' In fact, many occupiers or other residents who experienced housing problems complained that the lack of a response was what annoyed them the most, as expressed by Carla:

We always go to the Gebalis office. I've also sent emails to try to meet with the city councillor for housing, and I've sent registered letters. Once, I met this Gebalis director in a meeting and talked with her. She told me to send an email marked for her attention, and I did, but she never replied. They don't reply, that's the problem.

Interview with CARLA, 2019

In addition to not responding to the attempts to get in touch, the Lisbon City Council and Gebalis gave confusing signals, as described by Cátia and Nina, who were both occupying council apartments without authorisation:

I've been here for three years. They already took me to the other apartment twice and gave it back twice. The last time was just a while ago. They had just finalised the application process and my housing had been allocated. A family came to see this apartment, and I told them it wasn't vacant, that it was occupied. Then, when I went to renew my application, the official told me that an apartment had been allocated, and that they would give another one to that family, because this one had already been occupied.

Interview with CÁTIA, 2019

In October, they posted an eviction order on my door. I went to see the assistants at the city council and applied for social housing. Then nothing happened. At the end of the year, they said I should renew the candidacy. I went to the city council, and they told me that everything was fine, that the candidacy had already been renewed. Then they gave me a score of 73 – they communicated that with a letter sent to my occupied house. Then again, nothing. So, I don't know whether I should stay or leave. I'm staying, but it's difficult, as I don't know whether I can stay here in the future.

Interview with NINA, 2019

In other words, the families that occupy remain in limbo, without knowing whether they will have to leave or whether they will be able to stay. The responses given by the city councils were sometimes positive from the viewpoint of the occupiers, such as in the case of Loures when the regularisation of some occupations was being considered. Nonetheless, the communication channels between the occupiers and the city councils were characterised by informality: vague management practices which did not respect deadlines to communicate or the right to be informed about the services one is entitled to. A general problem was the lack of information; the families who faced housing exclusion were mostly left to find out for themselves where they should look for support. They were sent back and forth between various municipal agencies, constantly receiving the response that another agency would address their case (Auyero, 2010; Nygren, 2016). The lack of an adequate response or willingness to respond consequently forces the poor to keep waiting (Auyero, 2010), creating further confusion in an already complex and highly stressful situation.

4.2   Neoliberal Responses: In-the-Meanwhile Solutions, Self-responsibilisation and Competition

Other responses tended to fluctuate between caring responses, with the municipal employee seeking to identify a solution for the families, and self-responsibilisation, constructing the lack of access to council housing as the fault and responsibility of people facing housing precarity. These responses can involve the invention of alternative solutions, such as renting an apartment on the private market, and applying for a rent subsidy available in Lisbon that can cover up to a third of one's rent (*subsidio municipal ao arrendamento*) during one year, renewable for a maximum of one more year. Maria considered this to be insufficient: "I'm not a young girl anymore; in two years, I'll be 50. So, I'll rent for two years, and after that? Where do I go? On the street?" (Interview with Maria, 2018). Some were also proposed homeless centres, and when asked by Habita if that could be considered an adequate housing solution for a mother with three children, the municipal employees argued that that option was actually quite good, because 'it even had a kitchen and it offered meals.' In addition, they argued that it would be worthwhile because in this way, her score in the application process for council housing would increase (Fieldnotes, 11/02/2019).

An alternative to social housing was the Lisbon City Council programme Renda convencionada, a prize draw intended 'to create housing of intermediate value,' 'with rents up to 30% lower than the market prices' (Câmara Municipal de Lisboa, 2012). Yet very few homes have become available through it: from 2013 towards the end of 2018, Lisbon had allocated around 500 houses (interview ME3, October 2018), while the number of candidates tended to be huge: for example, more than 1,700 candidates applied for 14 homes for the 16th edition of the programme (Idealista, 2018a).

In Lisbon, some occupiers also tried to negotiate with Santa Casa da Misericórdia, but there was no clear understanding regarding the conditions under which a person could be entitled to Santa Casa's support. Moreover, in an interview, a Gebalis manager suggested to me that Santa Casa was also facing budget restrictions and was simply not able to respond to the (continuously) growing number of applications for support (ME7, Lisbon, 2018).

Another rather surprising but common suggestion by the city council was that the occupying mothers should go to live with their parents. Maria, who was 47 years old at the time of the interview, told me: 'The city councillor for housing told me I should go to my mother's. I said: My mother doesn't want me there. She said she would talk to my mother! I said, no, you're wasting your time' (Interview with Maria, 2018). These in-the-meanwhile solutions were proposed in contexts in which the housing manager in question was not able to devise any other solution, hoping that in this way, the situation would somehow improve. This sentiment is illustrated in this interview excerpt:

> There is also this educational approach and we try to help as much as possible so that the necessary score comes in. But if you ask me if we get an immediate solution for people, sometimes the solution people want is not the one we are able to give. When people are occupying a house, and there is going to be an eviction, they want a solution by tomorrow. And at Santa Casa, they go there, "I need a house". And there is emergency housing, temporary housing, a series of supports. But it's not often the answer that people want.
>
> ME8, Lisbon, 2019

By applying this 'educational approach', the 'caring responses' that were proposed as a solution began to shift towards self-responsibilisation: if the occupiers did not approve the proposed solution, it was because they were too demanding, hinting to the possibility that occupiers' housing exclusions might be their own responsibility or the result of their wrongdoings.

When pointing to the inadequacy of these responses, the managers tended to signal the lack of funding they face, stating that the vacant dwellings need to be renovated before they can be allocated, but no funds have been available. Some municipal employees specifically pinpointed the austerity policies, which did not anticipate funding for the renovation of social housing estates and which resulted in significant cuts to human resources (ME3, Lisbon, 2018). These comments highlight the effects of neoliberal and austerity urban policies in Portugal. Indeed, the budget for social housing began to decrease drastically in Portugal as early as 2003 (INE, 2015b: 7), well before the financial crisis. However, during my fieldwork, renovation work was either undertaken or planned for all of the council housing estates in Lisbon (ME2, Lisbon, 2018). This was because, since 2016, the City of Lisbon has been able to obtain funds for the rehabilitation of the apartment blocks on council estates (LP, Lisbon, 2018). Yet it is noteworthy that the balance of incomes and expenses related to social housing has been positive for both Lisbon and Loures: in Lisbon, the revenues from rents and from the sale of housing stock resulted in a positive balance of 4.3 million euros in 2015, which was further increased by revenues from the sale of housing stock that amounted to an income of 3.2 million euro (INE, 2015e). In Loures, the balance was much smaller but still positive at 940,000 euros (ibid.). These are small sums considering the investment needs, but they can nevertheless refute the argument that social housing would necessarily result in significant financial losses for the municipalities.

On the other hand, the officials pointed out that they have no control over the changes in legislation and that they have no power over the regulation of the markets: 'We can only try to build more homes, more quickly, to try to adjust the impact of the real estate pressure. Yet, if there are no funds, it is basically impossible' (ME2, Lisbon, 2018). Indeed, at the time of the fieldwork, real estate prices and rents were skyrocketing, which certainly resulted in increased pressure on social housing. Yet this explanation sidesteps the issue of the current management problems of the existing housing stock.

The lack of funding and resources is likely to contribute towards the conception of council housing as something that the families must 'deserve': it is not enough to be facing housing precarity, but one has to gain enough points in this competition of who is the 'most miserable' (fieldnotes, 24/07/2018). In an interview (ME3, October 2018), a Lisbon City Council official explained that council housing is allocated to people who are facing multiple deprivations: the most vulnerable groups in society – those who are already excluded from society – are the ones who manage to access council housing more easily. Consequently, due to the small number of council homes available, it would be difficult for employed people to obtain a council home. The official pointed out that for the Roma, it is generally challenging to find work, rent an apartment, or access healthcare in Portugal. This makes them much more vulnerable and justifies their prioritisation for access to council housing.[2]

The municipal employees acknowledged many shortcomings in the scoring system that they hoped to address in the new regulation, *Regulamento Municipal do Direito à Habitação* (RMDH, Municipal Regulation on the Right to Housing), which came into effect in November 2019 (Câmara Municipal de Lisboa, 2019b). These included the high score given to unemployment and to families with members with disabilities (ME4, Lisbon, 2018). While these are important considerations, these criteria have led to desperation for many single working mothers who are often surviving on low wages and precarious employment contracts but who, at the same time, cannot access council housing because they have a job. Yet the scoring matrix in the new regulation has remained essentially the same.

This state of play leads to considering council housing as a scarce resource that needs to be managed according to the notion of 'moral economy' (Wilde, 2020), which guided the everyday management practices, emphasising the need to assess each applicant carefully. In one interview, a municipal employee argued that:

> We, as a managing entity, a public entity, use taxpayers' money. There has to be some management because we don't have homes for everybody. There has to be justice and responsibility. There might be a family occupying a four-room apartment and, at the same time, another family waiting that might be in a worse situation.
>
> ME8, Lisbon, 2019

The notion of 'taxpayers' money' was used to underline the importance of this moral economy, to convey the idea that scarce resources would be wasted if someone who was in a 'better situation' were able to access a council dwelling.

---

2   The downside of this state of affairs is that it tends to fuel racist comments against the Roma – as was the case with Cátia – with many people on the council estates complaining that "all of the houses were given to the gypsies", with the common understanding being that as the Roma did not work, or did not declare that they were working, they easily gained access to council housing.

The notion of scarce resources was particularly emphasised about occupations. One official argued that 'an occupation compromises other families' rights to housing' (fieldnotes, Public Meeting of Lisbon City Council, 11/02/2018). In this reading, the practices of occupiers were unjust because they tried to bypass the application system, as described by one Lisbon City Council official:

> The [city] services have regulations, they have a long list of demands, and my opinion is that supporting, encouraging, or defending the regularisation of 10% of families who illegally occupy a council home, to the detriment of the 90% who are legally seeking access to housing, is reprehensible. Why? The slogan that is used, that housing is a right enshrined in the constitution, is valid for this 10% who bypass the rules and occupy abusively, but it is also valid for the 90% who apply for housing through the programmes. In my opinion, abusive occupations are indefensible because it is not known whether these people have a more serious socio-economic and family situation than the other 90%. Housing can only be allocated according to established rules.
>
> ME2, Lisbon, 2018

The municipal employees emphasised the illegality and informality of occupation, instead of considering the reasons behind the occupations. Murphy (2020) demonstrates how single parents who prioritised social housing and its security of tenure in Ireland, instead of opting for private rental housing, were framed as people who try to 'game the system' by the national housing agency. In a similar vein, the occupiers were thus perceived as people who try to 'jump the queue': their housing needs were questioned, and it was asserted that many of them already had other housing alternatives. The narrative of the need to obey the rules and wait for one's turn was particularly prominent, as described by one Gebalis manager:

> This question has to do with democratic countries, which means that we have legislation and people obey the existing legislation. This is not anarchy, right? When we need something, when we are hungry, we do not go to the supermarket to steal food, right?
>
> ME6, Lisbon, 2018

This manager thus strongly argued against illegal acts, contending that occupations would result in anarchy.

4.3   *Visible Fists: Evicting Families from Access to Housing*

In addition to municipal agencies not providing an adequate response, more disconcerting practices were reported. The Lisbon City Council persuaded some occupiers to leave Lisbon without informing them that this would exclude them from the applications for social housing in Lisbon. Some were even told that they could still continue to apply without giving their address, which is clearly against the existing regulations. As reported in chapter 3, Ema was persuaded to leave an occupied apartment only months before she would have been entitled to it due to the change in the council regulation in Lisbon.

Other women told me how they had been repeatedly contacted by the Lisbon City Council, affirming that they would be offered alternative housing but that they just needed to leave the occupied apartment. After leaving, they never managed to speak with the city councillor's assistants for housing as they neither answered the phone nor responded to their requests by email. Some families that applied for social housing were randomly excluded from the process because the authorities claimed that the families had provided false information on their applications. This was Paula's situation when she repeatedly applied for a council home: 'The Gebalis lawyer accused me of providing false information. She told me my neighbour had said that my daughter doesn't live with me, but with her grandmother. The lawyer decided to believe my neighbour, cancelling my application' (Interview with Paula, 2019).

These techniques of governance adopted by the state actors pertain to the realm of informality: the state itself is persuading the occupiers to leave by using extra-legal tactics. While it is conceivable that the state agents do not respond or offer adequate housing solutions due to their inability to do so, it is difficult to envisage why city council officials or Gebalis staff would deliberately exclude urban dwellers from accessing social housing. Rather than an intentional attack against the poor, this might result from a policy combination that at times might be contradictory and yield unforeseen consequences (Wacquant, 2009). In the context of the housing policies of the Lisbon Metropolitan Area, factors that might have contributed to excluding urban dwellers from access to housing, to social exclusion and marginalisation were administrative decisions that were seldom scrutinised and sometimes formulated ad hoc, as well as the political priorities of a specific time and a specific state agency. These unintended consequences of a disjointed policy formulation contribute to understanding why the state response might be inadequate. However, they do not explain why state agents deliberately exclude part of their population and make them invisible. The concept of 'moral economies' is helpful in this sense: due to the desire to do their work correctly and efficiently,

FIGURE 4.2 Carrying out an eviction. Condado, February 2019

safeguarding the 'scarce resources', the housing officials seek to find reasons to disregard some urban dwellers who come looking for their support.

In contrast, Susanne Soederberg (2016, 2017) argues that these readings conceal fundamental aspects of the production and governance of poverty, such as the 'monetisation of socio-spatial reproduction' and the active production of housing insecurity. Her theorisation provides important insights into the modalities of governance, focusing on how the exclusions are actually produced. In other words, the exclusions occur through the complex confluence of neoliberal housing policies, precarity, and governance and management practices that seek to exclude the urban poor and make them invisible. Similar processes occur in Lisbon and Loures: the poor are excluded from access to housing through high rents on the private market, as well as through insufficient access to social housing. Homelessness is also actively produced by criminalising and punishing residents who attempt to solve their housing problems through occupations. In fact, the local officers and social housing managers frame the occupiers predominantly as criminals.

In addition, from time to time, city councils evict occupiers. In Portugal, occupations are criminalised in the penal code. Article 215 *Usurpação de coisa imóvel*[3] (roughly translated as 'squatting in a property') states that occupations result in imprisonment for up to two years or in a fine of up to 240 days. It

---

3 See https://dre.pt/web/guest/legislacao-consolidada/-/lc/107981223/201708230100/73474133 /diploma/indice. Last accessed 06/10/2019.

also states that the criminal proceedings depend on a complaint, leaving it up to the owners of the property to decide whether they will press charges. The evictions from social housing are regulated by the LAA, the Law for Subsidized Renting, which gives a minimum of three days' notice for evictions in the case of 'occupations without a title' (Art. 35). It also states that the households that face housing shortages should be referred to 'legal solutions of access to housing' or to existing housing support services (*prestação de apoios habitacionais*, Art. 28, paragraph 6) prior to the eviction.

In Loures, the city council had in 2018 surveyed occupations without authorisation, using the upcoming renovation works as a justification to visit all of the apartments in Quinta da Fonte. During the fieldwork, the council officials were reviewing the situation, declaring that the solution could involve either regularisation of the occupation, or an eviction. They argued that as the occupation cases were diverse, they should be analysed individually to be able to define in which cases the occupying family should be allowed to stay (ME1, ME9, ME10, ME11, Loures, in 2018 and 2019). Local associations reported accounts of residents who had received an eviction notice but, on the other hand, some occupiers were invited to the city council to explain their situation and provide documentation on their family composition and income (author's fieldnotes, 23/01/2019).

Conversely, in the case of Lisbon City Council, the line was strict: occupations cannot be considered a solution. In fact, the municipality maintained that evictions should not be considered evictions in such cases, but rather *desocupações*, de-occupations: 'On the council estates, there are no evictions, there are de-occupations. In order to have an eviction, there has to be a contract' (ME3, Lisbon, 2018). Indeed, the City Council of Lisbon has a specific regulation on 'de-occupations' that stipulates how the residents of the occupied apartments should be evicted (Câmara Municipal de Lisboa, 2013). It states that all occupied municipal dwellings will be de-occupied; only in the case of occupations that preceded the entry into force of RRAHM in 2009 does the possibility exist to attribute the occupied dwelling to the occupier. Article 4, paragraph 3 states that the occupiers will be given a notice period of 90 days to leave the occupied dwelling. Yet paragraph 7A of the same Article adds that this does not apply to 'non-authorised occupations of vacant dwellings', which will be de-occupied immediately by the municipal police, and belongings taken to the municipal depository. It is also instructed that the 'non-authorised occupations should be subject to an obligatory criminal charge' (Article 4, paragraph 8).

In Lisbon, framing these evictions as de-occupations results in a different management procedure. This is exemplified in the way that a Gebalis employee referred to de-occupations during a community group meeting:

> They [de-occupations] are administrative processes, managed by Gebalis and the municipal police. They are executed in accordance with the law. More information can be found in the rescripts. In two months, the movement [evictions] will begin in the neighbourhood.
>
> Author's field notes, meeting of a community group, 15 March 2019

The direct violation of the right to housing was thus repackaged as an 'administrative process', something that can be communicated matter-of-factly in a

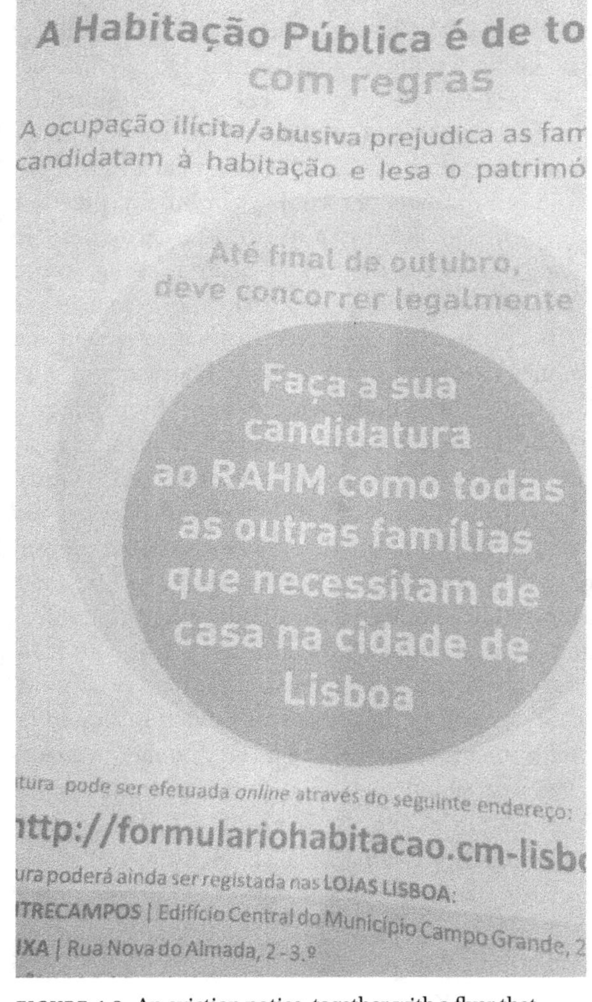

FIGURE 4.3   An eviction notice, together with a flyer that encourages the reader to apply for social housing. October 2018

neighbourhood meeting. This framing can also be used to justify the differential treatment that the occupiers are given when compared to other evictees:

> The law defines a three-day notice period, but the city council does not evict immediately. Gebalis does not evict right away. We always give people some time to try to find support, alternatives, but sometimes we ask ourselves if they try to look for help, or not.
>
> ME7, Lisbon, 2018

However, international law does not recognise a specific category of de-occupations; under the international framework, such as the International Covenant on Economic, Social and Cultural Rights (ICESCR, 1967), a de-occupation would clearly be considered a forced eviction, as it results in a 'permanent or temporary removal against their will of individuals, families and/or communities from the homes and/or land which they occupy, without the provision of, and access to, appropriate forms of legal or other protection' (OHCHR, 1997). As highlighted by UN-HABITAT & OHCHR (2014b, 2014a), in addition to being a direct violation of the right to adequate housing, forced evictions very often result in other severe human rights violations, such as the human right to food, water, health, work, property, security of the home and person, and freedom from cruel, inhumane and degrading treatment.

The UN also emphasises that while implementing some human rights obligations might require financial resources and time, this does not apply to forcibly evicting people. Therefore, the prohibition of forced eviction should be considered 'of immediate effect and not dependent on resources' (UN-HABITAT & OHCHR, 2014b). The states must take all measures to prevent the occurrence of evictions (UN-HABITAT & OHCHR, 2014b). In 'the most exceptional circumstances', evictions can be justified, but only 'after all feasible alternatives to eviction are explored with the affected community' and 'after due process protections are afforded to the individual, group or community' (UN-HABITAT & OHCHR, 2014b). In these cases, the eviction should be carried out 'in conformity with the provisions of the International Covenants of Human Rights' (ICESCR, 1967, paragraph 3), taking into consideration all the other human rights that the forced evictions interfere with. The 'basic principles that need to be met to comply with international standards include:
- Genuine consultation and participation of affected persons and communities;
- Adequate information and notification;
- Effective administrative and legal recourse;

- Due process when the actual eviction is carried out;
- Prohibition of actions resulting in homelessness and deterioration of housing and living conditions;
- Provision of adequate relocation to alternative housing and/or adequate compensation before evictions are carried out; and
- Non-discrimination of women, children, youth, older persons, Indigenous people, ethnic and other minorities, and other vulnerable individuals and groups' (AGFE & UN-HABITAT, 2011).

According to the Lisbon City Council, they provide adequate compensation: the officials and municipal employees state that the families are given a notice period and that they are always *encaminhados*, referred to different institutions, before the eviction, such as Santa Casa or the Social Security office for future support (ME2 and ME3, Lisbon, 2018). Yet the experience of evicted families demonstrates that the 'alternative support' is often far from adequate. Tita was forced to send her children to live with their grandmother, while she herself slept in the car. In addition, she was offered 450 euros by Santa Casa to pay the security deposit on a private rental apartment (fieldnotes, 02/11/2018). These actions thus resulted in a clear deterioration of the housing and living conditions of the family, as well as in the homelessness of the mother.

Claudia had received the notification in May, and she was evicted in November when she was pregnant with her third child. She also had to sleep in the car and was forced to send her children to stay with their grandmother. The city council did not offer her any support before or after the eviction. Claudia presented her case at the public meetings of the city council before the eviction and went there again after the eviction to try to negotiate. They suggested that she should try to rent a room for herself as, that way, her score for a council home might increase. Claudia was not happy with this proposal, however, as it might have meant living without her older children for months or years (fieldnotes, 28/11/2018). After this meeting, the municipal employee stopped taking her calls (fieldnotes, 28/01/2019). In Claudia's case, most of the 'basic principles' of a forced eviction (AGFE & UN-HABITAT, 2011) were thus breached: there was no genuine consultation; no adequate information or notification; no effective recourse; no due process of carrying out the eviction (presence of the police only, without any social worker); the eviction resulted in homelessness; and no alternative housing was offered, resulting in an extreme breach of the ICESCR and also of the Article 8 of the ECHR.

Aida, on the other hand, never received an eviction notice. Gebalis argued that it had been sent in August, but Aida had only occupied the apartment in September and was not contacted prior to her eviction in February. Nor was she offered any support by the city council (fieldnotes, 15/02/2019). In her case, all of the human rights breaches that occurred in Claudia's case also applied. Furthermore, the Lisbon City Council, along with Gebalis, have engaged in actions that can be considered, at the very least, questionable for managers of social housing, putting 'visible fists' (Auyero, 2010) into use, such as when engaging in domicide: breaking up the occupied council apartments that the families had spent time and money on fixing. During the fieldwork, I heard numerous accounts of the municipal police and Gebalis destroying the toilet bowls, bathtubs, mirrors, kitchen utensils, taps, lamps and so on, to discourage the families from returning after the eviction. The fact that this had often been carried out in front of children made this kind of action even more concerning.

Some municipal employees recognised the pain and humiliation of being evicted (ME6, ME7, Lisbon, 2018). Nevertheless, they argued that these evictions were justified because of the need to follow the rules. They also argued that the families had been informed that they had to leave and had been referred to Santa Casa (ME2, ME3, ME8, Lisbon, 2018 and 2019). Yet being informed does not help if a family has nowhere to go.

Despite the human rights conventions and the Portuguese Constitution, the Law on Subsidised Housing, the National Framework Law for Housing, and the municipal regulation in Lisbon do not take into adequate consideration the prohibition of occupations that result in homelessness or in the deterioration of housing conditions. Framing the evictions as a standard bureaucratic procedure, a 'de-occupation,' results in the notion that it is an acceptable practice, and the municipal employees in Lisbon tended to predicate their actions upon that notion. 'De-occupations' can thus be conceived as an example of 'informality as a modality of governance' (Roy, 2015). In its quest to follow the rules and regulations while watching over the 'scarce resources', the city council ends up governing through informality and extra-legality, using its 'visible fists (Auyero 2010) while committing serious human rights violations that result in 'domicides' (Porteous & Smith, 2001) and in the direct production of homelessness (Soederberg, 2018).

In September 2019, a new framework law on housing (*Lei de bases da habitação*, no. 83/2019) was enacted. The law stipulates that the state is the warrantor of the right to housing (Art. 3, paragraph 1), that everyone has the right to adequate housing (Art. 7, paragraph 1), and that the state is responsible for creating a system of access to housing that is compatible with the income of the families (Art. 7, paragraph 2). It also includes an Article on 'protection and follow-up in case of eviction' (Art. 13), stipulating that the state cannot prompt an eviction without ensuring a solution for rehousing (Art. 13, 4). Yet the following paragraph excludes occupations of public housing from this measure by stating that evictions are undertaken following the 'procedures established in the law' (Art. 13, 5).

5 To Conclude

This chapter has explored urban governance in relation to the management of council housing and the participation of the urban poor in housing governance. The analysis illustrated how, in both Lisbon and in Loures, residents were not allowed to participate during the resettlement processes because participation was not considered feasible in the context of strict deadlines. The objectives of urban redevelopment and the 'eradication of slums' thus took precedence over the living conditions of the residents to be relocated.

A clear path dependence can be detected when looking at the current participation structures. In Lisbon and Loures, they differed significantly in terms of the framings and existing initiatives: while the Lisbon City Council demonstrates pride in its participatory structures, in Loures, the municipal employees rightly admitted that little participation was possible. Yet, in terms of effective participation, the analysis demonstrated that the formal 'invited' spaces of participation did not present venues in which the residents of the council estates could effectively participate to make their voices heard. The forms of co-governance that were supposed to bring in the know-how of council residents tended to exclude direct participation, favouring the leading role of institutional actors.

Concerning the vacant council homes that were particularly prevalent in Lisbon, the analysis revealed how the municipal employees tended to shift the responsibility for poor management onto other actors, such as the council estate residents, arguing that the municipalities were unable to effectively manage the estates because the council housing residents did not fulfil their reporting obligations. In addition, problems such as a lack of resources and the massive pressure on the housing sector were indicated. While these arguments can be considered valid, my analysis deduced that the attitudes and practices of the housing managers played a strong role in creating these problems. Much more could be done in terms of securing an efficient use of existing council housing resources instead of presenting the shortcomings in council estate management as arising from the wrongdoings of the council housing residents. Moreover, the management could be undertaken much more efficiently if the participatory structures actually allowed for the participation of the council estate residents.

If the community groups were redesigned as a forum for more substantive participation where the residents of the council estates could set the agenda and bring up matters of interest to them, many issues, such as transfers between apartments that are either too big or too small, or the identification of vacant dwellings, could probably run more efficiently. This would require a profound change of mindset, however, giving the residents of the council estates a significant role in planning and organising the meetings. Likewise, the work conducted in the neighbourhoods should involve daily interaction with the residents, taking account of their concerns. Moreover, it would require a change of attitude so that the municipal employees would approach the residents facing housing shortages as important interlocutors instead of people to be educated.

This chapter has shown how, in the case of council housing managers of Lisbon and Loures, legal and extra-legal mechanisms of control and discipline converge with neoliberal forms of government, leading to the active production of marginalisation and housing exclusions. This combination of governance techniques involves (1) invisible elbows, that complicate the process of accessing council housing, (2) neoliberal responses that focus on self-responsibilisation and competition, and (3) visible fists, involving direct housing exclusions.

The naturalisation of entrepreneurialism – the logic of competition and the idea of scarce resources – in access to housing is used to justify the decisions to exclude some and include others on the basis of an evaluation of 'who needs housing the most.' Yet eliminating homelessness is not possible by decree or by elaborating a score matrix, as this will not change the situation of people experiencing homelessness.

In these actions, the state officials and authorities enter the realm of informality themselves, employing different extra-legal techniques but justifying these modes of governance by the need to respect the existing legislation and by the alleged illegality of occupations. The focus on the 'illegality' of occupations and the framing of evictions as 'de-occupations' leads the city councils to ignore the fact that in promoting evictions, they govern through informality and extra-legality, directly producing homelessness, further alienating these residents from the right to housing. These governance modalities cannot be justified only by the unintended consequences of policy formulation but rather also pertain to the realm of neoliberal strategies to exclude the urban poor. Yet the margin of manoeuvre of the housing managers is also strictly constrained by the neoliberal housing policies that have furthered market-based housing policies to the detriment of the promotion of social housing.

These types of policies and practices can be considered as reinforcing the subordination of urban dwellers, contributing to further their precarity and marginalization (Muñoz, 2017). The precarious and insecure housing context, combined with the unintelligible response by the state, undermines urban dwellers' capacities to organise or to try to devise long-term strategies. They thus push the residents to resort to more malleable tactics that allow for improvisation in fast-changing contexts. It is important to note that confusion and further insecurity also contribute to turning the occupiers against each other, undermining their capacity to organise collectively.

Makeshift Urbanism by Occupation

There are hundreds of thousands of families in the country without housing, or living in subhuman conditions. And it is clear that, despite the measures already taken or under study and the actions planned to encourage construction, there will be no possibility, even in the medium term, to fully solve, through new constructions, the serious problem of adequate housing for these families.

Consequently, the way forward in this situation and what the most elementary principles of social justice require is that, in order to alleviate this shortage in the short term, the full use of the country's housing stock will be promoted. As long as there are people without houses, it is not permissible that there are houses without people. This solution implies the establishment of legal and operational provisions that allow, in effective terms, to proceed to the immediate attribution of the vacant houses, namely in the cases in which there is a violation of the legislation in force.

Excerpt from Decree-Law no. 198-A/75 of 14 April 1975.[1]

∵

1 Occupations: Making the Urban from Below

This chapter will examine the strategy of dwelling occupations to directly enact the right to housing and to contest housing exclusion, conceiving occupations as a gendered, classed and racialised form of makeshift urbanism. I will examine occupations of council housing homes in Lisbon, adding some insights from council home occupations in Loures. Here, the emphasis of the analysis changes from the constraints upon agency and the relations between inequality and dispossession to the practices that seek to act against housing exclusions and contest evictions. Consequently, the analytical lens will draw on discussions on how practices of subalternised urban poor contribute to

---

1 Decree-Law No. 198-A/75 of 14 April 1975. "Legalisation of occupations". Available at: http://www1.ci.uc.pt/cd25a/wikka.php?wakka=novapol30. Last accessed 30/05/2021.

remaking and challenging the existing forms of the making of the city. Drawing from Esposito & Chiodelli (2023), Herbert (2018), Mahmood (2005, 2006), Simone (2019b), and Vasudevan (2015), the chapter explores how occupiers' agency unfolds in a specific situated context that includes constraints as week as opportunities. This agency is contextualised by the cycles of displacement and dispossession they face, which leads to extreme volatility and precarity. I consider this dispossession gendered, classed and racialised (vide chapter 3). While shifting the emphasis to analyse the agency and subjectivities of the occupiers in city-making, the constraints on agency and the relations of inequality are not ignored, as this and the following chapter continue to identify constraints in realising the right to housing, forming the cradle for the creation of variegated forms of agency. As Saba Mahmood argues, 'any discussion of the issue of transformation must begin with an analysis of the specific practices of subjectivation that make the subjects of a particular social imaginary possible' (Mahmood, 2005: 154).

The state actors play an important role in this process, which is why this chapter has a significant focus on the relations between the occupiers and the local municipalities. In addition to liaising with state actors, multiple other actors might be involved, with important roles in the process, such as relatives, politicians, academics, and social movement and NGO actors. The political and interpersonal relations are an essential part of the picture. Yet, in this chapter, I am also interested in asking what exactly is the capacity of occupations as a transgressive practice – up to what extent do they manage to question housing exclusions? What is their political efficiency?

In this chapter, the analysis focuses on urban dwellers' practices, including how and with whom they negotiate housing rights, whom they liaise with, and where they look for support. I identify specific features that characterise occupiers' agency. Firstly, the practice is occupation is framed as a last resort, the only option available, and it is building upon this sentiment that the women I interviewed had taken the decision to occupy. Furthermore, the temporal process of occupation is characterised by the following features: 1) the embeddedness in local networks; 2) the essential role of the material home-making practices; 3) the varied rhythm of hiding and reappearing to negotiate the right to housing with the State actors; and 4) building alliances, while 5) this takes place in the context of extreme volatility and precarity. These features will be the centre of attention in this chapter. I then compare them with insights provided by other accounts on need-based autonomous occupations in the global North (Esposito, 2022; Esposito & Chiodelli, 2023; Herbert, 2018b, 2018a).

In what follows, I will provide a brief contextualisation of occupations, as well as some of their historical background in Portugal. Thereafter, I will proceed to one of the key aspects of the struggle around occupations, exploring how diverse actors seek to assert the legitimacy and dominance of their framing of occupations. I will then examine occupations as a transgressive form of agency, focussing on its specific features.

2   Previous Occupations

The current occupations in council homes have important historical precedents. During the Portuguese revolutionary period in particular, many empty apartments and properties were occupied. The general revolutionary and participatory Zeitgeist of the time enabled transgressive action: in the context of the revolution, there was more openness towards different kinds of reasoning, and acceptance of diverse patterns of operation, including direct, participatory action (Downs, 1980; V. M. Ferreira, 1986) The 25th of April 1974 marked the start of the Portuguese revolutionary period, the PREC (*Processo Revolucionário em Curso*), when a military coup ended 48 years of dictatorship and authoritarian rule. From the first day onwards, people swarmed to the streets to celebrate the end of dictatorship, setting in motion a rich and unprecedented range of experiments of mass mobilisation, grassroots organisation and participatory democracy (Nunes & Serra, 2004; Queirós & Pereira, 2018). These plural movements addressed a myriad of issues (Santos, 1985): labour and production, social security, education, culture, justice, gender relations, access to land and, most importantly from the viewpoint of this study, housing. They were intimately linked to a profound process of transformation in the way of being, with an emerging awareness of 'the need to have more liberty, more rights, the urgency of the right to expression, to have voice, creating the capacity to claim equality' (Bandeirinha, 2011: 109).

This period was particularly important for housing struggles, supported by the SAAL (*Serviço de Apoio Ambulatório Local*, Mobile Service for Local Support), a state-assisted programme based on local organisation (Bandeirinha, 2011; Nunes & Serra, 2004; R. Santos, 2016). The occupation movement was another central initiative. It concerned both urban and rural properties and, in many cases, involved negotiation with previous owners of the buildings (private, state or municipality) and legalisation of the occupations (Downs, 1980; V. M. Ferreira, 1986; P. R. Pinto, 2015). In Lisbon and Setúbal, the newly built social estates (public and semi-public) were the first to be earmarked for occupation. However, the attribution processes tended to be lengthy, with unclear criteria and sometimes lasting for years. In the context of the revolution, neighbourhood committees and groups decided that they would no longer wait for the

FIGURE 5.1 Gathering in Rossio Square on 24 April 1974. By Estúdio Horácio Novais. CC BY-NC-ND 2.0

FIGURE 5.2 Gathering on 25 April 1974. By Estúdio Horácio Novais. CC BY-NC-ND 2.0

state to solve their housing problems (Downs, 1980). Between 26 April and 9 May 1974, they occupied approximately 2,000 social housing apartments in Lisbon, Setúbal, Oporto and Madeira (Bandeirinha, 2011). Women were active participants in the housing movements, often taking leading roles (Nunes & Serra, 2004).

The National Salvation Junta, a group of military officers designated to replace the government of Portugal after the revolution, was forced to react. It issued a condemnation of the occupations, but at the same time, it proposed legalising them. This group also attempted to establish a mid-term solution by aiming to create rules for occupations, such as rents to be paid (Downs, 1980; P. R. Pinto, 2015). A few weeks later, the first provisional government, in which Nuno Portas was the Secretary of State for Housing and Urbanism, launched a housing programme that included the SAAL (Bandeirinha, 2011; Portas, 1986). In September 1974, Decree-Law 445/74 was approved, which forced landlords to rent their vacant housing in an acceptable condition within a period of 120 days. This did not, however, pacify the urban dwellers, who were frustrated with their housing conditions, and this led to a new wave of occupations from November 1974 onwards (Downs, 1980).

The dwellers' activism gradually improved their capabilities to organise and take action. The central actors within their movements were specialists in housing and urban planning (architects, engineers), who worked with urban dwellers to articulate the technical, social and political aspects pertaining to housing issues (Nunes & Serra, 2004). In January 1975, the first meeting was held in what would become the Intercommission of Lisbon's Dwellers (*Intercomissões de Moradores de Lisboa*). This commission jointly planned strategies for the housing struggle and proposed 'popular control' of all of the vacant apartments (Downs, 1980; J. H. Santos, 2014).

In March 1975, there were significant institutional changes, including a change of government, and Nuno Portas was exonerated. The new provisional government enacted Decree-Law no. 198-A/75 on 'Legalisation of occupations' – quoted at the beginning of this chapter – which sought to consolidate its approach to occupations, yet faced challenges in seeking to please all of the different actors (Bandeirinha, 2011). The Decree-Law states that it would promote the legalisation of occupations made 'to satisfy the urgent needs of extremely disadvantaged people' but, conversely, also maintained that it would be 'necessary to prevent, in a definitive and very firm way, similar situations from being created in the future' (Decree-Law no. 198-A/75).

When the coalition government of conservative and 'moderate' wings of the military and the political 'centre' took control of the political process in November 1975), the revolutionary spirit began to vanish (Ferreira, 1986. It was further weakened by the approval of the new Constitution in April 1976. After the inauguration of the first constitutional government of Mário Soares in July 1976, the government chose to adopt a strategy of inflexibility and repression in relation to the occupations, but they nonetheless continued for years after the inauguration of the Soares government (J. H. Santos, 2014). The residents' committees, with the organisational capacity acquired during the revolutionary period, resisted evictions. Oftentimes, it was necessary to use numerous police officers to undertake evictions, and the eviction process sometimes lasted several days. The strict stance against occupations culminated in 1977 when the government declared that those involved in fighting against evictions would be prosecuted, with a maximum sentence of two years' prison service for those involved in resistance actions, and heavy fines for the residents' associations or committees that supported the evicted. Nevertheless, the local mobilisations frequently managed to stop the evictions of occupying families and, in many cases, occupations continued to be legalised (P. R. Pinto, 2015).

These two years were extraordinary in many respects. During the revolutionary period and in the context of participatory democracy, occupations acquired the status of legitimate activity. Even though the junta and the first provisional government considered occupiers to be problematic and sought to regulate and prevent their occupations, the occupiers' reasoning and their modus operandi continued to be framed as valid and justified. At times, the government even aligned with the occupiers' position and arguments, as illustrated in the extract from the Decree-Law on the legalisation of occupations. The positioning of the first provisional government was revolutionary in a Lefebvrian sense, aiming to promote the use value of the urban property, to the detriment of its exchange value. However, since the return to 'normality', which was characterised by representative – as opposed to participatory – democracy and centrist governance, there has arguably been an attempt to eliminate all experiences that appeared to be alternatives, erasing the memory of social and political participation (Nunes & Serra, 2004). Nevertheless, the urban dwellers involved in the residents' committees acquired organisational capacities that left an imprint of consciousness concerning civil and social rights. The PREC has also been credited with pushing through many social and political reforms that were incorporated into the Portuguese Constitution of 1976, including the right of all citizens to decent housing (Accornero, 2019; Drago, 2017; P. R. Pinto, 2015).

It is also important to highlight that in the housing movements during the PREC, urban dwellers and 'experts', such as architects, sociologists and politicians, came together (Queirós & Pereira, 2018). In Lisbon, the Renters' Association of Lisbon, AIL, had a considerable role in defending the occupations and the residents' committees. At the time, AIL based its work on the slogans 'As long as there are people without homes, there cannot be houses without people' and 'Housing is everyone's right: vacant houses are a crime!'[2] (H. Santos, 2014: 149).

The occupation movement vanished after the 1970s, but this did not end all occupations. In fact, occupations of vacant public housing continued – not through collective organised action, but mainly through the action of individual families. At the same time, occupations have been regulated through different laws and regulations over the years. Current legislation and regulations are tough on occupiers, enabling immediate eviction and criminal charges, although the latter are often not pursued.

During my fieldwork, the Lisbon City Council was conducting a study on the status of its council apartments, but the results were not made public. An official on the Lisbon City Council told me that 'They have always existed' but, significantly, she estimated that they had doubled in number in recent years (ME2, Lisbon). Likewise, the Loures City Council had initiated a procedure in the neighbourhood of Quinta da Fonte that involved visiting all of the apartments on the council estate one by one.

3   Framing Occupations – a Crime, or a Last Resort?

The experience of the PREC exemplifies how the way in which occupations are framed in the mainstream public debate has a significant impact on the occupiers' chances of making their claims heard. Framing occupations is thus an important part of the struggle and claims that legitimise and de-legitimise occupations by diverse actors. Diverse actors involved with occupations and evictions seek legitimacy for their narratives and interpretations of occupations. The state agents typically aim at consolidating the dominant reading of occupations as an informal, illegal activity, while the occupiers often seek to challenge this reading, bringing forward alternative framings. However, these differences are not clear-cut, as will be illustrated in this chapter. In the context of housing exclusion, many families, especially single mothers who see vacant council homes, have decided to occupy them. I argue that this can be considered a transgressive, 'invented' (Miraftab, 2004) form of home- and city-making, in the context that other options have dried up.

The women and men who occupied argued that the occupation was necessary due to their economic precarity, as illustrated in the biographies of Cátia,

---

2 'Enquanto houver pessoas sem casa, não pode haver casas sem gente' and 'a habitação é um direito de todos – casas devolutas é um crime'.

FIGURE 5.3 'We don't break in, we inhabit'. Lumiar, September 2019

Sara and Ema. By far, the most common reason for occupying encountered in this study was economic hardship, as Claudia explained:

> For a single mother, it's difficult to pay 200, 300 euros for a home. If I earn 500 euros and pay 300 euros for a home, I'm left with 200 euros. Then you have to buy a bus pass for the kids to go to school, 48 euros for two. I only have 150 euros for food until the end of the month. It's complicated.
>
> Interview with CLAUDIA, 2018

This is not to say that other kinds of occupations would not exist: in some cases, council homes have been occupied for private rental business, holiday homes, and drug trafficking, as was recounted by NGO workers and council estate residents in interviews and meetings with Habita (interviews with Ema, 2019; Miriam, 2018; NGO6, 2018; fieldnotes 30/10/2018 and 12/04/2018).

Yet occupiers encounter difficulties in attaining legitimacy for their framing. The municipal employees and local politicians in Lisbon recognised the existence of diverse kinds of occupations, but tended to emphasise those that were not carried out for housing purposes, strongly condemning all occupations (LP, ME2, ME3, ME4, ME6, ME7, ME8; in 2018 and 2019), and emphasising their illegality: 'We cannot let the people stay in those apartments because we have no legal basis for it' [...] 'the abusive occupations are a crime' (ME8, Lisbon, 2019).

Indeed, the effective housing needs of occupiers were often questioned as here by one of the municipal workers:

> That last person who was 'de-occupied' was an authorised cohabitant of a council home, as was her mother-in-law. So she already had a municipal dwelling. She could either return to her parents' home, or to her mother-in-law's home. Sometimes they are already overcrowded, but that doesn't justify the person occupying an apartment.
>
> ME2, Lisbon, 2018

In comparison, in Loures, the municipal employees contended that different cases exist (ME1, ME9, ME10, ME11, Loures, in 2018 and 2019).

However, some managers and local officers also showed an understanding towards the motivations of the occupiers:

> In relation to abusive occupations, what I can say at the moment is that they are understandable. Obviously, abusive occupations are a crime, and they must be regarded as such. However, with the crisis and the transformation of the city, we all suffer a lot, and the people in the [social housing] neighbourhoods suffer even more. There's overcrowding, the families have grown a lot, and people are unable to leave. They compete for municipal housing, there's not enough of this type of housing for everyone, they can't get a home, and then there are people who despair and end up committing this crime.
>
> ME8, Lisbon, 2019

This municipal employee, while framing occupations as a crime, also sided with many of the arguments presented by the occupiers, illustrating that within the city council, there is awareness of the challenges that the occupiers face. However, managers and local officials interpreted 'justice' and 'responsibility' as complying with the municipal regulations and the national housing legislation, with everyone being subject to the same application system. The state agents thus frequently emphasised respect for the rules as well as for refraining from illegal acts. According to this line of thought, justice is not predominantly related to the clauses of the Portuguese Constitution or to the human rights commitments of the Portuguese state. In fact, state agents interpreted the attempts to satisfy the basic needs enshrined in the Constitution as 'stealing' and 'anarchy'.

In addition to the local politicians and municipal employees, many organisations that defend housing rights do not accept the occupiers' cause as legitimate, arguing that officials cannot defend illegalities and therefore, hiding behind the presumed informality of the occupation. An AIL representative revealed during an interview (NGO1, 2018) that their legal nature is that of a 'cooperative that provides services for its members'. He recognised that the poorest segments of the population do not have the means to access their services, but did not consider that a significant challenge because this 'part of the population that is very poor, mostly elderly' generally reaches out to the public sector for support. One of the few associations defending occupiers at the time of my fieldwork was the Association Habita. In an interview documented in a journal article (R. Cachado et al., 2019), one of its members, Rita Silva, argued that:

> We support these people who occupy if they have no alternatives, and there are several hundred empty apartments in many municipalities, especially in Lisbon ... degraded houses, and considering that they [occupiers] fix these homes. Here it [the occupation] is considered a taboo, the worst sin you can commit. But what we really should be worrying about is the lack of alternatives that the households face. That's what makes them occupy.
>
> (R. CACHADO et al., 2019: 41)

Finding support for the occupiers' cause has thus not been straightforward. Nevertheless, there have been some important achievements in terms of legitimising their cause. These include the publication of articles in two of the main newspapers in Portugal: 'Having a place for my kids to sleep is a necessity' in *Público* (Moreira, 2018), and 'High rents lead families to occupy vacant houses. 'Either I occupy or live on the street" in *Diário de Notícias* (Reis, 2019). In November 2018, Radio Renascença produced a long report titled 'Ocupa Mothers' (*Mães Ocupas*, (Palma & Bourgard, 2018), in which it interviewed mothers who were either occupying or who had recently been evicted. The report argues that the precarious economic situation of the families, combined with high rents, pushes them towards considering occupation as a means of resolving their housing problem.

Some Catholic priests have also taken a stand in defending the occupiers, like the President of the Episcopal Commission for Pastoral Social, D. José

Traquina, who stated in a newspaper interview that the feminisation of poverty is one of the defining characteristics of poverty in Portugal and that the state and municipal institutions have a 'culture of indifference and *descarte*' [disposal, throwing out], which 'greatly affects the poor' (Sapo, 2018).

Occupiers, as well as the actors who support them, duly tended to face difficulties in gaining legitimacy for their cause in the public debate. One reason for this is that few people outside the council housing estates are familiar with the challenges related to the management of council homes. Most people do not realise how many council homes are vacant, sometimes for years. Similarly, many people are unaware of the council housing occupations, as well as of the diverse forms of brutality that the state officials inflict upon the occupiers. They sometimes purposefully destroy council apartments after evictions, albeit not admitting it. This results in setting the word of a municipal police agent or a Gebalis manager against the word of a resident who has been evicted.

It can be assumed that when the context normalises the neoliberal capitalist market economy and representative democracy, it becomes more difficult to assert the legitimacy of any highly transgressive and directly participatory action. To address this situation of precarity and lack of formal response, many residents respond by devising their own strategies to access housing. The following sections will demonstrate the types of experimentation and improvisation that families resort to when facing housing exclusion. The focus will be on the specific strategy of occupation as well as the different practices and tactics it involves.

4 Practices of Occupation

4.1 *Local Networks*

After someone decides to occupy, the process begins by looking for suitable apartments. People who intend to occupy typically either identify vacant apartments in the neighbourhood where they are already living, or they search for housing in a neighbourhood where relatives or friends are living. As Maria recounted: 'I went into that building to look around. There were two [vacant] apartments, but they both had an alarm, so I didn't go for them. I then asked a guy who lives here, and since he's my friend, he told me about this one' (interview with Maria, 2018). Some others rely on outsider support to identify and 'open' the apartments. Networking, in the sense of establishing contact with relevant actors, such as neighbours, was therefore considered to be crucial in identifying and gaining access to a vacant apartment. A longer occupation may be achieved by using one's networks, that is, finding the right persons for support. In some neighbourhoods, diverse groups have begun to control the vacant apartments, trying to establish a business out of 'selling' apartments to people who want to occupy. This service might incur heavy costs, as described by Anabela: 'They might charge 300 euros, or more. In Chelas, even 1,000 euros. There's a group of boys there, they open and sell' (interview with Anabela, 2018). According to the occupiers, the municipal police are aware of the occupations as well as the practices of 'selling' council homes.

In this context, the occupiers improvise with the means available to them. They establish 'strange alliances' (Simone 2019b: 37) with lawyers, diverse associations, neighbourhood gangs and neighbours, trying to construct bases on which they can operate. Extra-legal actions are mostly considered a necessity: occupiers might be concerned about the presumed illegality of the action, but prefer to think that they are justified because other options are not available. Instead, they focus on concrete issues, such as how to obtain their basic necessities.

After locating a vacant apartment, residents must figure out how to gain entry. In Lisbon, this normally involves removing a steel plate that the city council installs to protect the door, followed by breaking in, and finally by replacing the existing lock. Some women I spoke to had managed to remove the steel door by themselves, while others had hired other people to open the door. Nonetheless, some central issues need to be considered before they break in. Firstly, it is important to begin sleeping in the apartment immediately and to move some belongings in. This ensures that the entry is not considered to be a 'blatant entry' (*entrada flagrante*) by the police, and consequently the occupiers will not be evicted immediately. If members of the city council or Gebalis managers arrive, the occupier should request three days to leave the apartment. To minimise the risk of neighbours reporting the occupation, it is always preferable to know at least some of the people who live in the building, and to try to talk to them in advance.

However, one can end up simply being unlucky, as described by Célio:

> One day, I had put the steel door out on the balcony, to clean the house. It was very windy that day. The door was propped up, the wind caught it, and it fell down with a bang. So that's what gave us away, rather than other people. At 11:30 at night, everyone was frightened by the noise, right? They came to the window to see. This kind of thing makes it more difficult [to occupy].
>
> Interview with CÉLIO, 2019

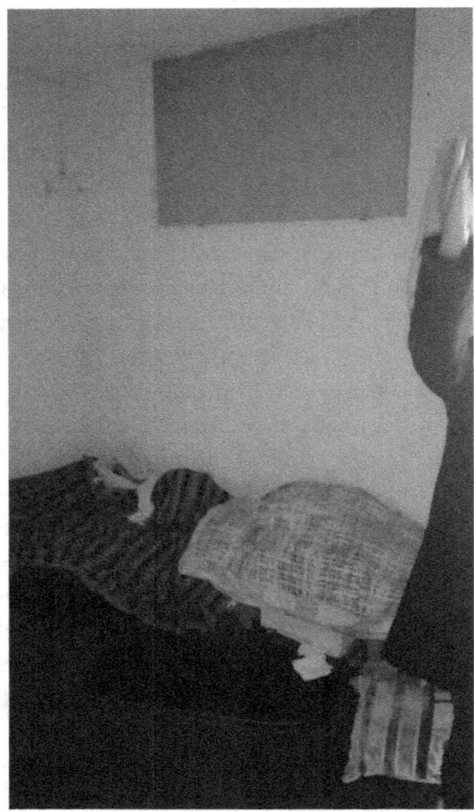

FIGURE 5.4 A closed council home that has been opened and occupied, but not renovated. April 2019

4.2   *Home-Making through Improvised Materialism*

Upon entry, most apartments tend to be in poor condition. Some apartments had been completely destroyed, lacking doors, windows, a floor, or any bathroom and kitchen facilities. The occupiers related how they had installed taps, toilet bowls and showers; they had painted the apartments and put in flooring, electrical wiring and bathroom fixtures. Another challenge lay in gaining access to water and electricity because in order to draw up a contract, the water company EPAL and the electricity company EDP generally demand to see the rental contract or other legal documents that attest to the persons' right to inhabit a particular apartment. Even so, some occupiers are more fortunate:

'I got water and electricity through the internet. They only asked for my ID, nothing else' (interview with Claudia). Others capitalise on their networks to search for people who can help to draw up a legal contract, such as contacts working for the water company: 'I have a friend at EPAL. I send the documents and the address to him, and he helps to make the contract' (Neida, field notes, 10/12/2018). Nevertheless, many others who were faced with the impossibility of establishing a legal contract resorted to making *puxadas*, illegal connections to water or electricity grids:

> I spent half a year without water at home, going to fetch it from the neighbours. Then, through word of mouth, I found someone who could make the connection for me – he's a construction worker and knows how to do these things. So I got water illegally. We have to commit some illegalities in order to survive.
>
> Interview with SARA, 2019

In this latter case, the management practices of institutions such as EPAL and EDP limit the options of the occupiers, rendering it difficult to establish a legal contract, and pushing the occupiers into further levels of presumed informality.

4.3 *Rhythms of Hiding and Making Pressure: How to Negotiate with the City Councils*

The Lisbon City Council claims to be fighting occupations, and its *Regulamento das Desocupações* stated in Article 4, paragraph 1 that the 'Managing Entity proceeds to evict all unauthorised occupations'. In this light, it is rather intriguing that most of the occupiers explained that they had already been in contact with the city council regarding their occupation. In line with the idea of rhythms of endurance (Simone, 2019b), urban dwellers thus proceeded in this ambiguous situation to experiment with diverse initiatives and solutions to determine the results they could yield. The occupiers I met can be characterised as highly proactive in their attempts to further their housing cause by interacting with the city councils, Gebalis and other public entities. The occupiers generally tried to open up a negotiation channel with the city council or with Gebalis. Occupiers even attended the public meetings of the city council and the municipal assembly to explain their situation and their reasons for occupying. These public meetings are recorded and currently available on

FIGURE 5.5   Before eviction. Occupied home, with renovated kitchen and living
              room. October 2018

YouTube.[3] Members of Habita often attended these meetings together with
the occupiers to support them.[4]

---

3   For example, Public meeting of the City Council of Lisbon, 25/07/2018: https://www.youtube
    .com/watch?v=Ae9Wblu6jmw&list=PLcypZqRAr2vwCK6xebfcYfEgx6Z_LF6OW&index=10.
    Last accessed 30/05/2020.
4   In April 2018 and in the months that followed, the Lisbon City Council began to restrict
    Habita's participation, demanding that those who do not intervene should wait in a separate

FIGURE 5.6 City council meeting in Loures, February 2018

Yet despite their efforts to negotiate with the authorities, it was rather rare for them to receive a response. One family explained this as follows:

> We got into this house a while ago. The police came and recommended that we should get in touch with the city councillor. We contacted Gebalis, which advised us to contact the city council, which told us in turn that we should contact Gebalis. We sent an email to the city councillor and received one back stating that they were analysing our case. This was six months ago.
>
> Fieldnotes, meeting organised by Habita, 27/02/2018

When occupiers managed to extract a reply from the city council, it was often a suggestion to send (yet another) application for social housing. In their negotiations, the occupiers generally had three primary aims:

1)   to remain in the occupied apartment.
2)   to have their eviction suspended, and
3)   to access alternative housing.

Regularisation of an occupation was difficult to achieve in Lisbon, and the city councillor also stated in public meetings that no occupations would be regularised. Nevertheless, rumours constantly circulated about people having

---

hall and assist the meeting from the screen in the hall. This was met with protest, and a few months later, Habita was again able to participate.

their occupations regularised. The most common allegation was that the Roma managed to have their occupations regularised because they 'caused so much confusion', which was affirmed in some interviews. However, during my fieldwork, I never met anyone in Lisbon whose occupation had been regularised with a rental contract. By contrast, in Loures, after the city council had paid a visit to all of the council homes in Quinta da Fonte, some opportunities opened up to allow regularisation. After those visits, some occupying families received a letter from the Loures City Council, calling them to a meeting to discuss their situation.

It was also sometimes possible to have an eviction suspended in Lisbon. Sara, for instance, had managed to have her eviction suspended by negotiating:

> I occupied this place in October 2017, when my son was born. Not even a month had passed when I went to open the door and saw two police officers wearing municipal police vests. They started asking questions and I immediately started to cry, explaining my situation. They said, look, we're just doing our job, we have to deliver the [eviction] notification; the only thing we can advise you to do is to go to Gebalis headquarters and explain the situation. The next day, I went to the Gebalis headquarters, explained my situation, and got to talk to a senior officer. She told me not to worry, that she was going to suspend the eviction order, to give me time, at most until January, she said. They have never contacted me again since then, and I have never called them. I've been here, quiet, pretending that there's nothing special about my situation.
>
> Interview with SARA, 2019

Many occupiers affirm that it is fundamental to 'know how to talk' to convince both the police and the council housing managers to delay or suspend an eviction. They stated that in interacting with city councils or Gebalis, it was essential to *chatear* – pester, or *fazer pressão*, which means to put pressure on the council housing managers and other authorities. Sara explained this as follows: 'You have to know how to defend yourself. You have to show you are not a person who says "yes" to everything they say. You have to pester them' (Interview with Sara, 2019). This meant that one could not merely wait patiently for a city council to respond; instead, one should always call, run from one office to another, and demand a solution. One should not stop, as Ema emphasised: 'When they see that I'm going around [to different agencies], they calm down. It's when I relax that they surprise me: at that moment, they'll send me an eviction notice' (Interview with Ema, 2019). This applied even when someone had already been given a council home: the tenant needed to continue to exert pressure so that the foreseen renovation work would actually start, and when they started it, it was better to accompany them constantly (interview with Paula, 2019).

For Sara, it was essential to travel to Gebalis to discuss her case. Even when that tactic did not result in a definite decision, she managed to buy herself time. In other cases, occupiers sometimes managed to turn back the municipal police officers who were there to evict them or to deliver the eviction notice or, in a rare case such as Sara's, managed to extract a promise – always verbal and informal – that their eviction had been suspended for some time. This offered them a welcome opportunity to remain in their apartment a while longer.

Even so, the uncertainty of the arrangement continued to cause anxiety, as Carla stated:

> So, we've been at this impasse for three or four years. We don't have to leave, but Gebalis hasn't proposed what we should do either. On the one hand, we've been told that this kind of process takes years at Gebalis so, in one respect, it's good because as long as we just wait, we'll stay here. On the other hand, it's exasperating not to have a final solution. The waiting takes a long time.
>
> Interview with CARLA, 2019

The occupiers therefore had to resort to elaborate tactics and carefully consider which situations warranted their continuing efforts to contact authorities, and which required them to merely 'keep quiet', like Sara, who preferred not to contact Gebalis out of fear that she might be evicted. Often, it was essential to wait and allow time to pass because sometimes, there was an unofficial moratorium on the eviction: the city council in question knew the home had been occupied, but allowed them to stay, while at the same time, the council claimed they had no means to legalise the occupation.

Given the difficulty in regularising occupations in Lisbon, many negotiations centred on the possibility of accessing alternative housing solutions. These negotiations were predominantly conducted alongside a conventional tactic that virtually all occupiers used: applying for council housing through the formal application process, year after year, which is a rather time-consuming process, with the need to submit a long list of official documents. The process involves many 'invisible elbows' (Auyero, 2010): To obtain these documents, applicants are often obliged to wait long hours in diverse state agencies, and this forces them to request days off work. Moreover, as the processes are long and drawn out, the information they had submitted in the original application – such as their employment status, wage or family composition – might be outdated, which could result in an exclusion during the application process. This is what had happened to one woman who complained at a meeting organised by Habita:

> This year, I finally got 102 points for my application. The city council asked me to bring all the documentation within 10 days. It took time to get all the documents, running from one place to another. What had changed is that my son and I were working part-time, while I was unemployed at the time of sending my application. What had changed is that me and my son were working part-time, while at the time of sending my application, I was unemployed. Afterwards, I submitted a new application and got 72 points [not enough to access a council home].
>
> Fieldnotes, meeting organised by HABITA, 30/11/2018)

These time-consuming bureaucratic processes, in which some applicants felt that they were being treated unjustly and arbitrarily, undermined the dwellers' confidence in the administrative processes of the city council and reinforced their sense of being excluded and not entitled to services. In some cases, these invisible elbows managed to achieve their purpose, as described by Auyero (2010): to put the urban poor in their place, to force them to accept their sub-alternisation. They also resulted in occupiers investing considerable time and energy, with many of them also trying to juggle between keeping a precarious job and sustaining a family with that salary.

4.4   *Building Alliances*

In addition to the municipal employees and other council estate residents, the occupiers frequently sought support from other actors. At times, this interaction involved forms of patronage between the occupiers and some politicians. For example, members of the CDS, a party led by Assunção Cristas at the time of my fieldwork, organised meetings in the social housing estates and collaborated with neighbourhood associations. Habita interpreted this effort as an attempt to gain votes. In one meeting in Condado in which I participated, members of the CDS offered to make a list of families with housing problems, subsequently handing the list over to the city council (Fieldnotes, 24/04/2018). Assunção Cristas also often attacked the city councillor for housing in public council meetings I attended (Fieldnotes, Public Meeting of Lisbon City Council, 26/04/2018), questioning why so many homes were vacant and why it was taking so long to renovate the apartments. The City Councillor for Housing duly replied that the CDS had voted against the renovation plan, and another city councillor pointed out that Assunção Cristas had been among the main architects of the legislation undermining the rights of the tenants, like the infamous 'New Urban Rental Regime' and the changes in the law for subsidised renting.

Some neighbourhood associations also got involved. In some cases, they sought to establish direct contact with the city councillor's office to suspend evictions or 'legalise' occupations. For instance, Claudia affirmed that one neighbourhood association protects the occupiers that become its members. When she occupied the apartment, she realised that the neighbourhood association had already 'promised' the apartment to another person and had already informed the city council that this person would occupy the vacant council home in question (Interview with Claudia, 2018).

Habita was also frequently contacted with requests to help stop an eviction. In these cases, Habita typically wrote to or called the city councillor's office for housing, succeeding at times to have an eviction suspended. Obviously, this involved giving the name and address of the person who was at risk of eviction, which emphasises the impression that many occupations are known to the city councils.

Other people managed to suspend an eviction by opening a legal case, using the *providência cautelar* (protective order) procedure, which should suspend an eviction until the case has been analysed and a court decision has been made. Yet Habita often witnessed cases in which the city council nevertheless proceeded with an eviction, claiming that they did not have knowledge of the protective order, or knowledge that there was a pending process on the institution of a protective order.

These narratives, although difficult to verify objectively, reinforce the idea that neighbourhood associations, lawyers, or social movement organisations can significantly impact on the negotiations, even if the city councils would not admit to this being the case. Liaising with a wide network of actors was thus mostly beneficial for the occupiers although, in practice, it was impossible to foresee which one, or which combinations of contacts, would bring about the desired results.

Habita also tried to play a concrete role in supporting the mobilisation of occupiers to collectively challenge the narrative of occupations as a criminal activity. One action in this sense was the open letter that the occupier women groups from Lumiar and Chelas wrote to the Lisbon City Council, in which the women explained their concerns and argued the following:

In competitions, our score always falls short, and it is clear that the scoring system is not working as it should. Among us are those who have been waiting for almost 20 years. In the current context, social housing cannot be directed only at the 'poorest'. Single mothers, or even a couple, working to earn the minimum wage, are unable to access housing on the private market. Among us are others who have already been called in to deliver the documents to receive a home for social housing, but at the last minute, arbitrarily, the social worker decided to cancel the application. We need protection from the work of some assistants who, instead of trying to understand a family's situation, strive to find any reason to make the family ineligible for social housing.

We want to emphasise that Lisbon City Hall has had many empty apartments for years, more than a thousand apartments, and that we have seen these apartments around us for years: they are beside us, next door, on the top or bottom floor. These houses are abandoned, deteriorating year after year, while we wait and despair about social housing that never materialises. Some of us have started to live in these apartments; we solved our housing problem, as the city council, for years and years, has not helped us to solve it. We took care of the abandoned apartments, which were vandalised. Hence, we ask: What is the bigger crime? To leave apartments empty and deteriorating, or for families in extreme situations of desperation to go into these houses, move in, and take care of them?

The Lisbon City Council, however, did not reply to this open letter, retreating again into silence and forcing applicants to wait as a modality of governance.

5   To Conclude

When comparing with insights provided by Esposito and Herbert on need-based occupations in the contexts of Naples, Italy, and Detroit, the United States, similarities and differences emerge. As in Naples and in Detroit, this form of occupation in Lisbon is essentially driven by housing precarity, which in turn is caused by a variegated assemblage of factors, ranging from the personal characteristics of the occupiers to forms of public housing governance, triggered by the broader urban development dynamics such as financialisation and neoliberalisation of housing. The occupiers present occupations as the last option available in a context where they cannot access housing through other forms. However, following Mahmood (2005), this does not necessarily mean an extinction of possibilities to enact agency, when agency is conceived not as resistance but as a capacity for action in a context of subordination and sub-alternisation. However, the notion of 'everyday forms of resistance' does not adequately characterise occupations for housing purposes because it occults the decisive purpose a person has when s/he occupies. In the biographical interviews I conducted, occupations emerged as carefully considered deci-sions, which implied the recognition of their illegality as well as the rejection of the subalternised position that the state actors suggested for the occupi-ers. The decision to occupy thus had a transgressive quality.

While in Lisbon, the occupiers maintain that they cannot access housing through other means, the act of occupying still necessitates taking the very concrete decision to do so, as well as careful organisation and plenty of work to both prepare the occupation and sustain it, using the tactics of networking locally, homemaking, negotiation, hiding and building alliances. Hence, as in the case of Naples (Esposito, 2022), while housing needs drive occupations this does not lead to the necessary characterisation of these forms of occupation as 'survival squatting' as Herbert (2018) or Pruijt (2013) suggest. This situatedness of the occupation practice in the context of extreme housing precarity neces-sarily encourages the adoption of more transgressive modes of agency when attempts to solve their housing problems through more conventional methods have failed to yield results. Yet the context itself does not produce occupations, and this is the crucial distinction that highlights the existence of agency in this situation.

In terms of public approach to occupations, the context of Lisbon diverges strongly from Naples and Detroit, where the abundance of vacant housing has increased the legitimacy of occupation practices, justified by the need to care for the vacant housing stock. In Lisbon, despite the existence of vacant and degraded housing, public opinion tends to strongly condemn the occupations, and there is little hope that an occupation without authorisation could be reg-ularised by the authorities. On the contrary, and unlike in Naples and Detroit, the occupiers in Lisbon are extremely likely to suffer an eviction without the provision of adequate housing alternatives.

Embeddedness in local networks is key in all three contexts. While in Lisbon and Naples, local networks are needed to identify vacant dwellings, in Detroit, the embeddedness is established later through interaction with neighbours and proving the intention to care for the occupied dwelling and its surround-ings. The material practices of homemaking, turning shelter into a home, also acquire a fundamental role in the three cities. Occupiers care for the prop-erty and its surroundings (Herbert, 2018: 248), fix the often degraded homes, creating liveable conditions and, essentially, transforming the precarious housing into the 'home-as-desire' (Esposito, 2022: 7) that they wish for themselves.

The rhythms of hiding and putting pressure also characterise occupations in these three cases, albeit in very different ways. Herbert (2018) describes occupations in Detroit as having an under-the-radar quality, in which the occupiers attempt to blend in with other residents without attracting attention to themselves. However, this might undermine social services' outreach efforts (Herbert, 2018: 808). In the context of Naples, the social legitimacy of need-based occupation enables blending in with other residents, but as in Detroit, blending in is also a strategy to avoid unnecessary attention by the authorities, a strategy that Esposito and Chiodelli (2023: 1449) characterise as 'camouflaging agency'. In Lisbon, hiding and blending in is another tactic the occupiers apply but this tactic is carefully counterbalanced with the more prominent tactic of negotiation with the council housing authorities. Other actors, such as housing and neighbourhood associations and lawyers, are also brought in to support the negotiations. The prominence of negotiations seems to be a particularity of the Lisbon context. In this precarious context of city-making, the notion of rhythms of endurance (Simone, 2019b) contributes to illuminating the dynamics involved in occupations, highlighting the importance of improvisation, adaptation, negotiation, and networking (Vasudevan, 2015). In Naples, hiding acquires a more prominent role as the occupiers believe they will eventually be legalised through the amnesties of occupations without authorisation, periodically undertaken by the authorities (Esposito & Chiodelli, 2023: 1448). In Detroit, occupations are instead a temporary sheltering strategy, with the wish that they can eventually leave the occupied house and have access to a formally rented or bought home (Herbert, 2018b).

These contexts are in stark contrast to Lisbon, where regularising occupation is very challenging to achieve, despite an amnesty being declared prior to the implementation of the Lisbon Council housing regulation in 2009. The negotiations thus centre more on avoiding an eviction and possibly obtaining a council housing dwelling at another location. To further their cause and improve their situation, occupiers sought to take advantage of their stocks of capital, meaning mainly their networks, through various everyday tactics. During this process, they had to carefully assess when they needed to visit the state agencies and attend meetings to 'put the pressure on', and when it was better to wait quietly and hope that the city councils had forgotten that they existed. These practices reflected their detailed analyses of the most appropriate political moment to attempt to press for lasting solutions. In this way, the occupying families manage – albeit only temporarily and very precariously – to resolve their situation of housing exclusion, by directly enacting their right to housing.

The act of occupying contributes to constructing the urban, and directly enacts the right to housing, fostering social transformation. Occupiers demand a response and recognition from the state agents, who would otherwise let them wait quietly and render them invisible. In addition, the act of occupying questions prevailing norms and regulations: the occupiers make visible the inherent problems in the management of council estates with many apartments left vacant. They also contribute to questioning the practices of capitalist housing governance, in which it is preferable to leave homes vacant, respecting their owners and their exchange value, rather than ensuring that all homes will serve their social purposes, contributing to the realisation of everyone's right to housing.

These practices are transformative in that they produce results. However, the results are not necessarily the ones that the occupiers had hoped for, as occupations can frequently result in eviction and further marginalisation. Occupations signify a promise to contribute directly to creating a different kind of 'everyday'. However, the condemnation and stigmatisation they face undermine their transformative potential and their capacity to produce new democratic practices.

Social Movements against Evictions: the Habita Association's Contribution to the Struggle

1 Social Movements against Evictions

As this book has shown, the occupiers' actions are strongly influenced and constrained by many other groups of actors. Housing movements and housing activists are a specific group that interact intensely with people facing housing exclusions, seeking ways to further their cause and support their struggle against homelessness. Habita is one of these activist social movement actors. As Table 2 demonstrates, Habita received close to three hundred families in their weekly sessions of *atendimento* (individual support). This chapter concerns the activities and practices of the Habita association, also including insights from other housing-related associations from the Lisbon Metropolitan Area that were interviewed and/or encountered during the fieldwork, such as AIL (*Associação dos Inquilinos Lisbonenses*), APPA (*Associação do Património e População de Alfama*), *Associação Renovar a Mouraria, Vizinhos de Areeiro*, SOS *Racismo, Rede de Solidariedade*, and Stop *Despejos*.

One of the most well-known organisations in Europe fighting against evictions is the Spanish PAH, *Plataforma de Afectados por la Hipoteca* (Platform for People Affected by Mortgages). The strategies and principles of PAH's practice have been analysed in many academic works (Casellas & Sala, 2017; Di Feliciantonio, 2017; García-Lamarca, 2017), by PAH's members themselves (Colau, 2011; Colau & Alemany, 2014), as well as by other social movement organisations, such as Habita. This can be largely attributed to the fact that PAH has had considerable success on many fronts, although falling short on others. It has built up a strong movement, geographically wide and with a huge number of mobilised people, with 226 different groups around Spain (PAH, 2020); it has been successful in resisting evictions; had a strong influence on banking practices; and its role has been considerable in legitimating occupations and resistance (Martínez, 2019). Yet despite launching many campaigns to promote certain policies and legislation, these have often been unsuccessful, such as in the case of making non-recourse debt compulsory by law, or the provision of homes at 'affordable rental prices' (Martínez, 2019). PAH is an important reference for Habita, and its partner in the European Action Coalition for Housing. Many aspects of Habita's method have been inspired by PAH. Nonetheless, it

FIGURE 6.1   Habita banner during the 25 April demonstration in 2019. "Affordable rents, but only with an unrealistic income"

was noted at Habita that the countries were different, and that this needed to be considered. PAH's practices needed to be adapted to the context of the LMA (Interview A1, 2018).

One of Habita's main concerns was how to support the mobilisation of people facing housing exclusions and deprivations so that they would become motivated to engage in collective action, building a collective, instead of fragmented and individualised, front, and create wider social movements. For this to happen, some authors argue for the importance of political opportunities or, alternatively, extremely harsh state action that undermines the victories of the past (Bayat, 2015; McAdam, 1999; Tilly, 1978). Others emphasise the importance of framing the struggle (Benford & Snow, 2000); for example, the articulation of claims through the language of human rights can be effective for promoting collective action (Holston, 2008). Still others draw attention to the more subjective aspects, such as the ability to see the threat as collective (Das & Walton, 2015), or to build up a collective identity (Simone, 2013; Spivak, 2005). The disruption of the 'neoliberal model of personal responsibilisation' (Di Feliciantonio, 2017) has been highlighted as one of the centrepieces of PAH's strategy in the fight against evictions (Casellas & Sala, 2017; Colau, 2011;

TABLE 2   Habita's strategies

Strategy	Form
A) Open struggle and political perspective	Invented
B) "Occupy – Resist – Live"	Invented
C) Campaigning and media	Invented
D) *Atendimento*	In-Between
E) Negotiation with public authorities	In-Between
F) Legal channels and court cases	Invited
G) Building rights and policies	Invited
H) Networking	Invited

Di Feliciantonio, 2017). Authors emphasise the potential of PAH's practices to disrupt the logic of neoliberalism, and particularly to question the dominant practices of neoliberal housing policy (García-Lamarca, 2017; Gonick, 2016). In particular, the more personal aspects of coalescence into collective action have a direct link to the processes of subjectification analysed in Chapter 3.

Many of the constraints on participation in collective action can be considered to stem from the neoliberal policies that privilege the owners and exchange-value of housing, to the detriment of the use-value and of the rights of the urban poor who face housing exclusions. Housing exclusions and precarity undermine the opportunities for political participation. The constraints are also gendered and racialised, with the implication that participation by single, low-income mothers is particularly stymied. However, linking individual practices of quiet encroachment to larger mobilisations has been proposed as the key to achieving political change (Pradel-Miquel, 2017).

The best ways to support the mobilisation of these families were under constant contemplation at Habita: new strategies were experimented with and tested, engaging in 'theoretical practices' (Osterweil, 2013) and, considering Habita's long experience, some of them had already been evaluated as more effective than others. Much deliberation was undertaken on the circumstances that single, homeless mothers, for example, faced in trying to participate in meetings and in mobilisation in general. By and large, Habita's experience seemed to prove that social movements can have a significant impact in promoting mobilisation against evictions and housing exclusions (Fieldnotes 27/02/2018, 26/06/2018, 12/03/2019). These theoretical practices were important in contributing to learning through housing activism (Lira & March, 2021).

Moreover, this chapter presents a detailed examination of the analysis that informs Habita's strategies, as well as of the strategies themselves. The strategies are analysed following Meyer and Staggenborg's (2012) framework, which sees the strategies as composed of tactics, demands, targets, and arenas. Yet the framework seems to lack the notion of the analysis needed for coming up with a strategy. While I agree with the idea of a strategy not only being an intentional instrument but also a legacy that 'produces itself, shapes the context and the subjects' (Caciagli, 2019), I also contend that the theoretical practice, including analysis, research, and theorising(Osterweil, 2013), tends to be an integral part of building strategies. In analysing strategies, therefore, at least 'demands', 'tactics', 'arenas', 'targets', the cultural and social context, and the analysis proceeding from the formulation should be considered.

In addition, I will build upon Miraftab's (2004) conceptualisation of 'invited' and 'invented' spaces of participation, categorising strategies into 'invited', 'invented', and 'in-between' strategies. At Habita, evictions are seen as belonging to four main categories: evictions from private rental housing, evictions through demolitions of settlements of informal origin, evictions by the bank, and evictions from social housing. A member of Habita (Interview A1, 2018) explained that these typologies were considered relevant because they differed in their historical backgrounds, in their legal frameworks, and in the sense of the actors promoting the eviction (a city council, a bank, or a landlord). They also involved different interests and population groups with diverse characteristics in cultural, social and economic terms.

By focusing on the case of Habita, this chapter will explore what kind of roles social movements can play in supporting people who face housing exclusion. What kind of strategies are used, and what kind of contradictions emerge in these interactions? And finally, to what extent can social movements have a significant impact on curbing housing rights violations and contributing to the creation or transformation of life worlds?

2   Housing Movements in Portugal

Historically, Portugal has often been depicted in terms of the absence of a strong, organised civil society, including social movements and citizen organisations and associations (B. de S. Santos & Nunes, 2004). Many have interpreted the country as having abandoned the promises of participation in the revolution of 1974, resulting in a situation in which, despite the change in the political regime and the advanced framework of rights, the relationship between state and citizens continues to be authoritarian, with little space for public debate and deliberation (Matos, 2016; B. de S. Santos & Nunes, 2004). Consequently, many protests in Portugal can be seen as responses to decisions on which the citizens have not been consulted or listened to (Matos, 2016).

The analyses of more recent urban social movements in Portugal focus mainly on the wane of the anti-austerity protests during the years 2010–2013 (Accornero & Pinto, 2015; Baumgarten, 2013, 2017; Cardoso et al., 2017; Matos, 2016; Matos & Sabariego, 2020; Seixas et al., 2015). A few analyses include social movements related to housing (Mendes, 2018; Sequera & Nofre, 2018; Tulumello, 2019), in addition to the analysis of more specific processes such as the Caravan for the Right to Housing (Falanga et al., 2019; Kühne, 2019). Although the emphasis of these studies tends to be on Lisbon's city centre, some authors also mention movements that operate on the outskirts of the city (Allegretti et al., 2018; Seixas et al., 2019; Seixas & Guterres, 2019b, 2019a).

As referred to in the methodology section, before starting the actual field research phase, I completed a mapping of different social movements and associations that work for the right to housing in the Lisbon Metropolitan Area and found that many of them tend to focus on the housing struggles of white Portuguese families in the centre of Lisbon. Habita is an exception in this sense, considering that it has its origin in the struggle against demolitions of informal neighbourhoods in the whole Lisbon Metropolitan Area. These neighbourhoods have a strong representation of both Afro-descendant and Roma populations due to their post-colonial origin as well as structural and institutional racism. Later, Habita's actions developed to challenge all kinds of forced evictions, conceiving them as a problem extending to the general population after the global financial crisis. In this regard, Habita is quite unique in the Portuguese setting, as the other housing organisations have more specific focuses, such as problems faced by tenants, inhabitants of neighbourhoods of informal origin, or people affected by mortgages.

It is noteworthy that Habita, in terms of numbers, is extremely small: in recent years, its core group of activists has consisted of five to ten active members, most of whom are women. Yet Habita increased its strength considerably by building alliances with other movements. During my fieldwork, the active group included only one male member. Most of the active members could be classified as 'activists', rather than 'affected people', in the sense of not facing an acute housing shortage. A few of them are also academics. Habita's organisation tends to be informal and organic. Many issues, such as reflection on current and previous practices, future strategies and actions to take, as well as the sharing of information, take place mainly at the weekly coordination meetings, combined with an exchange of emails, WhatsApp messages and phone calls. In addition to the core group, Habita receives support from other members who engaged in specific tasks, such as organising the monthly debates. Networking with other activist organisations, both nationally and internationally, constitutes vital support for Habita's action.

Habita's fight for the right to housing is referred to at least by Mendes (2018) and Tulumello (2019). Tulumello's (2019) main argument related to Habita's and other 'emerging social movements" practices is to question their ability to establish an alternative to dominant economic development models in the context of the normalisation of austerity policies. Mendes (2018), on a similar tone, analysing the 'new urban social movements in the city', considers that without a strong link combining urban struggles such as demonstrations and occupations with institutionalised political struggle, their impact might be limited. Based on my findings on Habita's work, I agree with Mendes but draw the opposite conclusion: this combination is exactly what Habita is engaging in, both through its own actions as well as with its various networks, as analysed in another article (Saaristo & Silva, 2024). All the above-mentioned accounts fail to reflect upon the prominent role of women in these movements, except Nunes & Serra (2004), who, in their analysis of occupation movements during the Portuguese revolutionary period (1974–1975), pay attention to the close connection of the housing struggle with women's traditional sphere, the home. The omission of women's role in these analyses is unsurprising considering that women often tend to be left out of urban theory-making (Peake, 2016).

Yet gender and ethnicity have played central roles in the urban social movements focusing on housing. Patriarchal practices also continue to be present within the movements, posing challenges to women activists (Miraftab, 2006; Seppälä, 2016), although in many cases, women have become central agents against evictions (Brickell, 2014; S. C. Motta, 2013; Patel et al., 2016; L. Podlashuc, 2011). In some cases, separate women's housing movements have been formed to fight against the patriarchy both within the movements and in the wider society (Marinas Sánchez, 2004). Immigrant women's important role in housing struggles has been highlighted in Italy (Colella et al., 2017; Grazioli & Caciagli, 2018) and in Spain (Gonick, 2016; Martínez López, 2017). Some authors highlight the centrality of women in the resistance movement with the concept of the feminisation of resistance, suggesting that subjects who simultaneously face multiple oppressions are in a position to re-imagine emancipatory politics, produce and embody difference, and create and experiment with new subjectivities (S. C. Motta, 2013; Seppälä, 2016). In some cases, these include specific forms of 'feminised resistances', such as the politicisation of motherhood (S. C. Motta, 2013). In this way, they can create deeper solidarities to more effectively battle against neoliberalism (Carty & Mohanty, 2015). The feminisation of the struggle against homelessness in the Lisbon Metropolitan Area was evident during my fieldwork. In addition to Habita's activists, most people who sought support from Habita were women, as exemplified in Table 2.

3 Theoretical Practices

3.1 *Real Estate Speculation, Housing Financialisation and Neoliberal Housing Policies*

In addition to considering the strategies, drawing attention to the analysis, research and theorising that social movement actors engage in is essential. The theoretical practices inform the construction of the action frames, as well as the consecutive design of the strategies. To contextualise the frames and strategies employed by Habita, it is essential to present how the activists and NGO workers perceived the causes of current housing exclusions, leading to the identification of priorities and the most urgent issues in the housing struggles.

The increasing connections between the finance and real estate sectors have been highlighted by many authors, notably by Aalbers et al. (2020), with their concept of the 'real estate-finance nexus'. Correspondingly, Habita and the EAC considered that in the current policies, housing is instead considered an asset or a commodity: 'Housing, a profitable investment for capital, has become a key target of speculation for banks and real estate companies over the past three or four decades' (Brochure by the EAC & Habita, August 2018: 7). Several authors have also pinpointed the tourism sector as being deeply intertwined with this nexus, with these three sectors playing a fundamental role in the Portuguese economy (Caldas et al., 2020; J. Rodrigues, 2018). Particularly since 2008, Lisbon has been promoted as an ideal destination for tourists, linking it to real estate investment (A. Gago & Cocola-Gant, 2019), following the logic of 'urban entrepreneurialism' (Harvey 1989), with its promotion of consumer culture. This struggle is related to touristification, especially in the city's central areas from which tenants have been displaced because of the investment opportunities for the real estate sector (A. Gago & Cocola-Gant, 2019).

Yet activists and NGOs emphasise that they are not against tourism as such but that its negative impacts need to be controlled with protective policies so that the historical neighbourhoods are not transformed into 'houses without people' (Interview A2, 2018). Unfortunately, the most vulnerable tend to be the most affected: Airbnb has centred in neighbourhoods where there have traditionally been more rental homes for the poor and immigrants (Cócola-Gant, Debate Habita, 22/02/2018). For Habita, 'to deny these elements is to defend particular interests that have used housing for speculation and for businesses that lack ethics, equality and social justice' (Habita at the parliamentary hearing on Housing Framework Law, 26/02/2019). Thus, Habita argues that gentrification and evictions must be considered if housing is to be recognised as a fundamental right. Habita and the EAC also link 'debtfarism' (Soederberg, 2014) to real estate speculation and financialisation, highlighting how the promotion of debt for survival, combined with austerity urbanism (Peck, 2012), have contributed to accumulation by dispossession:

> However, after the global economic crisis of 2008 ..., a wave of indebtedness spread across the world. Debt, combined with austerity policies, the loss of social income and the contraction of the European economy, gave rise to more predatory policies on the part of banks and large real estate groups. They took advantage of the opportunity to invest in housing and obtain important control over the housing stock available.
>
> Brochure by the EAC & Habita, August 2018, p. 7

The activists and housing association representatives studied made it clear that the role of the state actors has been crucial in the process of the financialisation of the city and speculation on its land and real estate: 'The origins of the housing crisis are above all political. Initiatives like golden visas have facilitated the co-optation of the city. They are even selling the palaces' (Fieldnotes, 14/03/2018). They criticised the withdrawal of the state from housing production as well as for a lack of market regulation:

> Housing and also affordable housing are being increasingly pushed towards the market. Public intervention is shrinking, as if the market was an entity with no relationships with the state. Financialisation is increasing, which worsens human rights issues.
>
> Habita's turn to speak at the meeting with the United Nations High Commissioner for Human Rights in Portugal, 29.04.2019

In this neoliberal form of urban governance, housing commodification and financialisation have been strongly supported by the municipalities and the central government, with diverse policies that promote real estate speculation and the financialisation of housing, like golden visas and tax exemptions (Tulumello & Dagkouli-Kyriakoglou, 2021). Rental law changes such as NRAU, facilitated a considerable number of evictions from private rental accommodation (A. Gago, 2018). A landlord can now make the excuse of carrying out extensive renovation work to evict a tenant, even in the case of long-term or elderly tenants (Interview A2, 2018). Therefore, new tenants have not managed to move into the historical neighbourhoods as the renovated buildings tend to be designated only for tourist accommodation. The state has thus facilitated financialisation and real estate speculation by liberalising the rental laws, reducing tenant protection, as well as many other pieces of legislation that promote the same objectives. The Lisbon City Council has also actively promoted Lisbon as a desirable tourist and investment destination.

In addition, the activists pointed out in the interviews (NGO2, 2018) and in the debates (Debate Habita, Ana Gago, 22/02/2018) that in many historical and self-built neighbourhoods, in the context of the financial and economic crisis, the city councils promoted speculation and gentrification by selling properties. They have thus acted as 'market-makers' (Çelik, 2021), unlocking land values. The Lisbon City Council has sold its properties, liberating them for the real estate investment markets, and with favourable policies, it has facilitated the entry of financial actors. Through the *Reabilita primeiro, paga depois* ('Renovate first, pay later') programme, the Lisbon City Council sold more than a hundred empty buildings between 2013 and 2016. According to the programme, new owners were given a timeframe of around two years to renovate the buildings, and only after that had to pay the purchase price (Bivar et al., 2017). In the historic neighbourhood of Mouraria,

> What we see today are, in fact, buildings that have largely been renovated for tourism … The luxury segment of apartments for foreigners has grown in the last year. The legislation confers many benefits the foreigner who buys a residential property here in Portugal. The real estate sector also takes advantage of this and is now growing considerably [...] there are actually many people who have had to leave their homes.
>
> Interview NGO2, 2018

In contrast, the Loures City Council has tried to promote the demolition of informal neighbourhoods, such as Bairro da Torre, to free up the land for other, more lucrative purposes. However, at the moment of the fieldwork, it only demolished homes whose residents had been resettled.

3.2   *Racism and Gender-Based Violence*

Racism is denounced by the activists, both at the institutional level and in intrapersonal interactions. The marginalisation, stigmatisation and criminalisation of poor residents have been singled out as a factor that contributes to the naturalisation and impunity of human rights violations in informal neighbourhoods and council estates (Alves, 2016; O. Raposo et al., 2019). The report by the *Caravan for the Right to Housing* (2018, unpublished) campaign states that racism was a problem in all of the neighbourhoods visited by the Caravan. The Afro-descendants and the Roma tend to be in low socioeconomic situations in Portugal. While Afro-descendants are often invisibilised, the Roma are almost regarded as outcasts and heavily excluded from society, as was pointed out by one of Habita's activists: 'The Blacks are seen as broom pushers, invisible, but with the Roma it's even worse – they're seen as "difficult foreigners"' (Interview A5, 2019). The exclusion of the Roma has deep roots: until the 25 April revolution in 1974, the Roma did not attend school and did not have any legal documents. In Alentejo, the Roma population has been continuously pushed from pillar to post without giving them any opportunity to settle (Interview A5, 2019).

In addition, the activists argued that in some municipalities, the authorities deliberately implement discriminatory policies, such as the demolition of neighbourhoods inhabited by ethnic minorities, because they assume that many of their electorates have racist worldviews and will thus support such policies (Interview A1, 2018). A certain kind of racism persists in the policies and practices of many municipalities:

> We are dealing with various issues here – the issue of discrimination against a group of people that have been persecuted historically, marginalised, especially by the institutions. There is a continuity [of colonial history] ... It's a racist society, one that doesn't care ... People who do everything they can to integrate themselves into society, to be able to have a dignified life, fulfilling their duties like any other people ... They consider it natural that the police, at the request of the city council, enter the neighbourhood and ... demolish people's homes without warning, without providing an alternative. And society sees it as natural, as if it was nothing. Some people even applaud, they even say it's very good, that this is what must be done.
>
> Interview A4, 2018

The activist interviewed thus identified that a profound silencing of the colonial past (Trouillot, 1995) still exists and has implications for the current practices. Moreover, the lack of adequate training of municipal employees can also result in institutional racism as there is no specific preparation for technicians or teachers who work in poor neighbourhoods:

> Racism exists; it may not be expressed directly, but it's implicated in many actions. Many people in the neighbourhoods can become marginalised because they are not heard. [...] Teachers ... are not selected

according to their skills, personality, or ability to work in a certain type of school. To work in a school like this one … teachers should have special preparation so that they would not have racist attitudes and could fight against discrimination.

Interview ME1, Loures, 2018

In addition to racism, gender-based violence is considered a significant challenge by many associations and activists (Fieldnotes, 25/06/2018, 25/10/2018, 14/01/2019). They stated that the institutions have often exacerbated the impact of gender-based violence through individual pathologisation (S. Motta, 2016), a specific kind of self-responsibilisation that depicts the person in question as guilty for having caused the violence inflicted upon them. When the authorities detect there is often a lack of response by the social services in the sense of provision of alternative housing (Interview with Sara, 2019, fieldnotes 21/07/2018). Overcrowding in social housing also tends to exacerbate domestic violence as people are not able to leave their parental homes for economic reasons (Interviews NGO3, NGO6, A4, 2018). Direct threats against women at risk of eviction or homeless women to withdraw custody of their children are equally reported (Fieldnotes 04/12/2018, NGO6, 2018, Interview with Nina, 2019), as are actual withdrawals of custody (Fieldnotes, 18/04/2019). The activists maintain that there is a need to establish efficient mechanisms of support for victims so that in situations of violence, women and children can access safe alternative housing and do not face additional stress caused by the authorities (Interview A1, 2018).

4   Building Political Subjectivities

4.1   *Constraints on Participation*

Responding to the above-mentioned problems was a fundamental objective at Habita. Internal and external mobilisation, meaning becoming internally organised and then generating mobilisation beyond the neighbourhood, as well as the mobilisation of the media, have been identified as key practices of resistance against evictions (Cabannes, 2010). In line with the importance of community organisation and mobilisation to prevent evictions, Habita has also sought to support the mobilisation of people at risk of eviction. In the family assemblies, Habita's members affirmed that the ability to defend the right to housing depends on the strength of the group: 'If people do not participate, we won't be able to defend each other' (Fieldnotes, Family Assembly, 24/07/2018). Yet mobilising those at risk of eviction is considered the most difficult challenge in the struggle, both by the social movement activists and the people at risk. First, there were practical constraints on participation that stemmed from the women's precarious situation and their role as the caretaker of the family. A simple lack of time was often mentioned: 'We women have a lot on our shoulders; we have to feed the children, work, buy clothes; this [housing] is not the only problem women have!' (Fieldnotes, meeting at Habita, 27/11/2018). Some also felt that the results of participation did not really compensate for the additional arrangements they needed to make to attend the meetings. Habita was not able to offer the clear solutions that some were hoping for, as argued by Carla:

> At the end of the day, I'm always at home with the kids, organising dinner, so it's very complicated [to go to meetings]. [...]. I don't know, I only went a few times, and that time, there were very few people. What I understood, from what I heard from Dona X, is that people want things done. I think people go there with their problems and they hope Habita will help find solutions to them. Then they get there and don't understand the point so well, because we go there to exchange experiences, and maybe that's why they end up not going.
>
> Interview, CARLA, 2019

The decision to participate in collective mobilisation might thus be weighed against the extra effort needed to enable participation in meetings. However, despite their lack of time, many occupiers tended to maintain that defending housing rights through collective action was necessary: 'People [who occupy] should get moving (*mexer-se mais*), not just wait until they are evicted and then hope everyone will go there to support them. Otherwise, we can't stop any evictions' (Interview with Maria, 2018). Yet many other issues emerged that constrained occupiers' participation in collective action.

An interesting case was the mobilisation of families that Habita promoted in Lumiar in 2018, where an initially strong movement of occupier families later fell apart due to nonparticipation, as explained by Paula:

> I think it was a very interesting process to begin with. One thing was that people were very united, and when they were called, they showed up. Then I started to notice what you usually notice in any kind of struggle, that I even see at work, that everything is very nice at first, but then, 'Oh, I don't feel like it today. I'm sure someone else [at the protest] will do it for me.' But then, when something happens, they're sure to say, 'Oh, I'm very worried, I have the police here!'
>
> Interview with PAULA, 2019

The idea often conveyed to me was that the person I talked to would go and participate, but they assumed nobody else would:

> I honestly don't like being idle. I'm unlike the typical Portuguese person who says, 'Look, this is just the way it is', and others respond, 'OK'. No, I'm going to fight. I'm up for it, but I don't see the solidarity. When there are demonstrations, things like that, I see most people, as has already happened, laughing at me. 'What are you going there for? Let it be,' And I [reply], 'It's because you all think that way, that we are the way we are' Then they complain, but they also do nothing to change the situation.
>
> Interview with SARA, 2019

According to Ema, only 10 years ago it was easier to get people to defend each other in countering evictions:

> Author: Why were you saying that when they tried to evict you the first time, people were more proactive? Was there more mobilisation at the time?
>
> Ema: Yes, people were more united with each other. Nowadays, everyone only thinks about themselves.
>
> Author: What do you think has happened?
>
> Ema: I don't know. It's like, people are very isolated. [They think] 'Oh, that one is being evicted, I have nothing to do with it. Better her than me.' It wasn't like that before. It was, 'She's being evicted, let's get together, let's make a noise, let's fight for her rights.' Nowadays, I don't see that here anymore. 'They are evicting her, look, let them evict her. At least they aren't coming to my door.' Or they even do the opposite here: 'Let's file a complaint about that person.' So that she'll be evicted and they'll be left alone. That's the problem now.
>
> Interview with EMA, 2019

These excerpts from the interviews can be interpreted in the context of the neoliberal capitalist society, where the society is understood as a company and the subject as an entrepreneur, following the fundamental principle of competition (Foucault, 2008; Dardot & Laval, 2013). The process of applying for social housing in Lisbon construes access to social housing as a competition, in which the residents compete for who is the 'most wretched' (*o mais contadinho*, fieldnotes, 24/07/2018); for example, having disabilities or being unemployed gets a higher score (Câmara Municipal de Lisboa, 2009). As the availability of social housing is minimal only the 'most wretched' have a chance in this race.

Additionally, the entrepreneurial subject valorises self-help and emphasises the responsibility of the individual (Dardot & Laval, 2013), resulting in an ideology in which people are socialised into taking care primarily of themselves, and participation in collective struggles can even be considered ridiculous, as pointed out by Sara.

The conception of housing as predominantly private, a financial asset, and the competition for social housing against other people with housing problems render it more difficult to perceive housing as something that everyone should have access to. It can be assumed that the logic of entrepreneurship and individual responsibilisation renders more complicated the task of building political subjectivities that could be used to form a collectivity (Simone, 2013; Spivak, 2005) or an overarching framework (Simone, 2013) for the struggle. The fragmentation of struggles was clear in the way that many of those occupying sought to find ways to argue that their situation was different from that of the other occupiers. They could, for example, say that they were not 'really' occupying, that someone had left them the apartment to take care of. Therefore their situation was different from the 'ordinary' occupiers (Interview with Carla, 2019). Despite often emphasising that with their income, it was impossible to have access to housing at current market prices, and recognising that many others were in the same situation, this did not translate into a strong notion of a collective problem. The idea of *união*, the sense of being united, was considered necessary both by activists and affected persons but difficult to achieve. This demonstrates how the existence of grievances alone will not suffice to motivate participation in the collective struggle.

Moreover, many people end up naturalising their housing exclusions due to already being segregated living in a neighbourhood perceived to be far away from the 'city' (Interview, NGO6, 2018). The territorial stigmatisation that self-built and council housing neighbourhoods face affects the preparedness to participate in collective struggles, as explained by this activist, born in a neighbourhood of informal origin himself (Interview A4, 2018).

> The way in which rights are violated in these neighbourhoods is mostly due to the ideology, the propaganda. The people who are victims of this violence, many of them, in many cases, end up internalising what it said about them. So they often end up becoming their own worst enemy. And this is one of the first difficulties in these types of situations, in order to be able to resist, to be able to organise, to face problems. So afterwards, this gives way to all kinds of arbitrariness.
>
> Interview, A4, 2018

This subjectification as 'less equal than others' (García-Lamarca, 2017) ends up limiting the sense of entitlement: people might be so used to living on the other side of the 'abyssal line' (Santos, 2014, 2017) where claiming rights is not realistic, that they end up considering their exclusion as normal. The sense of entitlement to rights can also become diminished in the case of having an immigrant background: 'These people [residents of stigmatised neighbourhoods] do not feel like they are wholly accepted; they feel like they do not entirely belong to Portugal' (Interview, NGO6, 2018). In fact, many young people with an immigrant background do not have Portuguese nationality even if they were born and have since lived in Portugal because Portuguese nationality is acquired through the principle of *jus sanguinis*, which inevitably causes diverse types of exclusions (Alves, 2018; O. Raposo et al., 2019; Rodrigues, Anabela Fernandes et al., 2017).

Misunderstandings between activists, municipal employees, and residents facing housing deprivations sometimes contributed to exacerbating biased attitudes between these groups of actors. For instance, groups of occupiers who began to publicly claim that Habita would 'legalise' their occupations, which contributed to the souring of Habita's relationship with the Lisbon City Council (Interview with Paula, 2019). Due to this, some municipal employees allegedly began to exert pressure on some neighbourhood associations to refuse to collaborate with Habita (Interview, NGO6, 2018). Some occupiers also claimed that Lisbon City Council employees had warned them not to participate in Habita's activities if they wished to access council housing. While these stories are difficult to verify, they were pretty common.

These dynamics illustrate how coalescence into collective action faces numerous challenges and constraints: it seems to be discouraged by the state actors and sometimes also horizontally by others in similar situations. The most significant discouragement, however, seemed to come from within: having internalised the power relations and their place within them, people at risk of eviction discourage themselves from participating in the struggle. The interpretations of homelessness as a personal failure, irresponsibility, and shame – the neoliberal model of personal responsibilisation (Dardot & Laval, 2013; Di Feliciantonio, 2017) or the 'socialisation of guilt' (Casellas & Sala, 2017) – are often created by neoliberal institutional framings and management practices, and through how homeless people are depicted in the media and by the institutions. As entrepreneurial subjects, many homeless people and people at risk of eviction consequently create self-images in which homelessness or housing problems are constituted as their own responsibility. Consequently, homelessness is conceived as a personal failure. Following Foucault (2007), power operates here not only by repressing, but also by creating particular subjectivities and self-images (May, 2014). Becoming 'the entrepreneur of his own exist-ence' (Dardot & Laval, 2013) combined with subjectification 'as an outcast' (García-Lamarca, 2017), the urban dweller facing housing exclusion internal-ises their condition and stops questioning whether they should or could have the right to different kinds of situations. In addition, in the context of 'urban entrepreneurialism' (Harvey, 1989), housing is perceived primarily as an asset for the creation of wealth. Consequently, it is not framed principally as a right, but rather as a commodity: people must be able to *pay* for their housing. All of these aspects restrain the possibility to create a common identity and discour-age people from participating in collective action for housing rights.

4.2   *Breaking the Model of Personal Responsibilisation*

In meetings, Habita sought to challenge the framings of homelessness as a per-sonal fault and the conceptualisation of housing as a commodity. In the Forum da Habitação seminar in May 2018, a member of Habita explained that Habita wants to do transformative work, transforming the guilt that people feel, bring-ing in the notion that the policies are to blame, not the people (Fieldnotes, 05/05/2018). At Habita's meetings, the notions of personal shame, failure and being alone began to be challenged and replaced by notions of unity and hope for the future:

> When you're being put out onto the street, you react like, 'Oh no, what now?' But after people talk to you, they create another mood, a different feeling. It happened to me. First, it was, 'Now what?' Then, talking to you [and to the other activists and people at risk of eviction], your state of mind improves, right?
>
> Interview with CÉLIO, 2019

Aida explained how she had felt after being evicted, when a group of activists came to support her during her meeting with the representatives of Santa Casa:

> I started to cry, it was bad ... I started thinking about my house in Guinea-Bissau ... Then I looked at all of you, your faces, all there support-ing me, and I gained more strength to listen to what people were saying.
>
> Fieldnotes, 11/02/2019

Breaking the conceptualisation of housing problems as the responsibility of the failed entrepreneur thus helped to trigger participation in collective action. It was fundamental to try to break the subjectification of people fac-ing housing deprivations as outcasts, to challenge the socialisation of guilt, as well as the neoliberal model of self-responsibilisation (Di Feliciantonio, 2017; Sletto & Nygren, 2016). Challenging the neoliberal model of responsibilisation, or the socialisation of guilt, can be conceived as a dialectical process in which the initial understandings of personal responsibility, shame, and guilt are gradually questioned. When people at risk of eviction bring their situations to Habita's open-door sessions or family assemblies, they hear about other people in similar situations. They thus enter a space in which their experience receives acceptance and understanding. They are allowed to explain their housing problem in detail, without facing moral judgement regarding the decisions they have made in the past, or regarding their performance in life (to use a neoliberal idea of competition coming into all spheres of life, as described by (Foucault, 2008), or life being a competition). During the discussions about each person's particular case (at the assemblies and in *atendimentos*), the members of Habita and other people at risk of eviction share their experiences of similar situations. The activists argue that the situation cannot be interpreted as the failure of an individual but should rather be construed as an injustice affecting a vast number of people and that has to do with issues an individual person at risk of eviction has little power over. In this process, the dominant neoliberal interpretations of homelessness, property and evictions are questioned.

In this way, other kinds of self-images are offered for consideration, suggesting that 'I have failed because I cannot afford a house' can and should be replaced by 'the state should ensure that more public and affordable housing becomes available'. Other readings of a particular situation are brought to the table: for example, readings of injustice, racism, irresponsible urban and housing policies, relentless real estate speculation, and the failure of the state to address the needs of single mothers on a low income. This gives people at risk of eviction strength and support, and they gradually start challenging the ideas they have internalised about themselves and others. In this process, collective action frames (McAdam et al., 2001) were created, constructing a shared idea about the problem to be tackled. Perceiving housing primarily as a human right validates collective action for housing rights in a different way.

Unity and emotional support thus give strength and contribute positively to triggering interest in collective action. The activists attempted to create a sense of unity by emphasising that the housing crisis affects many people, and to fight against it, it would be important to be united (Fieldnotes, Family Assembly, 27/02/2018). They stated that collective action was the way that many had been able to negotiate alternative housing solutions or stop an eviction, or that the city council would give in because they knew that the residents were united and supported each other (Fieldnotes, Family Assembly 24/07/2018). For many people, Habita's approach changed their mindset about collective mobilisation, so that they began to embrace the idea of resisting together:

> I learned that if we come together, we can sometimes get answers that we can't get on our own. Not only solidarity with each other, but together we also manage to really demonstrate our discontent, because if we act in groups, I think that they are practically obliged to listen to us.
>
> Interview with PAULA, 2019

As a result, notions such as 'it is not worth struggling', and 'even if I go, the others will not participate' could gradually start being replaced by thoughts like 'I will fight for access to housing' and 'if we are unified and loud, they will have to listen to us'. In this sense, Habita's sessions worked as 'educational sites of resistance' (Caciagli, 2019), contributing to the formation of collective political subjectivities, and socialising the idea of participation in housing activism. Habita's work explored the transformative processes of both unlearning the subalternisation – involving the internalisation of inferiority and personal guilt – and learning about one's rights and the possibilities of collective mobilisation, echoing the ideas of the pedagogy of the oppressed (Freire, 1990) or Enrique D. Dussel's (2019) pedagogics of liberation, which analyse what kind of (pedagogical) processes can liberate an oppressed subject.

These changes do not occur in the same way for all; everyone has their own way of reacting to these stimuli. Not everyone is convinced by Habita's interpretation of the situation, and in this context, the general trust in and credibility of Habita matter – issues that are often undermined by how Habita's actions are framed by other actors such as social housing managers or politicians, as explained in this chapter. Even so, for most people affected, at least a seed of transformation was sown in that their sense of self-worth was reinforced: at the very least, they felt relieved and satisfied on account of the emotional support they had received, which gave them the fortitude to continue. For others, while they might not embrace the idea of a collective struggle, they sensed that they had received concrete advice on how to face the different institutions and how to manage to present their case. They thus felt stronger and better equipped to continue their personal struggle. Still, others declared that the collective struggle and union were meaningful and that in addition to helping themselves, they also received much from being able to help others in similar situations. They are the ones who embrace the idea of the collectivity and union around the struggle for the right to housing.

5   Strategising Collective Action

5.1   *Invented, Invited, and In-between Strategies*
Habita uses a wide variety of strategies and tactics to fight for the right to housing. As a joint brochure states, Habita, together with the EAC and Stop Despejos, works through:
– citizens' awareness and empowerment through community self-organisation and the training of activists;
– political and public pressure, through direct intervention or denunciation, to change systems, legislation, and policies;
– the formulation of political proposals and dialogue with institutional actors;
– supporting the various struggles within the area of housing and urbanism, namely direct actions of protest and resistance, and serving as a communication channel between tenants and the management authorities;
– organising academic and political debates, and with meetings residents of affected neighbourhoods.

> EAC, Habita and Stop Despejos, A financeirização da habitação na Europa, August 2018

I have grouped Habita's strategies for fostering mobilisation against evictions, drawing on Cabannes et al. (2010) and Miraftab (2004, 2009), into three main categories, organised according to whether they can be considered 'invented', 'invited', or 'in-between'. Invented strategies directly confront the status quo and the authorities, while invited strategies are those legitimised by government interventions (Miraftab, 2004). However, it needs to be considered that in practice many strategies fall between these two extremes, which are neither completely legitimised nor totally confrontational. I therefore consider it useful to add the category of 'in-between' strategies. In this study, invented strategies are considered transgressive strategies, or strategies with have a high degree of transgression, according to the degree to which they challenge entrenched practices. In contrast, the second group of strategies are characterised by a low degree of transgression. 'In-between' strategies contain moderate transgression (Table 2). With the 'degree of transgression' concept, I intent to demonstrate how Habita engages in a broad set of actions, alternating between and combining transgressive/invented, more conventional, invited, as well as in-between strategies.

These wider strategy groups will also be analysed within the framework proposed by Meyer & Staggenborg (2012), considering the demands, tactics, arenas and targets implicated in each strategy. In the interviews and meetings, when reflecting on the diverse strategies, activists also drew attention to other aspects that matter when evaluating strategies, namely the actors involved and the context in which the strategy is applied. In terms of the actors involved, Habita's meetings were predominantly female. Yet gender was not explicitly emphasised, and men were equally welcomed. The specific role of women in the housing struggle was nonetheless clearly recognised. Providing a home for one's children continues to be seen as primarily the responsibility of women, and mothers do not abandon their children easily, which prompts them to engage actively in the fight for housing, as argued by one activist:

> I think it's obvious, I mean, to begin with, many families are headed by a single parent and the single parent is the woman, right? ... So, you have a woman with a child who has to come forward to fight for the apartment; she feels that she must. The guy, if the situation doesn't suit him, sacode as calças [washes his hands of it], as they say, and leaves, doesn't he? But she won't ... This isn't necessarily a bad thing. As I saw here at Habita, these women are super tough, and even when there's a man around, he tends to stay in the shadows.
>
> Interview A5, 2019

Yet the strategies and framings used could not be regarded as particularly 'feminised' (S. C. Motta & Seppälä, 2016).[1] The challenges faced by single mothers were often mentioned but in conjunction with other structural problems. Domestic violence was seldom directly discussed, possibly because of the sensitivity of the issue.

The list of Habita's actions reported during my fieldwork illustrates that there have been a variety of activities and actions.[2] Highly transgressive, invented actions have been more common, with 52 cases, whereas 21 actions with a moderate degree of transgression are listed. However, the weekly *atendimento* sessions must be added to these 21 actions, significantly increasing the number of in-between actions. Nonetheless, Habita also engages in a significant number of actions with a low degree of transgression (26 listed actions). The variety of strategies interact and support each other, and while transgression gained importance, other strategies also made an important contribution.

---

1 This has changed since my fieldwork, as Habita has become involved with the MuDHA network (*Mulheres pelo Direito à Habitação*, Women for the Right to Housing).

2 I have aimed at including all of the most significant actions, but the list might not be all-inclusive.

5.2 *Conquering Space by Transgression*

Occupations and protests, political mobilisation and heightening political awareness form some of Habita's core strategies – while also constituting the actions that Habita tends to be most criticised for by the authorities, as well as by some academics. There is an emphasis on these kinds of activities in Habita, especially on the strategy of open struggles (strategy A). The tactics include promoting mobilisation and political awareness-raising through *assembleias de famílias* (collective meetings, 'family assemblies' for families at risk of eviction), and bigger and smaller protests and demonstrations. Family assemblies aim to promote emancipation through collective discussion and deliberation on possible solutions, targeting the families themselves above all. It is through these assemblies that Habita also seeks to promote the mobilisation and collective organisation of the affected families.

Fighting demolitions has been a core area of Habita's work, and is where its work actually began. In this field, Habita has built long-standing, influential work across municipalities (in Cascais, Almada, Seixal, but above all in Amadora and Loures), as described in Di Giovanni (2017) and Saaristo & Silva (2024). During my fieldwork, the struggle with the municipality of Amadora against the demolitions in the 6 de Maio neighbourhood was constant. Habita received alerts about demolitions on numerous occasions. The tactics used to stop demolitions involved mobilisation of the affected residents, negotiation with the city council and the central government, and trying to stop demolitions on the spot.

In this field, one of the tactics used was temporary occupations of state and city council offices after evictions and demolitions if all of the other negotiation channels had dried up, as occurred in April and November 2018 when Habita occupied the Ministry of Environment together with the inhabitants of 6 de Maio. These occupations are often seen as 'putting pressure on' [*fazer pressão*] the authorities so that they will speed up their processes, apply current legislation or policies, or demonstrate to the authorities that the current policies or legislation have unintended, negative consequences.

In addition, Habita is actively promoting larger-scale demonstrations. For example, in 2018, Habita began to contact various organisations and collectives to propose collective action for a demonstration on the Right to Housing. This duly resulted in the Demonstration on the Right to Housing held on 22 September 2018, together with more than 30 collectives and organisations. The primary demand during the demonstration was, in concrete terms, to provide more affordable housing for all and, in terms of framing, to question the notion of housing as a financial asset and as something that must be earned, promoting the idea of housing as a right. The arenas for these actions are

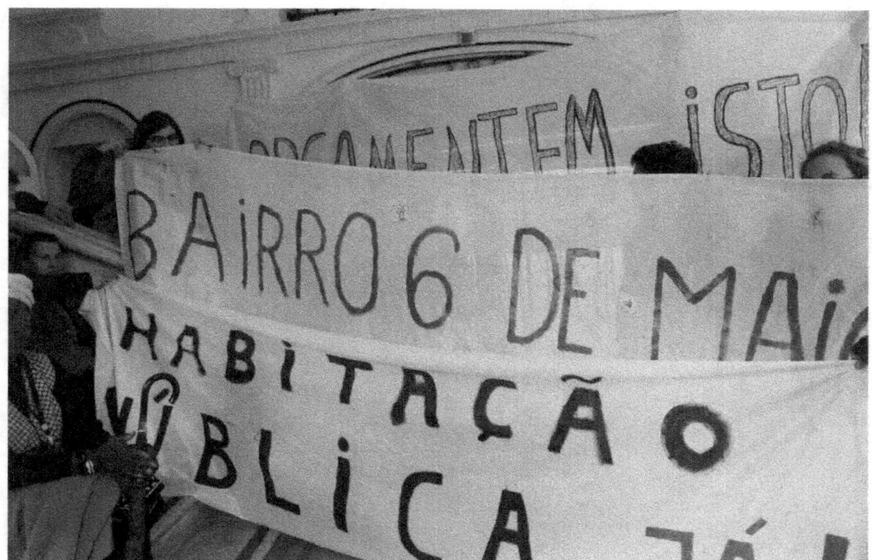

FIGURE 6.2   Occupation of the Ministry of Infrastructure, November 2018

varied: *assembleias de familias* typically take place on Habita's premises, while other meetings are organised in the neighbourhoods. In street demonstrations and protests, public space is used as an arena to gain visibility.

Strategy A partly overlaps with strategy C, Campaigning and Media, in which the tactics used include carefully constructed campaigns for housing rights, but also individual actions in response to evictions, such as open letters to authorities or press releases. It also includes contacting journalists to give interviews, and using social media to publish short videos and pieces of information on current events. For videos and campaigns, Habita often partners with Stop Despejos, a collective that it helped to initiate in December 2017.[3] In campaigns and open letters, the demands are related to specific policies, programmes, or problems, such as access to social housing, or challenges caused by real estate speculation. In contrast, social media and directly contacting the city council and / or ministries is usually used to demand more consideration for an individual case of housing exclusion.

For example, in the Mouraria neighbourhood in 2017, a real estate company, the owner of a building located in Rua dos Lagares, sought to evict all 17 families living in the building by sending them a letter of opposition to the renewal

---

3   See https://vimeo.com/stopdespejos. Last accessed 30/07/2020.

FIGURE 6.3   Demonstration for the Right to Housing, September 2018

of the contract. The municipal elections were set for October 2017, and Habita realised there was a political opportunity to put pressure on the Lisbon City Council to intervene. Habita organised a campaign with high visibility in June and July and managed to convince the city council to negotiate with the owner, with the result that the rental contracts were extended without increasing the rent for five subsequent years.

> At the time, it was only possible to do it that way because the municipal elections were just around the corner. In other words, all strategies are inserted in a context, and we have to see which strategies we're going to follow in a particular situation. But it was an interesting process, it really was. It probably wouldn't have the same outcome today, though, because we don't have an election coming up.
>
> Interview A1, 2018

The strategy of 'occupy – resist – live' (strategy B) is something that Habita has not yet been able to fully implement, unlike, for example, the PAH in Spain, which has used *recuperación* (recovery) of empty mortgaged buildings as a key strategy (Casellas & Sala, 2017; Gonick, 2016), or Brazilian occupation movements that have used occupations as a pre-planned strategy to claim housing rights (Cabannes et al., 2010; Earle, 2012; Piotto & Sanches, 2019; Sanches et al., 2019). Instead, Habita has focussed on defending families who occupy because of their lack of housing. Here, the demand centres around the framing of occupations. 'When there are people who have already been trying to gain access to housing through legal means for a long time, Habita considers it legitimate to occupy', as was argued in one of the family assemblies organised by Habita (Fieldnotes, 27/02/2018). Habita regards occupations not as a crime or as vandalism, but as a structural problem, resulting from the commodification of housing as well as from inadequate financing for and management of social housing, and consequently demands that the central state as well as the city councils bear their responsibility in terms of addressing the housing needs of these families, instead of evicting them. Street demonstrations, temporary occupations, campaigns, and the use of the media all primarily target the state actors, mainly the central government with its line ministries, as well as the city councils.

Habita was involved in the mobilisation of women occupying social housing apartments, by promoting many meetings in Lumiar and Chelas during 2018 and 2019, by organising family assemblies, and by encouraging collective participation in the public meetings of the City Council and the Municipal Assembly of Lisbon. The primary objectives were to raise awareness of the problem, contest the framing of occupiers as criminals, and trying to encourage the women to organise collectively to defend their housing rights. In addition, Habita defends individual occupation cases. For example, in February 2019, Aida and her three children were evicted from a council home they had occupied without any alternative housing being provided. After the eviction, Habita supported Aida in occupying – together with activists – the office of the City Councillor for Housing. In the resulting negotiation, Lisbon's Santa Casa agreed to pay for Aida's hostel room for the weekend (the eviction was undertaken on a Friday) and to meet with her the following Monday to discuss future support. The solution was a homeless shelter for mothers with small children (Fieldnotes, 15/02/2019). While this response cannot be considered adequate, it resulted in a place for Aida and her children to stay. The following April, Aida was notified that she had been allocated a council home. Yet the Lisbon City Council decided it would press criminal charges against her, a process that was still ongoing at the time of writing.

Habita's efforts have had many tangible outcomes in the concrete work of resisting evictions. During my fieldwork, Habita, often working together with Stop Despejos, managed to stop or suspend, through different tactics, many evictions from social housing and private rental accommodation, as well as the demolition of informal neighbourhoods. This happened through personal contacts (Habita contacting the city council directly) or by collective organisation (a petition to the City Council of Lisbon and participation in city council meetings), at times achieving a temporary suspension of evictions from social

FIGURE 6.4 Family assembly at Habita, October 2018

housing. For these achievements, acts of civil disobedience, such as protests and evictions, were often considered necessary:

> We have already seen that institutional work, such as meetings, hear-ings, and petitions in which we have participated, has its role but fails to promote fundamental changes. We understand that another type of complementary action is necessary and urgent: direct action, such as occupation and sit-ins in public institutions, or the blockade of evictions, hand-in-hand if required are essential forms of pressure that can help to boost social movements, promote public discussion, and contest the legitimacy of evictions in a country that assumes the right to housing but without promoting alternatives, where the only interests defended are those of the market
>
> Habita, Activity Plan 2018–2019

Inventing new spaces of participation using transgressive tactics, if necessary, was thus considered fundamental by many activists. They recognised that in this struggle, formal rights were often the preserve of landlords, real estate companies, municipalities, or the state:

> An eviction is a massive act of violence that is legitimised by the law today and that is too normalised in our society. Only disobedience can restore reason, and only disobedience can stop this social scourge that is defended by politics and powerful economic interests … I think what we have to demonstrate (and they fear it! I know) is that we are ready not to be politically correct, prepared to do something unpredictable, that we can disrupt political campaigns, the opening of events and cocktail parties, and that we are ready to disobey … Of course, this action has to be weighed in the balance, and always done with thought and a strategy.
>
> Habita member, fieldnotes, 19/06/2018

As a result, if the activists quietly obeyed and stayed within the invited, legitimised, and formal spaces of participation, the reasons for exclusions and inequalities would not be questioned.

5.3 Building Bases with Support and Negotiation

In the category of in-between strategies, with a moderate degree of transgression, D and E definitely belong to Habita's primary modi operandi. Strategy D, *atendimento*, written in Portuguese due to lacking a good equivalent in English, has been one of Habita's core activities. It consists of weekly open sessions, targeting families facing housing problems. Habita's members then try to support them in finding ways to defend themselves. Habita's premises were the main arena for this. *Atendimento* can be considered an in-between strategy in the sense that while providing information and advice, it is not a contested activity – the response that Habita often considers most effective has to do with mobilisation and contesting the policies and legislation that are considered unjust:

> We try to give information about the various steps that people can take to defend themselves. But then, we always say that this fight is not a legal fight but a collective fight.
>
> Habita member, fieldnotes, 05/05/2018

Atendimentos are probably the strategy that has been most discussed internally (within Habita), with considerable reflection on how this activity stands in relation to the objective of mobilisation. Habita has been criticised by some other actors for this strategy, labelling the association as *assistencialista*, an entity that creates dependency.

> An assistentialist movement will always be limited in its possibilities for
> growth. [...] We can take as examples the AIL (Associação dos Inquilinos
> de Lisboa, the Lisbon Tenants' Association) or Habita, as opposed to the
> PAH. Both of these do not try to support those seeking help in forming
> community-based organisations to for their own interests. Instead, they
> give technical or legal assistance, or external mobilisation for specific
> cases. These are solutions that have been revealed to be weak in dealing
> with the size and characteristics of housing problems.
>
> Interview, A3, 2018

Yet some other associations contested this idea and highlighted the need to
provide information:

> We must support people. That is why we opened the doors of the asso-
> ciation, to help them get organised, to look at the letters they receive,
> and many people have approached us for these reasons. We ask people
> to bring their contracts to see what they've signed, to tell them what
> their rights are, and how they can be prepared if something happens in
> the future.
>
> Interview A2, 2018

The 'example of the PAH', referred to above largely concerns one of the PAH's
principles: that mobilisation and mutual support are essential. As described
by the PAH, it does not wish to be acknowledged as 'anti-eviction professionals
but rather to help build collective processes that allow us all to take on the daily
injustices we face' (Colau, 2011). This was something that Habita also reflected
upon frequently: 'In the *atendimentos*, we talk with the people, they leave
more motivated, but then we never talk again', as was pointed out in one of the
meetings (Fieldnotes, 12/03/2019). Yet in *atendimentos* as well as in assemblies,
Habita was able to support the families in developing negotiation strategies
with the city councils. Paula described how this worked out in her case:

> But at the time, I didn't know where to turn, because I even went to the
> office of the City Councillor for Housing, but I never managed to talk
> to anyone! Not even with a secretary. It was always over the phone, but
> I didn't know how to find them. Habita gave me the possibility, in addi-
> tion to being able to fight for my cause, to support other people, but also
> to know where to go to find the municipal employees!
>
> Interview with PAULA, 2019

In this way, the assemblies and *atendimentos* served many purposes. They made it possible for those at risk of eviction to learn about their rights and how to protect them but also provided them with concrete steps on how to approach the city councils and put pressure on them. The *atendimentos* and assemblies worked as an antechamber of action: there can be no action without prior organisation, mobilisation and awareness-raising of the problems involved. They thus fortified and empowered the people at risk of eviction, something many families needed in order to continue their housing struggle.

Habita has been very active in furthering the negotiations between the authorities and the people at risk of eviction in various ways (strategy E). Habita helps residents to prepare themselves to speak in public meetings held by the city council or city assembly, in which the residents can, by previous registration, present a problem or a challenge related to the city council's policies. The city councillor responsible for the sector then answers the residents, and other city councillors might also intervene. In addition to making an intervention, Habita also advises the residents to go to the meeting because doing so might result in a chance to speak directly with the advisors of the city council for housing, or with the city councillor themself. It is considered fundamental to go to the sessions together, as a collective, to show that the group is organised (Fieldnotes, Meeting of Assembleia de Bairros, 11/03/2018).

Other direct negotiation tactics include sending letters, trying to schedule meetings with the city councillors, their advisers or social housing managers, and using personal contacts to negotiate. Personal contacts with the

FIGURE 6.5   Habita's group giving support to a woman who was evicted, during her
intervention at the municipal assembly, October 2018

authorities are often considered to yield favourable results, as they can "break the ice" and establish an initial contact between a resident and a municipal employee (Interview A5, 2019). The demands typically concern specific situations brought to Habita's attention, such as threats of eviction or demolition, which Habita tries to stop. Here, as well, the targets of the strategy are normally the city councils or the government.

5.4   *Operating in Invited Spaces*

This group includes diverse strategies, bound together by their perceived acceptability in the eyes of the authorities. The legal channels and court cases (strategy F), while a legitimate form of action, also encompass a certain degree of transgression due to the aims of the legal action. This strategy often targets the decisions made by the Portuguese state or municipal authorities. During my fieldwork, Habita was not very active in this field since it did not have a lawyer to support such actions, although the situation has changed since my fieldwork. Initiating legal processes was thus considered costly and slow, so other forms of action were preferred. Moreover, previous results of these kinds of actions had not been very promising. For example, in 2016, Habita made a collective complaint to the Portuguese Ombudsman and the Special Rapporteurs on Adequate Housing, denouncing the way the municipality of Amadora was implementing the PER programme, which involved violent demolitions and leaving many inhabitants of the target neighbourhoods homeless. This resulted in a recommendation by the Ombudsman to the Minister of Environment, in which the Ombudsman proposed that the current occupied territories should be integrated into the PER, and all of the inhabitants who were forced to leave their homes due to demolitions should be rehoused (Provedor da justiça, 2016). This recommendation was also cited in the report by the (ECRI, 2018). Yet these recommendations had little impact as the city council in question refused to take them into account.

Still, the possibility of taking legal action was always given due consideration. For example, during my fieldwork, a workshop on how to use the International Covenant on Social, Economic and Cultural Rights to defend housing was organised. In addition, other associations hired lawyers to make a *providência cautelar*, a protective order. Although Habita had used this tool, particularly in the case of demolition threats in the neighbourhoods of informal origin, it did not consider this strategy very effective:

> A protective order will not grant anybody housing. By law, no one has the right to a home via occupation. Now, there may be a political decision

to legalise a situation. This decision can only happen if there is pressure
from us.

Fieldnotes, Family Assembly, 24/07/2018

Habita engages in building policies (strategy G) in various ways. Building policies (strategy G) are engaged in by Habita in various ways. In its activity plan
for 2018–2019, Habita defined its demands in terms of policy changes:
- There can be no evictions without solutions (a solution is defined as ade-
  quate housing in terms of quality, size and value, respecting the person's
  roots in the community).
- Amendment of the new rental law to protect tenants and the stability of
  contracts: long-term and automatically renewed.
- Controlled rents (with maximum ceilings).
- Provision of public and collective housing (cooperatives, etc.).
- New expropriation law.
- New law for the municipalities to exercise pre-emptive rights at fixed and
  non-market prices.
- End of regime for non-habitual residents.
- Combat Golden Visas.

The tactics for implementing this strategy are varied. To inform its policy recommendations, Habita collects information on residents' situations and analyses existing policies and policy plans. Habita shares its knowledge directly
with decision-makers by participating in parliamentary hearings, organising
petitions and open letters, contacting the politicians in charge directly, and
organising debates that bring together activists and academics. Furthermore,
Habita organises debates on policies and other housing-related issues, and
participates in the debates and events organised by others.

Most social movement activists that I interviewed considered that they had
played a fundamental role in promoting new policies on housing and improving draft bills, in proposing policies and existing policies, such as the New
Generation of Housing Policies (Secretaria de Estado da Habitação, 2017) –
especially its programme *1° Direito* – the Housing Framework Law, the new
municipal regulation of housing policies in Lisbon, and in pushing to undertake a new, nationwide survey on rehousing needs (IHRU, 2018). For example,
Habita launched a petition to cancel the debts that had resulted from the
change to the Law on Subsidised Renting (LAA) for tenants on various council
estates. The law was subsequently changed. Habita has also tried to highlight
the plight of homeless single mothers so that the Lisbon City Council officials
would better consider their situation in the scoring system for social housing

applications. Municipal employees told me in interviews (ME8, Lisbon, ME10, ME11, Loures, 2019) that due to pressure from Habita, they had decided to examine the situation of single mothers and their children more closely.

Habita also networks actively with other organisations (strategy H), belonging to the Morar em Lisboa platform[4] with other associations, participating and co-organising actions with the Stop Despejos collective,[5] and being an active member of the European Action Coalition for the Right to Housing and the City (EAC).[6] It organised the EAC's annual meeting in Lisbon in September 2018. Habita has also undertaken study visits to other organisations that promote housing rights.

A good example of an initiative implemented together with various actors is the Caravan for the Right to Housing, initially proposed to Habita by the network of neighbourhoods of informal origin – *Assembleia de Bairros*. Many academics also joined the initiative and Habita secured a small grant from the Guerrilla Foundation for this purpose.[7] This led to the organisation of the Caravan for the Right to Housing in September 2017, which visited dozens of neighbourhoods in the Lisbon and Porto Metropolitan Areas and the Azores in order to promote participation and inclusion in the discussion on policies so that the right to the city, to housing and to essential goods would become an effective right. This promoted meetings with the Ombudsman, parliament members, and the President of the Institute of Social Security. At the international level, the process triggered a visit by ECRI (the European Commission against Racism and Intolerance) and another by the UN Special Rapporteur on adequate housing (in 2019). The Caravan resulted in a document entitled *For the Right to Housing*, handed to the Secretary of State for Housing, Ana Pinho, in December 2017 (Falanga et al., 2019; Kühne, 2019). Its impact on creating visibility was considered significant as it promoted the connection between populations and communities with diverse housing problems, giving visibility to the national housing problem (Habita's Activity Report, 2017). In 2018, resettlements finally began again in Bairro da Torre (Loures) and Bairro da Jamaica (Seixal).

The strategies with a low degree of transgression, such as building policies and contributing to policymaking, were considered significant. The participation in debates and parliamentary hearings was crucial for increasing awareness of the housing problems among the general population. The diverse

---

4   See moraremlisboa.org. Last accessed 25/05/2019.
5   See stopdespejos.wordpress.com. Last accessed 30/07/2020.
6   See https://housingnotprofit.org/. Last accessed 25/05/2019.
7   See http://guerrillafoundation.org/. Last accessed 30/07/2020.

strategies thus complement each other in the sense that all of them are important in different ways and acquire greater or lesser importance depending on the context and the actors involved. While building policies and networks have yielded many interesting results, political mobilisation and protest create pressure for change. Within these strategies, diverse tactics were used in different contexts, according to what was considered the most promising in light of the political environment.

6   To Conclude

Although various strategies have been identified as important in Habita's struggles, the transgressive strategies acquired a unique role in pushing issues forward. A fair amount of civil disobedience was often needed to 'increase the political will' to promote transformations. Yet arguably, what seems to produce the most favourable results from the social movement perspective is the balance of the diverse categories of strategies. Depending on the timing, political opportunities and restrictions it provides, it is fundamental to pick a strategy that is the most appropriate for the moment. Furthermore, the strategies support each other mutually, with the combination of strategies increasing the chances of success. Diverse combinations of strategies with varying degrees of transgression have been used to point out gaps, problems, and inconsistencies in current housing policies and legislation, and to promote empowerment and transformation at the personal level.

The analysis has shown that the social movements have had a fundamental role in supporting the mobilisation of people at risk of eviction – even if challenges are encountered along the way – and that they have taken a decisive role in contributing to the design of policies and programmes. The massive scale of current housing problems in Portugal has been made visible in the political and everyday debate. Awareness has been created of the plight that many low-income single mothers face in the current system, in which their salaries are clearly insufficient to cover the current costs of housing and other expenses. The activists have contributed to the emancipation and transformation of the life worlds by creating awareness of human rights and justifying the individual and collective struggle. These social movements have thus, in many ways, contributed to challenging the structures and relations of inequality, creating more space for participation and democratic deliberation.

CHAPTER 7

Conclusion: Subjectivities of Evictions and Occupations

In this book, my objective has been to explore the diverse subjectivities implicated with council housing occupations and evictions in the Lisbon Metropolitan Area, asking what factors contribute to the formation of these subjectivities and the forms of agency and city-making applied. Examining housing precarity and its contestation gains relevance in the current context, in which homelessness is growing and evictions are increasing in number. Housing exclusions are an important factor causing poverty (Desmond, 2016), worsening living conditions and prospects for the future. As Dotsey & Chiodelli (2021) insightfully argue, this housing precarity is, however, enrooted in a plethora of broader issues. It is crucial to understand how diverse population groups are differentially affected by capitalist and neoliberal urban governance processes, to enable the design of inclusive urban policies. Considering the inability of states to provide or guarantee adequate housing for all, the various improvised tactics through which the urban poor and the 'urban majority' (Simone, 2013, 2018) seek to secure some form of housing for themselves become increasingly important. Throughout history, both in the global South and in the global North, land and dwelling occupations have emerged as a central tactic for resisting housing exclusions. Yet, as they are predominantly conceptualised as belonging to the realm of 'informality' (Roy, 2003), they are frequently criminalised without taking into consideration the claims they seek to advance. However, such claims can often be considered legitimate in terms of international human rights commitments (Convention for the Protection of Human Rights and Fundamental Freedoms as Amended by Protocol No. 15 as from Its Entry into Force on 1 August 2021, 2021; ICESCR, 1967; OHCHR, 1997; UN-HABITAT & OHCHR, 2014b).

In this journey, I have argued that the analysis has to necessarily depart from an in-depth contextualisation, involving an examination of the historical, political and societal dimensions and processes that frame and condition the formation of subjectivities in a specific time and place for a person with particular characteristics in terms of gender, social class, ethnicity as well as social and cultural capital. To do so, it was necessary to begin with a wider contextualisation of the diverse dynamics of housing crises in Portugal and its metropolitan areas. To approach these housing crises analytically, I tackled forms and definitions of urban neoliberalism, departing from critical, neo-Marxist conceptualisations of neoliberalisation as an elite project that promotes market-based regulatory responses and commodification to expand capitalist profit-making.

The long-term housing struggles in Portugal have been linked to the lack of emphasis of the dictatorship on housing accessibility, which left strong marks in the Portuguese housing provision, and on the other hand, to rural-to-urban migration and migration from the former Portuguese colonies to Portugal, triggering the phenomenon of self-build housing (Beja Horta, 2006; Cachado, 2011). The 'new housing question' in turn, is contextualised by the increasing financialisation of the Portuguese economy, which is intrinsically linked with the financialisation of the housing sector through credit, liberalisation of the national banking sector and its insertion in international financial markets (A. C. Santos, 2019a). Since the beginning of the democratic era, the State has placed more emphasis on promoting homeownership. Housing was pushed into the realm of finance by the State by first making available multiple incentives for families to obtain mortgages. Later, since the global financial crisis of 2007/2008, the financialisation of housing has been further promoted through the facilitation of the entry of new types of investors, financial actors and real estate companies (J. Rodrigues et al., 2016; A. C. Santos, 2019a) that have operated through accumulation by dispossession, pushing elderly, migrants and low- and middle-income families out of the central areas of Lisbon and Oporto, and even out of the cities (Cocola-Gant & Gago, 2019).

The Portuguese economy has increasingly become strongly dependent on the 'financialisation-real estate-tourism' complex (Aalbers et al., 2020; Caldas et al., 2020; J. Rodrigues et al., 2016). Attracting private and speculative capital to the housing sector is privileged without attention to the effects of displacement and dispossession caused by capital accumulation. Foreign investors and funds are enticed by favourable legislation for real estate funds. Tax benefits and European Union resident permits are given to those investing in the country. Rents are allowed to rise in an uncontrolled manner. The urban policies promoted by the Portuguese central state and the city councils of Lisbon and Loures can be broadly conceptualised as urban entrepreneurialism, focusing on private-public partnerships, speculative activities and projects that boost the image of cities. Touristification has been promoted, especially in the Lisbon and Oporto metropolitan areas and the Algarve region, which has directly impacted housing prices and availability.

So far, the current housing and urban development policies tend to fail when it comes to providing affordable housing, as they avoid regulating private market rental and real estate prices and, on the contrary, act as facilitators and market makers of promoting further housing commodification and financialisation (A. C. Santos, 2019a; R. Silva, 2021). The measures that direct more state funding to the already booming housing market or that try to compete with fiscal benefits to induce private homeowners to rent their homes via programmes, such as the Programme for Affordable Renting, have been largely unsuccessful (L. Pinto et al., 2021). Since 2017, many policies related to housing have been launched. Notably the New Generation of Housing Policies and its programmes *1 ° Direito* on social housing and Affordable Renting, but also initiatives related to the Housing First model. The Recovery and Resilience Facility of the European Union provided Portugal with funding that can also be allocated to housing, and in 2021, the Government of Portugal (2021) announced that it would fund *1 ° Direito* with 1.25 billion euros in the coming six years, increasing the amount later to 1.80 billion, with the intent to provide 26 thousand dwellings.

Yet despite the efforts, the possibilities families have to access housing in Portugal are only deteriorating: in 2023, Portugal had the most unaffordable housing in the European Union, assessed by comparing the housing prices with the residents' income (Jorge et al., 2024). As social housing represents a trivial portion of the total housing stock, it cannot respond to the housing needs. Yet, at the same time, according to the latest census in 2021, the country has 723 thousand empty dwellings, out of which two-thirds are already suitable for habitation or would need only minor renovation works.[1] Nonetheless, occupations in Lisbon and Loures have targeted mostly vacant council and social housing dwellings, not privately owned homes. Contrary to Detroit as described by Herbert (2021), Lisbon is a booming, touristified city with an increasing population. The occupations of Lisbon and Loures are more comparable to the occupations in Naples, where council housing is targeted. However, the scale seems to be very different: in Italy, tens of thousands of council homes are occupied without authorisation (Nomisma, 2016), cited in Esposito & Chiodelli, 2023).

In these processes of capital accumulation, some population groups tend to be particularly affected by the processes of 'creative destruction' that urban transformation involves. Poor female workers have often been the major scapegoats (Federici, 2004; S. Motta, 2016). The ability to access housing is often intimately linked to the social markers and personal characteristics of the person facing housing exclusion, as exemplified in this book through the specific cases of Cátia, Ema and Sara, resulting in gendered, classed and

---

1   https://www.ocontador.pt/noticias/60,31052024/index.htm.

racialised forms of homelessness and housing exclusion. Contrary to the case of Detroit, in Lisbon and Loures, the occupiers are not necessarily the poorest of the poor but rather low-wage workers and single parents, especially mothers. Immigrants and racialised persons are more likely to work in the low-wage sectors and with precarious job contracts, such as being considered an independent service provider. The labour situation strongly impacts the ability to access housing, as the salary levels and type of job contracts affect the ability to pay rent and the possibility of buying or acquiring a mortgage to buy a dwelling. While an unemployed person might be able to access social housing in Lisbon and Loures, an employed one is necessarily considered 'too well-off' to be able to score high enough.

Similarly, a person's gender impacts the care responsibilities that they are likely to have. Large amounts of unpaid care work decrease the time available for paid work, thus limiting strongly the possible working hours, as they need to be compatible with, for example, children's school hours. In addition, a person's legal situation in a country largely defines the forms of public support available and the possibility of accessing credit. All this is important to detail because, as theorisations of both Southern urbanisms and feminist theories of agency highlight, all agency is intimately linked to and conditioned by the context in which it is inserted. All conditions of life influence the possibilities and probabilities of housing inclusion or exclusion. This is clearly illustrated through the examination of the life histories of Ema, Sara and Cátia (chapter 3), which illustrate exclusions that are gender, ethnicity and social-class-specific, exclusions that directly affect the housing availability for single mothers who work in the low-wage service sector.

Firstly, for all three, the cycle of housing displacement was initiated when they began their reproductive work: with their first pregnancies. For many, having a child is when the lack of an adequate and secure home starts to gain acuteness. When living alone or without dependents, a person can often adapt to housing conditions that are less than ideal. The need to care for another, vulnerable and dependent person adds another layer to the situation. It is this care responsibility that ultimately provokes the necessity to organise a safe space called home. This responsibility, a responsibility that feels all the more overpowering when faced without the support of relatives or the community. Sara and Ema both had to leave their home due to their pregnancies. In Sara's case, the pregnancy triggered gender-based violence: her partner saw her in a vulnerable situation, without housing alternatives, and took advantage of having more physical strength by starting to abuse her. In Ema's case, her mother took issue with the pregnancy and forced her to leave. Cátia did not relate experiences of violence, and she initially stayed together with her partner. Yet she found herself to be the sole provider of the small new family and discovered she alone was not in the position of paying the rent for a family home.

Secondly, Cátia, Ema and Sara have all felt the consequences and implications of housing policies that do not emphasise the provision of social housing. Due to the highly restrictive access criteria to social housing, these women do not qualify for council housing in Lisbon despite being sole carers of their children and earning low wages. In this sense, they are not 'miserable enough', as ironically stated by some housing activists: only by quitting working or acquiring a disability, the scores of their housing applications increase to the level at which they could be considered as eligible. Conversely, they also do not qualify for the homes made available through the 'Housing First' programme in Lisbon. In this case, they are not 'enough homeless' as the programme in Lisbon only contemplates the two first categories ETHOS uses to classify situations of homelessness: 'rooflessness' (sleeping rough or in an overnight shelter) and 'houselessness' (sleeping in a temporary emergency shelter). Cátia, Ema, and Sara have gone through a variety of grades and shades of homelessness, but mostly, their situation tends to fall into the ETHOS category 3: living in insecure housing. This category groups situations that are well-familiar to them, such as temporary accommodation with family or friends, living in unsafe housing because of domestic violence, or living under the threat of eviction due to non-authorised occupation. Yet the programme does not consider these forms of housing exclusion, rejecting support for Cátia, Ema and Sara.

Thirdly, all three had also been forced to move due to the unaffordability of private rental housing. They have alternated renting out apartments, houses and rooms with diverse types of contracts, including their housekeeping labour or renovation works they agreed to undertake. Nonetheless, these solutions have offered them little stability, as their salaries are no match for the exorbitantly high rental prices. This situation is exacerbated by of being the sole provider of the family, responsible for responding to all the needs and expenses of the family. So far, there is no sign that housing affordability will improve in Portugal. Much to the contrary, housing prices have more than doubled since 2015 (INE, 2023b), and housing-related expenses now constitute, on average 39% of Portuguese families' expenditures (INE, 2023a).

Fourthly, instead of supporting these women and their families, the State has acted as a direct promotor of homelessness by evicting them from the places they have made for themselves to survive. Eviction causes much distress, making attending school and work increasingly difficult. Families often lose many of their belongings in an eviction, rendering the new start even more challenging. These violent dispossessions force the families through cycles of displaced survival, which tend to increase in terms of psychological, social and economic impact. In this way, as argued by Soederberg (2021), housing exclusions and evictions contribute to the social reproduction of the urban poor, resulting in an expulsion from essential social and economic opportunities (Sassen, 2014). Furthermore, as the care responsibilities tend to fall on women, especially racialised women, they end up being doubly influenced (Federici, 2004; Fraser, 2016; Tronto, 2013).

I propose that the amalgamation of labour precarity and housing insecurity can be conceived as a mechanism of subalternisation, describing a situation in which subjects are excluded from their rights and then persuaded by diverse subjugation techniques to accept their exclusion. Thus, in addition to analysing neoliberalism as something 'from above', I considered it fundamental to explore the ways neoliberalism affects the making of subjects. This means adding a Foucauldian approach in which neoliberalism is seen as a mode or modality of government: how the – often exploited – subjects internalise the logics of competition and individualisation and how they manoeuvre these logics and strategise to create opportunities and access to resources (V. Gago, 2017). State actors can apply diverse governance techniques to force and convince subjects to accept the state of play, and Chapter 4 sought to examine these techniques, inquiring about their impact on access to housing. Instead of effectively supporting these subalternised groups in securing housing, the responses provided by the state actors, in this case, municipal employees, frequently alienate these residents from the right to housing. This fact often relates to the reality of sparse resources allocated for housing within the municipal budget. However, this alienation is also promoted through housing managers' personal views and biases and their everyday work practices. In my analysis, I argued that the previous experiences of participation during the resettlement of previously existent neighbourhoods, or the lack thereof, seem to have paved the way for the later naturalisation of hierarchical and paternalistic management of council housing. Instead of promoting emancipation, the current invited spaces of participation rather attempt to legitimate the prevailing status quo and to keep the power structures intact. Participation of council housing residents is solicited for tasks such as maintaining the buildings clean, but their inclusion in the present co-governance structures is not facilitated. The lack of adequate notice and sharing of information about the meetings, as well as filling the existing community groups with institutional representatives, rather than council housing dwellers, discourages and even effectively thwarts democratic self-management.

In their interaction with the occupiers, the municipal employees tend to use three main techniques of governance, as analysed in Chapter 4:

(1) Invisible elbows. Management issues, such as complex bureaucracy and the lack of accurate records, result in the existence of vacant council dwellings. Lack of communication with the authorities who refuse to answer phone calls or respond to e-mails consequently delays housing processes. Social biases and inflexibility among municipal employees exacerbate the problem, leaving many residents in uncertain and stressful situations regarding their housing status.

(2) Neoliberal responses that focus on self-responsibilisation and competition. Responses from municipal employees ranged from caring responses, in which municipal workers seek to identify alternative solutions, to blaming individuals for their housing precarity, often suggesting inadequate solutions like temporary rent subsidies or homeless shelters. The scarcity of social housing leads to stringent allocation criteria, prioritising the most vulnerable groups according to the assessment matrix. However, other groups facing housing insecurity, like single working mothers, end up excluded. Additionally, the framing of occupiers as queue jumpers highlights a moral economy and competitive perspective. Through self-responsibilisation, municipal employees emphasised 'fairness' and 'the need to follow the rules' despite the inadequate housing options available. In this way, they attempted to convince the occupiers that their housing exclusion was their own responsibility or the result of their wrongdoings and tried to exert pressure or coerce them to leave.

(3) Visible fists and active production of homelessness by proceeding to eviction or imposing criminal charges. Municipal agencies in Lisbon have engaged in troubling practices, including persuading occupiers to leave without informing them of their exclusion from social housing applications and using violence to evict them. This leads to the deterioration of living conditions and homelessness, with evictions reframed as administrative 'de-occupations' to justify harsh measures. Despite international human rights commitments and a new housing framework law, these practices persist, highlighting a governance approach that prioritises following bureaucratic rules over providing adequate housing solutions.

In these actions, the state officials and authorities often enter the realm of informality themselves, employing different extra-legal techniques. It is important to note how the state officials and authorities' discourse about occupations tends to highlight the need to obey the rules, emphasising the illegality of occupations in relation to the existing regulations of council housing. This contrasts strongly with the authorities' constant breach in respecting international human rights legislation, the Portuguese constitution and the housing framework law, which is taken for self-evident. Much more could be done in terms of securing an efficient use of existing council housing resources instead of presenting the shortcomings in the management of council estates as a result of the wrongdoings of the council housing residents.

The techniques used also illustrate how these forms of governance are remarkably similar to the forms of governance of homelessness in the so-called Global South. The informal techniques of governance described by Auyero (2010) in the context of Argentina are replicated in analogous forms in the context of the Lisbon Metropolitan Area. Specific moral economies are used to justify the decisions to exclude some and include others, based on an evaluation of 'who needs housing the most', categorising people as deserving and undeserving. Yet the elimination of homelessness is not possible by decree: even if their homelessness and attempts to access housing are criminalised, housing precarity does not disappear.

In the absence of spaces of effective participation and in the context of subalternisation produced by neoliberal urban governance, homeless urban dwellers need to resort to more invented forms of participation, switching to transgressive forms of agency. Dwelling occupations in Lisbon and Loures emerge as one of these practices. In what follows, I will detail both the similarities and differences between these occupations with 'individualised squatting' (Esposito, 2022; Esposito & Chiodelli, 2021) and 'survival squatting' (Herbert, 2018a, 2018b) as well as highlight some of the contributions subaltern or Southern urbanisms as well as feminist theorisations on agency can bring to explore these practices further. The following aspects seem to characterise occupations analysed in this book.

To begin with, these 'autonomous' occupations are deeply rooted in the existing housing conditions, and in this sense, they are profoundly gendered, racialised, and classed. In this sense, they are often framed as the 'last option available' by the occupiers, undertaken due to the lack of other housing options and economic hardship, which, as presented earlier, in many cases had gendered reasons. Consequently, I argue that in Lisbon and Loures, occupations can be considered a 'feminised' strategy of responding to a situation of homelessness, in the sense that women with children might be more inclined towards them than lone men. Due to the heightened insecurity women and children would face if they slept on the streets, occupations, along with other forms of accommodation that depend on networks and/or acquaintances, emerge as a more viable housing option for mothers with children. This, however, ends up concealing the homelessness of these women and children, removing them from the official homelessness statistics.

Nevertheless, the 'last option' argument tends to be thoroughly challenged by the state actors and the wider public, who focus solely on the illegality of occupation. This dominant interpretation of housing occupations significantly influences the legitimacy of occupiers' claims. Despite the prevalence of occupations that are undertaken because of housing needs, as in the case of single mothers needing homes, the dominant narrative often emphasises the criminality of all occupations, hindering public support. Some municipal employees acknowledge the economic struggles driving these occupations, but overall, adherence to legal regulations often overrides social justice and human rights considerations. Advocacy for occupiers' rights has gained some traction through media and supportive organisations, highlighting the need for a more humane and supportive approach to housing policy. In Lisbon, the City Council has not signalled any willingness to consider the regularisation of occupations in case the families do not fulfil the strict criterion of 'deserving' families as stipulated in the scoring matrix of the municipal regulation. In Loures, the latest developments involve negotiations with occupying families without any clear indication of the possible outcome of the process.

In the second place, it is interesting to highlight how these occupations are intimately inserted into the local networks. They depend on their neighbours' approval or, at the very least, tolerance. In many cases, family members live already in the neighbourhood. A typical case is an adult mother who has a family home in the same area yet has been unable to find housing for herself and her offspring. The intimate familiarity of the neighbourhood, its infrastructure, and its inhabitants significantly supports the process of identifying a vacant apartment. It also helps to assess whether that particular apartment can be considered available for occupation or whether, on the contrary, it might have already been appropriated by local gangs or other groups that claim the right to use that particular apartment. Neighbours also play an essential role in either denouncing the occupation to the authorities or, on the contrary, protecting the occupation by, for example, telling the visiting city council authority that the apartment in question is not available anymore.

Thirdly, I have analysed how these occupations intersect with practices of care for infrastructure. Due to the lack of proper management, many dwellings owned by the city councils have deteriorated over time, becoming de facto inhabitable. In Lisbon, this has resulted in the closing of the apartments with steel plates. Occupiers thus remove the steel plates, enter the apartments and begin a slow reparation process constructing and caring, transforming the occupied space into a home. These home-making practices are thus an essential part of the temporal process of occupation.

Moreover, in Lisbon and Loures, occupiers tend to develop an elaborate negotiation strategy, drawing from tactics of hiding and reappearing. These occupation cases cannot thus be analysed in terms of 'camouflaging agency' only, as my interviewees highlighted the importance of putting pressure on the city councils: going to their meetings, sending letters, and making phone calls. As the authorities' response oscillates between tolerant to repressive, the occupiers need to carefully assess when keeping quiet is more beneficial than trying to advocate for their housing rights.

Additionally, and linked to the previous characteristic, occupiers seek to build alliances. These occupations are thus individualised but not a form of agency that would occur in a vacuum. Collaboration with housing rights organisations, local politicians, and lawyers has sometimes yielded positive outcomes. However, this has been the case for only particular families: no action has so far managed to bring about a collective response to the housing precarity of occupying families. Even a recommendation by the Committee for Economic, Social and Cultural Rights (Habita, 2022) to suspend these evictions has largely gone unnoticed. In addition, forming an occupiers' movement is rendered difficult due to the importance of hiding.

Finally, living in an occupied apartment is characterised by extreme insecurity and volatility, as predicting actions or reactions of state actors is extremely difficult. The psychological toll of living in an occupied apartment is thus substantial, resulting in many cases in considerable risk of mental health problems for the occupying families.

In conclusion, the occupations analysed can be perceived as a transgressive and gendered form of city-making that subalternised urban dwellers opt for in the case of acute and intense housing exclusion. The housing situations of the occupying families are characterised by frequent displacement and dispossession. This precarity can be assumed to limit the spheres of possible action, producing a more fragmented, individualised agency, characteristic of this form of housing occupation. Neither 'resistance' nor 'everyday practices' depict these modalities of agency well, which can be rather characterised by improvisation, adaptation, and mobilisation of resources available at a given moment. In many senses, the process of occupying council homes in Lisbon and Loures can be characterised as quiet encroachment: the silent, protracted, but pervasive advancement of the ordinary people on the propertied and powerful to survive and advance their lives' (Bayat, 2015: S34). These occupations are non-collective actions promoted by dispersed individuals, justified by necessity, and involve many 'tactical retreats' (Bayat, 2013: 51) in the sense of choosing carefully where to occupy, hiding and reappearing again, and utilising a variety of negotiation tactics. They also share many characteristics of 'peripheral urbanisation' (Caldeira, 2017), as they build upon autoconstruction, or at least, 'autorenovation', and possess the specific temporality of autoconstruction, in the sense of being always in the making. The occupations analysed articulate with and unsettle official logic, but as Caldeira argues, not necessarily through direct contestation but rather in transversal ways, seeking to renegotiate the notions of illegality and irregularity, promoting new interpretations of the current laws and regulations.

Yet it is contestable whether these occupations can generate new modes of politics or 'produce new kinds of citizens, claims, and contestations' (Caldeira, 2017: 9). In this sense, they do not exhibit a transformative quality (Hume & Wilding, 2020), nor can they be depicted solely as a practice of 'resistance' (Mahmood, 2006) despite their evident transgressive character. Instead, they present a form of agency, a capacity for action to respond to oppressive conditions that force these women to subaltern positions. However, occupations are not passive survival responses; they but incorporate multiple motivations, aspirations and objectives that occupying women have for their future. Nonetheless, a needs-based occupation itself can be considered a political act in the sense that, through it, occupiers directly enact their right to housing, promoting social transformation and contributing to the process of constructing the urban. They also serve to illustrate diverse gendered, racialised and classed aspects of housing exclusion. However, as these occupations consist of fragmented, individual acts, the state agents can dismiss them easily as illegal, refusing to consider the questions that inform and produce occupations, such as housing and labour precarity. This clearly undermines the transformative potential of autonomous occupation.

Collective action might bring more strength to have occupiers' voices heard. However, for many occupiers, it is difficult to embrace an overtly public approach and expose themselves, as they tend to wish to keep the door open also for the possibility of being out of reach of the authorities. This study also investigated how housing movements, focusing on the specific case of Habita, have sought to support autonomous occupiers. Habita's strategies were explored by using the 'degree of transgression' as an analytical device, examining the activists' perception of the capacities of different categories of strategies – invented, invited, and in-between. The analysis presented a strong consensus on the idea that Habita cannot further its claims by operating through invited strategies alone. Invited strategies, such as building policies, are extremely relevant. Habita has registered various cases of successful policy proposals that were later adopted by the central state or the municipalities. In addition, in-between strategies with a medium degree of transgression are fundamental to building bases for the action by negotiation and mobilisation. Yet invented, transgressive strategies are also needed to conquer new spaces of participation regarding cases and issues that would otherwise not be heard. Hence, by temporarily occupying a ministry or the office of a city councillor, movement activists, together with the 'affected' residents, can take their claims directly to decision-makers and compel them to react. Consequently, while all strategies make an essential contribution, those with a high degree of transgression are crucial for contesting the current neoliberal order in which people experiencing homelessness tend to be made responsible for their housing exclusion.

Habita's family assemblies were presented in this study as an example of an educational site of resistance, potentially breaking the conceptualisation of housing problems and deprivations as the individual's responsibility and challenging the socialisation of guilt. The actions promote an alternative form of subjectification that emphasises the broader causes of housing exclusions and frames housing as a human right. This helps promote the socialisation of housing activism, triggering participation in collective action. This is crucial so that these occupation practices could be conceived as being connected to other struggles against evictions and for the right to housing. As Rolnik et al. (2022) write, there is an urgent need to scale up the struggles to face global actors that impact the right to housing across the world.

References

Aalbers, M. B. (2017). The Variegated Financialization of Housing. International Journal of Urban and Regional Research, 41(4), 542–554. https://doi.org/10.1111/ijur.12522.

Aalbers, M. B., Fernandez, R., & Wijburg, G. (2020). The Financialization of Real Estate. In P. Mader, D. Mertens, & N. van der Zwan (Eds.), The Routledge International Handbook of Financialization (pp. 200–212). Routledge. https://doi.org/10.4324/9781315142876-17.

Abrantes, P., & Roldão, C. (2019). The (Mis)education of African descendants in Portugal: Towards vocational traps? Portuguese Journal of Social Science, 18(1), 27–55. https://doi.org/10.1386/pjss.18.1.27_1.

Accornero, G. (2019). 'Everything was possible': Emotions and perceptions of the past among former Portuguese antifascist activists. Mobilization, 24(4), 439–453. https://doi.org/10.17813/1086-671X-24-4-439.

Accornero, G., & Pinto, P. R. (2015). Brandos costumes? Protesto e mobilização em Portugal sob a austeridade, 2010–2013. Estudos Ibero-Americanos, 41(2), 393–421. https://doi.org/10.15448/1980-864X.2015.2.21366.

Acuto, M., Dinardi, C., & Marx, C. (2019). Transcending (in)formal urbanism. Urban Studies, 56(3), 475–487. https://doi.org/10.1177/0042098018810602.

Agência Lusa. (2017, January 2). IHRU diz que não há dinheiro para concluir Programa Especial de Realojamento. Observador. https://observador.pt/2017/02/01/ihru-diz-que-nao-ha-dinheiro-para-concluir-programa-especial-de-realojamento/.

AGFE & UN-HABITAT. (2007). Forced Evictions – Towards Solutions? UN-HABITAT. http://www.unhabitat.org/pmss/listItemDetails.aspx?publicationID=2353.

AGFE & UN-HABITAT. (2011). Forced evictions Global crisis, Global solutions (pp. 1–142). UN-HABITAT. https://unhabitat.org/books/forced-evictions-global-crisis-global-solutions/.

Agier, M. (2015). Do Direito À Cidade Ao Fazer-Cidade. O Antropólogo, a Margem E O Centro. Mana, 21(3), 483–498. https://doi.org/10.1590/0104-93132015v21n3p483.

Aguilera, T., & Bouillon, F. (2013). Le squat, un droit à la en actes. Mouvements, 74(2), 132–142.

Allegretti, G., Tulumello, S., & Seixas, J. (2018). Repositionner le débat sur le droit à la ville à Lisbonne: Tendances contradictoires dans le secteur du logement. Sud-Ouest Européen, 46, 93–110.

Almada, F. J. T. Z. (2020). Os discursos sobre a Cova da Moura: Uma análise crítica e exploratória a partir de alguns conceitos de Frantz Fanon [Iscte – Instituto Universitário de Lisboa].

Alves, A. R. (2016). (Pré) textos e Contextos: Media, Periferia e Racialização. Política & Trabalho, 44, 91–107.

Alves, A. R. (2018). Realojar, despejar, guetizar. Arqueologias de uma violência obliterada: Habitação e racismo nos relatórios nacionais/internacionais (O Combate Ao Racismo Em Portugal: Uma Análise de Políticas Públicas e Legislação Antidiscriminação). Centro de Estudos Sociais, Universidade de Coimbra.

Alves, A. R. (2022). Quando ninguém podia ficar. Racismo, habitação e território. Livraria Tigre de Papel.

Alves de Matos, P. (2021). Bodies of and against austerity: Gendered dispossession, agency and struggles for worth in Portugal. Social Anthropology, 29(4), 992–1007. https://doi.org/10.1111/1469-8676.13107.

Alves De Matos, P. (2021). Disciplined Agency: Neoliberal Precarity, Generational Dispossession and Call Centre Labour in Portugal. Manchester University Press.

Alves de Matos, P. (2023). Distributed agency: Care, human needs, and distributive struggles in Portugal. Critique of Anthropology. https://doi.org/10.1177/0308275X231207732.

Amin, A. (2014). Lively Infrastructure. Theory, Culture & Society, 31(7/8), 137–161. https://doi.org/10.1177/0263276414548490.

Amin, A., & Lancione, M. (Eds.). (2022). Grammars of the Urban Ground. Duke University Press. https://doi.org/10.1215/9781478022954.

Antunes, G. (2018). Políticas de Habitação – 200 anos. Caleidoscópio.

Araújo, M., & Maeso, S. R. (2012). History textbooks, racism and the critique of Eurocentrism: Beyond rectification or compensation. Ethnic and Racial Studies, 35(7), 1266–1286. https://doi.org/10.1080/01419870.2011.600767.

Arendt, H. (1963). On revolution. Faber & Faber.

Arnstein, S. R. (1969). A Ladder of Citizen Participation. JAIP, 35(4), 216–224.

Ascensão, E. (2011). The post-colonial slum: A geography of informal settlement in Quinta da Serra, Lisbon. King's College, University of London.

Ascensão, E. (2013). Following engineers and architects through slums: The technoscience of slum intervention in the Portuguese-speaking landscape. Analise Social, 48(206), 154–180. https://doi.org/10.2307/41959853.

Ascensão, E. (2016). Interfaces of informality: When experts meet informal settlers. City, 20(4), 563–580. https://doi.org/10.1080/13604813.2016.1193337.

Auyero, J. (2010). Visible Fists, Clandestine Kicks, and Invisible Elbows: Three Forms of Regulating Neoliberal Poverty. European Review of Latin American and Caribbean Studies, 89(October), 5–26.

Auyero, J. (2011). Researching the urban margins: What can the United States learn from Latin America and vice versa? City and Community, 10(4), 431–436. https://doi.org/10.1111/j.1540-6040.2011.01370.x.

Auyero, J., & Swistun, D. Alejandra. (2009). Flammable: Environmental suffering in an Argentine shantytown. Oxford University Press.

Ba, M. (2017, September 7). A fábula de um país com racistas sem racismo. Público. https://www.publico.pt/2017/09/07/sociedade/opiniao/a-fabula-de-um-pais-com-racistas-sem-racismo-1784575.

Baiocchi, G., & Corrado, L. (2010). The politics of habitus: Publics, blackness, and community activism in Salvador, Brazil. Qualitative Sociology, 33(3), 369–388. https://doi.org/10.1007/s11133-010-9155-z.

Baker, A. G. (2017). Bailiffs at the Door: Work, Power, and Resistance in Eviction Enforcement. In Geographies of Forced Eviction: Dispossession, Violence, Insecurity (pp. 145–165).

Baksh, R., & Harcourt, W. (2015). Introduction: Rethinking Knowledge, Power, and Social Change. In R. Baksh & W. Harcourt (Eds.), The Oxford Handbook of Transnational Feminist Movements. https://doi.org/10.1093/oxfordhb/9780199943494.013.35.

Bandeirinha, J. A. (2011). O Processo SAAL e a Arquitectura no 25 de Abril de 1974. In O Processo SAAL e a Arquitectura no 25 de Abril de 1974. Universidade de Coimbra. https://doi.org/10.14195/978-989-26-1265-2.

Barata Salgueiro, T. (1994). Novos produtos imobiliarios e reestruturacao urbana. Finisterra, 29(57), 79–101.

Barnett, C. (2005). The consolations of 'neoliberalism'. Geoforum, 36(1), 7–12. https://doi.org/10.1016/j.geoforum.2004.08.006.

Bastia, T., & Montero Bressán, J. (2018). Between a guest and an okupa: Migration and the making of insurgent citizenship in Buenos Aires' informal settlements. Environment and Planning A, 50(1), 31–50. https://doi.org/10.1177/0308518X17736312.

Baumgarten, B. (2013). Geração à Rasca and beyond: Mobilizations in Portugal after 12 March 2011. Current Sociology, 61(4), 457–473. https://doi.org/10.1177/0011392113479745.

Baumgarten, B. (2017). The children of the Carnation Revolution? Connections between Portugal's anti-austerity movement and the revolutionary period 1974/1975. Social Movement Studies, 16(1), 51–63. https://doi.org/10.1080/14742837.2016.1239195.

Bayat, A. (2013). Life as politics: How ordinary people change the Middle East. Stanford University Press.

Bayat, A. (2015). Plebeians of the Arab Spring. Current Antropology, 56(Supplement 11), 33–43.

Bayat, A., & Biekart, K. (2009). Cities of extremes. Development and Change, 40(5), 815–825. https://doi.org/10.1111/j.1467-7660.2009.01584.x.

Beja Horta, A. P. (2006). Places of resistance: Power, spatial discourses and migrant grassroots organizing in the periphery of Lisbon. City, 10(3), 269–285. https://doi.org/10.1080/13604810600980580.

Benford, R. D., & Snow, D. A. (2000). Framing Processes and Social Movements: An Overview and Assessment. Annual Review of Sociology, 26, 611–639.

Benhabib, S. (1992). Situating the self: Gender, community and postmodernism in contemporary ethics (Reprinted). Polity Press.

Bhan, G. (2013). Planned Illegalities: Housing and the 'failure' of planning in Delhi 1947–2010. Economic and Political Weekly, 48(24), 58–70.

Bhan, G. (2014). The impoverishment of poverty: Reflections on urban citizenship and inequality in contemporary Delhi. Environment and Urbanization, 26(2), 547–560. https://doi.org/10.1177/0956247814542391.

Bhan, G. (2019). Notes on a Southern urban practice. Environment and Urbanization, 31(2), 639–654. https://doi.org/10.1177/0956247818815792.

Bhattacharyya, G. (2018). Rethinking Racial Capitalism: Questions of Reproduction and Survival. Rowman & Littlefield.

Bivar, M., Saldanha, M., Lopes, R., & Santos, S. (2017, September 29). Reabilita primeiro. Ganha depois. Esquerda.net. www.esquerda.net/artigo/reabilita-primeiro-ganha-depois/51169.

Blas, A., & Ibarra, P. (2006). La participación: Estado de la cuestión. Hegoa.

Blokland, T., Hentschel, C., Holm, A., Lebuhn, H., & Margalit, T. (2015). Urban Citizenship and Right to the City: The Fragmentation of Claims. International Journal of Urban and Regional Research, 39(4), 655–665. https://doi.org/10.1111/1468-2427.12259.

Blunt, A., & Dowling, R. M. (2006). Home. Routledge. https://helka.finna.fi/Record/helka.2000774.

Bogado, D. (2017). O Museu das Remoções da Vila Autódromo. Potência de resistência criativa e afetica como resposta sociocultural ao Rio de Janeiro dos megaeventos (Vol. 1). University of Sevilla.

Bogado, D., & Saaristo, S.-M. (2021). Subjective and symbolic disputes in the fight for the right to the city: Actions of the collective Stop Despejos for resistance of the 6 de Maio neighbourhood in Lisbon. In A. Allegri, A. Benatti Alvim, E. Helena Abascal, J. Sabaté, J. Pedro Costa, & M. C. Schicchi (Eds.), Research Tracks in Urbanism: Dynamics, Planning and Design in Contemporary Urban Territories (pp. 167–173). CRC Press.

Borja, J., & Carrión, F. (2017). Introducción. Ciudades resistentes, ciudades posibles. In J. Borja, F. Carrión, & M. Corti (Eds.), Ciudades resistentes, ciudades posibles (pp. 17–58). Editorial UOC.

Brenner, N., Peck, J., & Theodore, N. (2010a). After Neoliberalization? Globalizations, 7(3), 327–345. https://doi.org/10.1080/14747731003669669.

Brenner, N., Peck, J., & Theodore, N. (2010b). Variegated neoliberalization: Geographies, modalities, pathways. Global Networks, 10(2), 182–222.

Bretherton, J. (2017). Reconsidering Gender in Homelessness. European Journal of Homelessness, 11(1), 1–22.

Brickell, K. (2014). "The Whole World Is Watching": Intimate Geopolitics of Forced Eviction and Women's Activism in Cambodia. Annals of the Association of American Geographers, 104(6), 1256–1272. https://doi.org/10.1080/00045608.2014.944452.

Brickell, K., Fernández Arrigoitia, M., & Vasudevan, A. (2017). Geographies of Forced Eviction: Dispossession, Violence, Resistance. In K. Brickell, M. Fernández Arrigoitia, & A. Vasudevan (Eds.), Geographies of Forced Eviction: Dispossession, Violence, Resistance (pp. 1–23). Palgrave Macmillan. https://doi.org/10.1057/978-1-137-51127-0.

Bullock, H. E., Reppond, H. A., Truong, S. V., & Singh, M. R. (2020). An intersectional analysis of the feminization of homelessness and mothers' housing precarity. Journal of Social Issues, 76(4), 835–858. https://doi.org/10.1111/josi.12406.

Burawoy, M. (1998). The Extended Case Method. Sociological Theory, 16(1), 4–33.

Burgum, S., & Vasudevan, A. (2023). Critical geographies of occupation, trespass and squatting. City, 1–13. https://doi.org/10.1080/13604813.2023.2223854.

Busch-Geertsema, V., Edgar, W., O'Sullivan, E., & Pleace, N. (2010). Homelessness and homeless policies in Europe: Lessons from research. FEANTSA; European Commission.

Butler, J. (2011). Bodies in Alliance and the Politics of the Street. Eipcp.

Cabannes, Y. (2010). Putting the Cases in Perspective. In Y. Cabannes, S. G. Yafai, & C. Johnson (Eds.), How people face evictions (pp. 9–27). Development Planning Unit, University College London.

Cabannes, Y. (2013). Urban movements and NGOs: So near, so far. City, 17(4), 560–566. https://doi.org/10.1080/13604813.2013.795328.

Cabannes, Y., Yafai, S. G., Johnson, C., Cabannes, Y., Yafai, S. G., & Johnson, C. (2010). How people face evictions. Development Planning Unit, University College London.

Cachado, R. d'Ávila. (2011). Realojamento em zonas de fronteira urbana. O caso da Quinta da Vitória, Loures. Forum Sociológico, 21, 23–31. https://doi.org/10.4000/sociologico.425.

Cachado, R. Á. (2012). Uma etnografia na cidade alargada. Hindus na Quinta da Vitória em Processo de Realojamento. Fundação Calouste Gulbenkian.

Cachado, R. Á. (2013). O registo escondido num bairro em processo de realojamento: O caso dos hindus da Quinta da Vitória. Etnográfica, 17(3), 477–499. https://doi.org/10.4000/etnogra.

Cachado, R., Estevens, A., & Ascensão, E. (2019). 'Estamos numa febre de especulação pela procura de mais-valias': Entrevista com Rita Silva, Presidente da associação Habita. CIDADES, Comunidades e Territórios, 38, 36–44. https://doi.org/10.15847/citiescommunitiesterritories.jun2019.038.into2.

Caciagli, C. (2019). Housing Squats as "Educational Sites of Resistance": The Process of Movement Social Base Formation in the Struggle for the House. Antipode, 51(3), 730–749. https://doi.org/10.1111/anti.12515.

Cahen, C., Schneider, J., & Saegert, S. (2019). Victories from Insurgency: Re-Negotiating Housing, Community Control, and Citizenship at the Margins. Antipode, 51(5), 1416–1435. https://doi.org/10.1111/anti.12558.

Caldas, J. C., Silva, A. A. da, & Cantante, F. (2020). As consequências socioeconómicas da COVID-19 e a sua desigual distribuição. COLABOR.

Caldeira, T. P. R. (2015). Social Movements, Cultural Production, and Protests: São Paulo's Shifting Political Landscape. Current Anthropology, 56(Supplement 11), 126–136.

Caldeira, T. P. R. (2017). Peripheral urbanization: Autoconstruction, transversal logics, and politics in cities of the global south. Environment and Planning D: Society and Space, 35(1), 3–20. https://doi.org/10.1177/0263775816658479.

Câmara Municipal de Amadora. (2017). Execução do PER – dez. 2016. Câmara Municipal de Amadora. http://www.cm-amadora.pt/images/INTERVENCAO_SOCIAL/HABITACAO_SOCIAL/DOCS/execucao_per_dez2016.xls.

Câmara Municipal de Lisboa. (2009). RRAHM (Regime de Acesso à Habitação Municipal). In 1.o Suplemento ao Boletim Municipal N.0814, Assembleia Municipal de Lisboa.

Câmara Municipal de Lisboa. (2010). Programa Local de Habitação de Lisboa, CARTA DOS BIP/ZIP. Bairros e Zonas de Intervenção Prioritária de Lisboa. Relatório: Metodologia de identificação e construção da carta dos BIP/ZIP. Câmara Municipal de Lisboa.

Câmara Municipal de Lisboa. (2012). O PHL em Acção. O Programa Local de Habitação de Lisboa. Relatório da 3a fase: Concretizar. Câmara Municipal de Lisboa.

Câmara Municipal de Lisboa. (2013). Regulamento das Desocupações de Habitações Municipais. 2. o Suplemento Ao Boletim Municipal n.o 99.

Câmara Municipal de Lisboa. (2016). Estrutura e modelo de funcionamento de Co-Governação para os Gabinetes de Apoio aos Bairros de Intervenção Prioritária. Pelouro da Habitação e Desenvolvimento Local. http://habitacao.cm-lisboa.pt/index.htm?no=27510001.

Câmara Municipal de Lisboa. (2019a). Plano Municipal para a pessoa em situação de sem abrigo. 2019–2023. Câmara Municipal de Lisboa.

Câmara Municipal de Lisboa. (2019b, November 12). Regulamento Municipal do Direito à Habitação. Diário Da República, n.o 230/2019.

Câmara Municipal de Lisboa. (2020). Promover novos canais de comunicação com a sociedade civi. https://cidadania.lisboa.pt/.

Câmara Municipal de Loures. (2018). Loures investe três milhões de euros na Quinta da Fonte. https://www.cm-loures.pt/Conteudo.aspx?DisplayId=3951.

Cardoso, G., Accornero, G., Lapa, T., & Azevedo, J. (2017). Social Movements, Participation and Crisis in Europe. In M. Castells, O. Bouin, G. Caraça, J. B. Thompson, & M. Wieviorka (Eds.), Europe's Crisis (pp. 405–427). Polity Press.

Carreiras, M. (2018). Integração socioespacial dos bairros de habitação social na área metropolitana de Lisboa: Evidências de micro segregação. Finisterra, 53(107), 67–85. https://doi.org/10.18055/finis11969.

Carty, L., & Mohanty, C. T. (2015). Mapping Transnational Feminist Engagements: Neoliberalism and the Politics of Solidarity. In R. Baksh & W. Harcourt (Eds.), The Oxford Handbook of Transnational Feminist Movements (Issue March 2018, pp. 1–41). https://doi.org/10.1093/oxfordhb/9780199943494.013.010.

Casellas, A., & Sala, E. (2017). Home Eviction, Grassroots Organization and Citizen Empowerment in Spain. In K. Brickell, M. Fernandez Arrigoitia, & A. Vasudevan (Eds.), Geographies of Forced Eviction: Dispossession, Violence, Insecurity (pp. 167–191). Palgrave Macmillan. https://doi.org/10.1057/978-1-137-51127-0.

Castela, T. L. L. (2011). A Liberal Space: A History of the Illegalized Working-Class Extensions of Lisbon [University of California, Berkeley]. In UC Berkeley Electronic Theses and Dissertations. http://dx.doi.org/10.1016/j.physbeh.2008.04.026.

Castelo, C. (2011). Uma incursão no lusotropicalismo de Gilberto Freyre. Blogue de História Lusófona, Setembro, 261–280.

Cattaneo, C., & Martínez, M. A. (2014). Introduction: Squatting as an Alternative to Capitalism. In C. Cattaneo & M. A. Martínez (Eds.), The Squatter's Movement in Europe: Commons and Autonomy as Alternatives to Capitalism (pp. 1–24). Pluto Press.

Çelik, Ö. (2021). The roles of the state in the financialisation of housing in Turkey. Housing Studies, 0(0), 1–21. https://doi.org/10.1080/02673037.2021.1928003.

CERD. (2017). International Convention on the Elimination of all Forms of Racial Discrimination. In Concluding observation on the fifteenth to seventeenth periodic reports of Portugal: Vol. CERD/C/PRT. United Nations Committee on the Elimination of Racial Discrimination. https://doi.org/10.1163/9789004279926_019.

Chatterjee, P. (2004). The politics of the governed: Reflections on popular politics in most of the world. Columbia University Press.

Chiodelli, F., Coppola, A., Belotti, E., Berruti, G., Clough Marinaro, I., Curci, F., & Zanfi, F. (2021). The production of informal space: A critical atlas of housing informalities in Italy between public institutions and political strategies. Progress in Planning, 149, 100495. https://doi.org/10.1016/j.progress.2020.100495.

Cho, U. (2003). Global capital and local patriarchy: The financial crisis and women workers in South Korea. In D.-S. S. Gills & N. Piper (Eds.), Women and Work in Globalizing Asia (pp. 52–69). Routledge. https://doi.org/10.4324/9780203166925.

Clarke, A., & Parsell, C. (2020). The Ambiguities of Homelessness Governance: Disentangling Care and Revanchism in the Neoliberalising City. Antipode, 52(6), 1624–1646. https://doi.org/10.1111/anti.12671.

Coates, R., & Nygren, A. (2020). Urban Floods, Clientelism, and the Political Ecology of the State in Latin America. Annals of the American Association of Geographers, 110(5), 1301–1317. https://doi.org/10.1080/24694452.2019.1701977.

Cocola-Gant, A. (2018). Tourism Gentrification. In L. Lees & M. Phillips (Eds.), Handbook of Gentrification Studies (pp. 281–293). Edward Elgar Publishing.

Cocola-Gant, A., & Gago, A. (2019). Airbnb, buy-to-let investment and tourism-driven displacement: A case study in Lisbon. Environment and Planning A, 0(0), 1–18. https://doi.org/10.1177/0308518X19869012.

COHRE. (2010). Briefing Paper: The impact of forced evictions on women (Issue October). Centre on Housing Rights and Evictions (COHRE). https://issuu.com/cohre/docs/cohre_briefpaper_impactforcedevicti.

Colau, A. (2011). How to stop an eviction. The experience of the Plataforma de afectados por la hipoteca (Platform for people affected by mortgages). Plataforma de afectados por la hipoteca. http://www.afectadosporlahipoteca.com.

Colau, A., & Alemany, A. (2014). Mortgaged Lives From the housing bubble to the right to housing. Journal of Aesthetics & Protest Press.

Colella, F., Gianturco, G., & Nocenzi, M. (2017). Immigrant women and housing issues: A symbolic magnifying glass for social and cultural changes in Italian civil movements*. International Review of Sociology, 27(1), 37–60. https://doi.org/10.1080/03906701.2017.1303968.

Constance-Huggins, M. (2011). A Review of the Racial Biases of Social Welfare Policies. Journal of Human Behavior in the Social Environment, 21(8), 871–887. https://doi.org/10.1080/10911359.2011.588531.

Convention for the Protection of Human Rights and Fundamental Freedoms as Amended by Protocol No. 15 as from Its Entry into Force on 1 August 2021 (2021).

Costa, P. (1993). Cidades e Urbanização em Portugal: Uma Sociologia, Geografia ou Economia Urbanas? (pp. 1–25). SOCIUS – Centro de Investigação em Sociologia Económica e das Organizações, Universidade Técnica de Lisboa. http://pascal.iseg.utl.pt/~socius/index.htm.

Council of Europe. (2018). Report to the Portuguese Government on the visit to Portugal carried out by the European Committee for the Prevention of Torture and Inhuman or Degrading Treatment or Punishment (CPT) from 27 September to 7 October 2016: Vol. CPT/Inf (2 (Issue January). https://www.refworld.org/docid/5a951b3e4.htm.

Cristino, S. (2018, December 11). Na Picheleira trabalha-se com medo e há espaços municipais que albergam 'salas de chuto' ilegais e carros furtados. O Corvo. https://ocorvo.pt/na-picheleira-trabalha-se-com-medo-e-ha-espacos-municipais-que-albergam-salas-de-chuto-e-carros-furtados/.

Dadusc, D., Grazioli, M., & Martínez, M. A. (2019). Introduction: Citizenship as inhabitance? Migrant housing squats versus institutional accommodation. Citizenship Studies, 23(6), 521–539. https://doi.org/10.1080/13621025.2019.1634311.

Dardot, P., & Laval, C. (2013). The New Way of the World: On Neoliberal Society. Verso.

Dardot, P., & Laval, C. (2018). Foucault, Neoliberalism and Europe. In D. Cahill, M. Cooper, M. Konings, & D. Primrose (Eds.), The SAGE Handbook of Neoliberalism

(Issue 2018, pp. 193–200). SAGE Publications. https://doi.org/10.4135/9781526416001.n16.

Das, V. (1989). Subaltern as Perspective. In R. Guha (Ed.), Subaltern Studies VI: Writings on South Asian history and society. Oxford.

Das, V. (2011). State, citizenship, and the urban poor. Citizenship Studies, 15(3–4), 319–333. https://doi.org/10.1080/13621025.2011.564781.

Das, V., & Poole, D. (2004). State and Its Margins. Comparative Ethnographies. In V. Das & D. Poole (Eds.), Anthropology in the margins of the State (pp. 3–33). School of American Research Press.

Das, V., & Randeria, S. (2015). Politics of the Urban Poor: Aesthetics, Ethics, Volatility, Precarity: An Introduction to Supplement 11. Current Anthropology, 56(11), 3–12.

Das, V., & Walton, M. (2015). Political Leadership and the Urban Poor. Local histories. Current Anthropology, 56(Supplement 11, Oct), 44–54.

De Soto, H. (1986). El Otro Sendero: La Revolución Informal. Editorial El Barranco.

della Porta, D., & Diani, M. (2006). Social Movements: An Introduction. Blackwell Publishing.

Desmond, M. (2016). Evicted: Poverty and profit in an American City. Crown Publishers.

Desmond, M., & Kimbro, R. T. (2015). Eviction's fallout: Housing, hardship, and health. Social Forces, 94(1), 295–324. https://doi.org/10.1093/sf/sov044.

Di Feliciantonio, C. (2017). Social Movements and Alternative Housing Models: Practicing the "Politics of Possibilities" in Spain. Housing, Theory and Society, 34(1), 38–56. https://doi.org/10.1080/14036096.2016.1220421.

Di Giovanni, C. (2017). Uma história do Habita: Como se fez um colectivo activista. Le Monde Diplomatique – Edição Portuguesa. https://pt.mondediplo.com/spip.php?article1308.

Diani, M., & McAdam, D. (2003). Social Movements and Networks: Relational Approaches to Collective Action. Oxford University Press. https://doi.org/10.1093/0199251789.003.0001.

Dizon, H. M. (2019). Philippine housing takeover: How the urban poor claimed their right to shelter. Radical Housing Journal, 1(1), 106.

DN/Lusa. (2017, September 16). Robles responsabiliza Cristas por despejo de mil famílias. Diário de Notícias.

Doshi, S. (2013). The politics of the evicted: Redevelopment, subjectivity, and difference in Mumbai's slum frontier. Antipode, 45(4), 844–865. https://doi.org/10.1111/j.1467-8330.2012.01023.x.

Dotsey, S., & Chiodelli, F. (2021). Housing precarity: A fourfold epistemological lancet for dissecting the housing conditions of migrants. City, 25(5–6), 720–739. https://doi.org/10.1080/13604813.2021.1979802.

Downs, C. (1980). Comissões de Moradores and urban struggles in revolutionary Portugal. International Journal of Urban & Regional Research, 4(2), 267. https://doi.org/10.1111/j.1468-2427.1980.tb00363.x.

Drago, A. (2017). Is This What The Democratic City Looks Like? Local Democracy, Housing Rights and Homeownership in the Portuguese Context. International Journal of Urban & Regional Research, 41(3), 426–442. https://doi.org/10.1111/1468-2427.12491.

Dussel, E. D. (2019). Pedagogics of liberation: A Latin American philosophy of Education. Punctum books.

Earle, L. (2007). Housing, Citizenship and the Movimento Sem Teto of São Paulo. 1–20.

Earle, L. (2012). From insurgent to transgressive citizenship: Housing, social movements and the politics of rights in São Paulo. Journal of Latin American Studies, 44(1), 97–126. https://doi.org/10.1017/S0022216X11001118.

ECRI. (2018). Relatório da ECRI sobre Portugal (quarto ciclo de controlo). European Commission Against Racism and Intolerance.

Engels, F. (1873). The Housing Question. Martin Lawrence, Ltd. https://doi.org/10.1136/bmj.2.3016.450-b.

England, K., & Ward, K. (2016). Theorizing neoliberalization. In S. Springer, K. Birch, & J. MacLeavy (Eds.), Handbook of Neoliberalism (pp. 50–60). Routledge, Taylor & Francis Group. https://doi.org/10.4324/9781315730660-13.

Esposito, E. (2022). Deprivation-based squatting as a choice from necessity: The housing pathways of low-income squatters in public housing in Naples, Italy. Cities, 124, 103623. https://doi.org/10.1016/j.cities.2022.103623.

Esposito, E., & Chiodelli, F. (2023). Beyond proper political squatting: Exploring individualistic need-based occupations in a public housing neighbourhood in Naples. Housing Studies, 38(8), 1436–1458. https://doi.org/10.1080/02673037.2021.1946017.

European Action Coalition for the Right to Housing and to the City. (2019). Housing, Financialization Trends, Actors, and Processes. Rosa Luxemburg Stiftung. https://www.rosalux.eu/publications/housing-financialization/.

Eurostat. (2020a). General government expenditure by function [data set]. https://ec.europa.eu/eurostat/.

Eurostat. (2020b). House price index [data set]. https://ec.europa.eu/eurostat/.

Eurostat. (2020c). Housing cost overburden rate by income quintile – EU-SILC survey [data set]. https://ec.europa.eu/eurostat/.

Eurostat. (2020d). Housing cost overburden rate [data set]. https://ec.europa.eu/eurostat/.

Falanga, R., Tulumello, S., Alves, A. R., Jorge, S., Kühne, J., & Silva, R. (2019). The 'Caravana pelo Direito à Habitação': Towards a new movement for housing in Portugal? Radical Housing Journal, 1(1), 171–187.

Falzon, M.-A. (2009). Multi-Sited Ethnography: Theory, Praxis and Locality in Contemporary Research. Ashgate.

Fanon, F. (1963). The Wretched of the Earth. Grove Weidenfeld. https://doi.org/10.4324/9780203073186.

Farha, L. (2017). Report of the Special Rapporteur on adequate housing as a component of the right to an adequate standard of living, and on the right to non-discrimination in this context. Mission to Portugal. In Human Rights Council, 34th Session: Vol. A/HRC/34/5. United Nations Human Right Council. https://www.ohchr.org/EN/HRBodies/HRC/RegularSessions/Session34/Documents/A_HRC_34_51_Add.2_EN.docx.

Farouk, B. R., & Owusu, M. (2012). 'If in doubt, count': The role of community-driven enumerations in blocking eviction in Old Fadama, Accra. Environment and Urbanization, 24(1), 47–57. https://doi.org/10.1177/0956247811434478.

Farris, S. R. (2013, July 10). Neoliberalism, Migrant Women, and the Commodification of Care. The Scholar & Feminist Online. https://sfonline.barnard.edu/neoliberalism-migrant-women-and-the-commodification-of-care/.

FEANTSA. (2017). What is ETHOS? European Typology of Homelessness. In European Typology on Homelessness and Housing Exclusion (p. 13).

FEANTSA & Foundation Abbé Pierre. (2018). Third Overview of Housing Exclusion in Europe. FEANTSA; Foundation Abbé Pierre.

Federici, S. (2004). Caliban and the Witch. Autonomedia.

Federici, S. (2021). Patriarchy of the wage: Notes on Marx, gender, and feminism. PM Press.

Ferguson, S., & McNally, D. (2015). Precarious migrants: Gender, race and the social reproduction of a global working class. In L. Panitch & G. Albo (Eds.), Transforming Classes: Socialist Register 2015 (pp. 1–23). Merlin Press.

Fernandes, R. C., & Pinto, S. P. (2018, April 7). 2000 famílias despejadas do centro histórico de Lisboa em 4 anos.pdf. Sapo. https://sol.sapo.pt/noticia/607256/2000-familias-despejadas-do-centro-historico-de-lisboa-em-4-anos-.

Fernandez, R., & Aalbers, M. B. (2016). Financialization and housing: Between globalization and Varieties of Capitalism. Competition and Change, 20(2), 71–88. https://doi.org/10.1177/1024529415623916.

Ferreira, A. F. (1988). Política(s) de Habitação em Portugal. Sociedade e Território, 59, 54–62.

Ferreira, J. P., Silva, N. B., & Costa, J. F. (2019). O preço da habitação: As determinantes do valor na área metropolitana de Lisboa. In A. C. Santos (Ed.), A nova questão da habitação em Portugal: Uma abordagem de economia política (pp. 171–197). Actual.

Ferreira, V. M. (1986). A Cidade e o Campo. Uma leitura comparada do movimento social, 1974–1975. Revista Crítica de Ciências Sociais, 18/19/20.

Ferreri, M. (2023). Radical difference in 'transitional commoning': Hidden histories of London's squats to co-ops. City, 1–17. https://doi.org/10.1080/13604813.2023.2213123.

Fields, D., & Raymond, E. L. (2021). Racialized geographies of housing financialization. Progress in Human Geography, 45(6), 1625–1645. https://doi.org/10.1177/03091325211009299.

Fine, B., & Saad-Filho, A. (2017). Thirteen Things You Need to Know About Neoliberalism. Critical Sociology, 43(4–5), 685–706. https://doi.org/10.1177/0896920516655387.

Florea, I., Gagyi, A., & Jacobsson, K. (2018). A Field of Contention: Evidence from Housing Struggles in Bucharest and Budapest. VOLUNTAS: International Journal of Voluntary and Nonprofit Organizations, 29, 712–724. https://doi.org/10.1007/s11266-018-9954-5.

Forment, C. A. (2015). Ordinary Ethics and the Emergence of Plebeian Democracy across the Global South: Buenos Aires's La Salada Market. Current Anthropology, 56(Supplement 11), 116–125.

Foucault, M. (1982). The Subject and Power. Critical Inquiry, 8(4), 777–795. https://doi.org/10.1515/9783110815764.387.

Foucault, M. (2007). Security, Territory, Population: Lectures at the College de France, 1977–78 (M. Senellart, Ed.). Palgrave Macmillan.

Foucault, M. (2008). The Birth of Biopolitics: Lectures at the Collège of France, 1978–1979 (M. Senellart, F. Ewald, & A. Fontana, Eds.). Palgrave Macmillan.

FRA. (2018). Second European Union Minorities and Discrimination Survey Being Black in the EU (EU-MIDIS II). European Union Agency for Fundamental Rights (FRA). https://doi.org/10.2811/51938.

Fransen, L., Del Bufalo, G., & Reviglio, E. (2018). Boosting Investments in Social Infrastructure in Europe: Report of the High-Level Task Force on Investing in Social Infrastructure in Europe (European Economy Discussion Papers, Issue January). European Commission. https://doi.org/10.2765/794497.

Fraser, N. (1992). Introduction. In N. Fraser & S. L. Bartky (Eds.), Revaluing French feminism: Critical essays on difference, agency, and culture. Indiana University Press.

Fraser, N. (2013). Fortunes of feminism: From state-managed capitalism to neoliberal crisis. Verso.

Fraser, N. (2016). Contradictions of Capital and Care. New Left Review, 100, 99–117.

Freire, P. (1990). Pedagogy of the oppressed. Penguin Books.

Freyre, G. (1933). Casa grande e senzala. Schmidt Editor.

Gago, A. (2018). O aluguer de curta duração e a gentrificação turística em Alfama, Lisboa [Universidade de Lisboa; Escola Superior de Hotelaria e Turismo do Estoril]. https://doi.org/10.1007/s12272-014-0538-7.

Gago, A., & Cocola-Gant, A. (2019). O alojamento local e a gentrificação turística em Alfama, Lisboa. In A. C. Santos (Ed.), A nova questão da habitação em Portugal: Uma abordagem de economia política (pp. 143–169). Actual.

Gago, V. (2017). Neoliberalism from below: Popular pragmatics and baroque economies. Duke University Press.

García-Lamarca, M. (2017). From Occupying Plazas to Recuperating Housing: Insurgent Practices in Spain. International Journal of Urban and Regional Research, 41(1), 37–53. https://doi.org/10.1111/1468-2427.12386.

García-Lamarca, M., & Kaika, M. (2016). 'Mortgaged lives': The biopolitics of debt and housing financialisation. Transactions of the Institute of British Geographers, 41(3). https://doi.org/10.1111/tran.12126.

Ghertner, D. A. (2011). Gentrifying the State, Gentrifying Participation: Elite Governance Programs in Delhi. International Journal of Urban and Regional Research, 35(3), 504–532. https://doi.org/10.1111/j.1468-2427.2011.01043.x.

Gibson, N. C. (2012). What Happened to the 'Promised Land'? A Fanonian Perspective on Post-Apartheid South Africa. Antipode, 44(1), 51–73. https://doi.org/10.1111/j.1467-8330.2010.00837.x.

Gilligan, C. (1993). In a Different Voice: Psychological Theory and Women's Development. Harvard University Press. https://doi.org/10.4159/9780674037618.

Gonick, S. (2016). From Occupation to Recuperation: Property, Politics and Provincialization in Contemporary Madrid. International Journal of Urban and Regional Research, 40(4), 833–848. https://doi.org/10.1111/1468-2427.12392.

Gorjão Henriques, J. (2017, August 26). Há uma preferência "óbvia" dos senhorios em arrendarem casa a brancos. Público. https://www.publico.pt/2017/08/26/sociedade/noticia/ha-uma-preferencia-obvia-dos-senhorios-alugarem-casa-a-brancos-1782904.

Gorjão Henriques, J. (2018). Racismo no país dos brancos costumes. Tinta-da-china.

Gorjão Henriques, J. (2019a, May 20). Oito polícias de Alfragide condenados, nove absolvidos. Vítimas vão receber indemnizações. Público. https://www.publico.pt/2019/05/20/sociedade/noticia/julgamento-alfragide-decisao-1873346.

Gorjão Henriques, J. (2019b, June 17). INE chumba pergunta sobre origem étnico-racial no censos. Público. https://www.publico.pt/2019/06/17/sociedade/noticia/censos-1876683?fbclid=IwAR1AEs39FInS8hXc-UXKutnN-XdCchVVXoQkyhn9FqqpozsTCoXnXnl3LkQ.

Government of Portugal. (2017). ESTRATÉGIA NACIONAL PARA A INTEGRAÇÃO DAS PESSOAS EM SITUAÇÃO DE SEM-ABRIGO 2017–2023. Diário Da República, 1.a Série – N.o 142–25 de Julho de 2017, 142(26 de julho), 3924–3931.

Government of Portugal. (2018, April 26). Governo aprova pacote legislativo de políticas de habitação – XXI Governo – República Portuguesa. https://www.portugal.gov.pt/pt/gc21/comunicacao/noticia?i=governo-aprova-pacote-legislativo-de-politicas-de-habitacao.

Government of Portugal. (2021, February 19). PRR tem 1250 milhões para gastar em Habitação em seis anos. https://www.portugal.gov.pt/pt/gc22/comunicacao/noticia?i=prr-tem-1250-milhoes-para-gastar-em-habitacao-em-seis-anos.

Graddy, G. (2010). Politics of Scale. In D. Mulvaney (Ed.), Green Politics: An A-to-Z Guide (pp. 328–331). SAGE Publications, Inc.

Gramsci, A. (1978). Some aspects of the southern question. In Q. Hoare (Ed.), Selections from Political Writings (1921–1926). Lawrence and Wishart.

Grazioli, M. (2017). From citizens to citadins? Rethinking right to the city inside housing squats in Rome, Italy. Citizenship Studies, 21(4), 393–408. https://doi.org/10.108 0/13621025.2017.1307607.

Grazioli, M., & Caciagli, C. (2018). Resisting to the Neoliberal Urban Fabric: Housing Rights Movements and the Re-appropriation of the 'Right to the City' in Rome, Italy. Voluntas, 29(4), 697–711. https://doi.org/10.1007/s11266-018-9977-y.

Green, M. (2002). Gramsci cannot speak: Presentations and interpretations of Gramsci's concept of the subaltern. Rethinking Marxism, 14(3), 1–24. https://doi .org/10.1080/0893569022101242242.

Guerra, I. (2010). A Cidade Sustentável: O conceito permite renovar a concepção e a prática da intervenção? CIDADES – Comunidades e Territórios, 20/21, 69–85. https://doi.org/10.7749/citiescommunitiesterritories.dec2010.020-21.art05.

Guerra, I. (2011). As politicas de habitaçao em Portugal: A procura de novos caminhos. CIDADES, Comunidades e Territórios, 22, 41–68.

Guha, R. (1988). Preface. In R. Guha & G. C. Spivak (Eds.), Selected Subaltern Studies (pp. 35–36). Oxford University Press.

Habita. (2022, December 21). Habita consegue nova suspensão de despejo através de queixa a ONU. Habita! Associação Pelo Direito à Habitação e à Cidade. http:// habita.info/habita-consegue-nova-suspensao-de-despejo-atraves-de-queixa-ao -alto-comissariado-para-os-direitos-humanos-das-nacoes-unidas/.

Haila, A. (1988). Land as a Financial Asset: The Theory of Urban Rent as a Mirror of Economic Transformation. Antipode, 20(2), 79–101. https://doi.org/10.1111 /j.1467-8330.1988.tb00170.x.

Haila, A. (2016). Urban land rent: Singapore as a property state. John Wiley & Sons Inc.

Hale, C. R. (2006). Activist Research v. Cultural Critique: Indigenous Land Rights and the Contradictions of Politically Engaged Anthropology. Cultural Anthropology, 21(1), 96–120. https://doi.org/10.1525/can.2006.21.1.96.

Hanisch, C. (1970). The Personal is Political. In S. Firestone & A. Koedt (Eds.), Notes from the Second Year: Women's Liberation. Editors.

Haraway, D. (1988). Situated Knowledges: The Science Question in Feminism and the Privilege of Partial Perspective. Feminist Studies, 14(3), 575. https://doi.org /10.2307/3178066.

Harrison, H., Birks, M., Franklin, R., & Mills, J. (2017). Case Study Research: Foundations and Methodological Orientations. Forum: Qualitative Social Research, 18(1). http:// dx.doi.org/10.17169/fqs-18.1.2655.

Harvey, D. (1978). The urban process under capitalism: A framework for analysis. International Journal of Urban and Regional Research, 2(1–2), 101–131. https://doi .org/10.4324/9781351068000.

Harvey, D. (1989). From Managerialism to Entrepreneurialism: The Transformation in Urban Governance in Late Capitalism Published by. Geografiska Annaler. Series B, Human Geography, 71(1), 3–17.

Harvey, D. (2003). The New Imperialism. Oxford University Press.

Harvey, D. (2008). The Right to the City. New Left Review, 53(53), 23–40. https://doi.org/10.1080/13604819608713449.

Harvey, D. (2010). Organizing for the anti-capitalist transition. Interface: A Journal for and About Social Movements, 2(1), 243–261.

Herbert, C. W. (2018a). Like a Good Neighbor, Squatters Are There: Property and Neighborhood Stability in the Context of Urban Decline. City & Community, 17(1), 236–258. https://doi.org/10.1111/cico.12275.

Herbert, C. W. (2018b). Squatting for Survival: Precarious Housing in a Declining U.S. City. Housing Policy Debate, 1–17. https://doi.org/10.1080/10511482.2018.1461120.

Herbert, C. W. (2021). A Detroit Story: Urban Decline and the Rise of Property Informality (1st ed.). University of California Press. https://doi.org/10.2307/j.ctv1honvkn.

Holston, J. (1998). Spaces of insurgent citizenship.pdf. In L. Sandercock (Ed.), Making the Invisible Visible: A Multicultural Planning History (pp. 37–56). University of California.

Holston, J. (2008). Insurgent Citizenship: Disjunctions of Democracy and Modernity in Brazil. Princeton University Press.

Hoover, J. (2015). The human right to housing and community empowerment: Home occupation, eviction defence and community land trusts. Third World Quarterly. https://doi.org/10.1080/01436597.2015.1047196.

Hume, M., & Wilding, P. (2020). Beyond agency and passivity: Situating a gendered articulation of urban violence in Brazil and El Salvador. Urban Studies, 57(2), 249–266. https://doi.org/10.1177/0042098019829391.

ICESCR. (1967). International Covenant on Economic, Social and Cultural Rights. https://doi.org/10.1017/CBO9780511575372.009.

Idealista. (2018a, January 15). Há mais de 1.700 candidatos a 14 casas do Programa Renda Convencionada. Idealista. https://www.idealista.pt/news/imobiliario/habitacao/2018/01/12/35294-ha-mais-de-1-700-candidatos-a-14-casas-do-programa-renda-convencionada.

Idealista. (2018b, November 22). The increase in rental prices in Lisbon slows down (but are still at their highest for eight years). Idealista. https://www.idealista.pt/en/news/property-rent-portugal/2018/11/22/210-increase-rental-prices-lisbon-slows-down-are-still-their.

IHRU. (2015a). 1987–2011. 25 anos de esforço do Orçamento do Estado com a habitação. Instituto de Habitação e da Reabilitação Urbana.

IHRU. (2015b). Estratégia Nacional para a Habitação. Challenges and Changes (Issue June). Instituto da Habitação e da Reabilitação Urbana.

IHRU. (2018). Levantamento Nacional das Necessidades de Realojamento Habitacional. Instituto da Habitação e da Reabilitação Urbana.

INE. (2011). The Population Census. https://censos.ine.pt/.

INE. (2015a). Alojamentos familiares clássicos (Parque habitacional – N.o) por Localização geográfica (NUTS – 2002); Anual (1) [data set]. https://www.ine.pt/.

INE. (2015b). Fogos de habitação social (N.o) por Localização geográfica (NUTS – 2013) e Destino dos fogos; Anual [data set]. Instituto Nacional da Estatística. https://www.ine.pt/ngt_server/attachfileu.jsp?look_parentBoui=272427615&att_display=n&att_download=y.

INE. (2015c). Fogos de habitação social (N.o) por Localização geográfica (NUTS – 2013) e Destino dos fogos; Anual. [Data set]. https://www.ine.pt/.

INE. (2015d). População residente (N.o) por Local de residência (NUTS – 2013), Sexo e Grupo etário; Anual (2) [data set]. https://www.ine.pt/.

INE. (2015e). Receitas e despesas com o parque de habitação social, por NUTS II – 2015 [data set].

INE. (2016). Quadros do Destaque. Caraterização da Habitação Social em Portugal. Instituto Nacional de Estatística. https://www.ine.pt/xportal/xmain?xpid=INE&xpgid=ine_destaques&DESTAQUESdest_boui=250034590&DESTAQUESmodo=2&xlang=pt.

INE. (2019). Estatísticas da Construção e Habitação. Instituto Nacional de Estatística.

INE. (2023a). A HABITAÇÃO CONCENTROU CERCA DE 39% DA DESPESA MÉDIA DAS FAMÍLIAS EM 2022. Instituto Nacional de Estatística. https://www.ine.pt/xportal/xmain?xpid=INE&xpgid=ine_destaques&DESTAQUESdest_boui=598753053&DESTAQUESmodo=2.

INE. (2023b). Índice de preços da habitação (Base–2015) [Dataset]. https://www.ine.pt/xportal/xmain?xpid=INE&xpgid=ine_indicadores&contecto=pi&indOcorrCod=0009201&selTab=tabo.

Ismail, S. (2019). 'Imali Nolwazi' ('we need money and knowledge') – a rallying cry from the South African Homeless Peoples Federation. Radical Housing Journal, 1(April), 151–169.

Jorge, S., Ferraz, A. C., Pestana Lages, J., Veiga, I., Carolino, J., Higuera, R., Saaristo, S.-M., Mendes, L., & Viegas, S. (2020). Crise pandémica e crise na habitação. Mulheres em foco (J. Pestana Lages & S. Jorge, Eds.). DINÂMIA'CET-Iscte. https://comoficarem casa.pt/guia/.

Jorge, S., Oro, A. V., & Roseta, H. (2024, May 15). 4. Preço das casas e rendimento das famílias – evolução no século XXI. O Contador. https://www.ocontador.pt/direito-a-habitacao/historico/00000063,00000016/index.htm?4-preco-das-casas-e-rendimento-das-familias-evolucao-no-seculo-xxi.

Karaliotas, L., & Kapsali, M. (2021). Equals in Solidarity: Orfanotrofio's Housing Squat as a Site for Political Subjectification Across Differences Amid the "Greek Crisis". Antipode, 53(2), 399–421. https://doi.org/10.1111/anti.12653.

Keil, R. (2016). Urban neoliberalism: Rolling with the changes in a globalizing world. In S. Springer, K. Birch, & J. MacLeavy (Eds.), Handbook of Neoliberalism (pp. 385–397). Routledge, Taylor & Francis Group. https://doi.org/10.4324/9781315730660-46.

Kern, L., & Mullings, B. (2013). Urban Neoliberalism, Urban Insecurity and Urban Violence. Exploring the gender dimensions. In L. Peake & M. Rieker (Eds.), Rethinking Feminist Interventions into the Urban (pp. 59–92). Taylor & Francis Group.

Krausova, A. (2020). Latin American Social Movements: Bringing Strategy Back In. Latin American Research Review, 55(4), 839–849. https://doi.org/10.25222/larr.1398.

Kühne, J. S. C. (2019). Em Movimento na Área Metropolitana de Lisboa: Uma Etnografia da Caravana pelo Direito à Habitação. Universidade Nova de Lisboa.

Kuttab, E. (2014). The Many Faces of Feminism. Palestinian Women's Movements Finding a Voice. In S. Nazneen & M. Sultan (Eds.), Voicing Demand: Feminist Activism in Transnational Contexts (pp. 219–251).

La Coordinadora de Vivienda de Madrid. (2017). La Vivienda no es delito (L. Barrio Recio, M. Lowezka Lovera González, T. Youngman, & V. Canabal Fernández, Eds.). El Viejo Topo.

Lages, J. P. (2022). Habitação em pandemia: Os desafios da COVID-19 a partir da experiência de mulheres em situação de precariedade habitacional. CIDADES, Comunidades e Territórios, 45. https://doi.org/10.15847/cct.26604.

Lamb, V., Schoenberger, L., Middleton, C., & Un, B. (2017). Gendered eviction, protest and recovery: A feminist political ecology engagement with land grabbing in rural Cambodia. Journal of Peasant Studies, 44(6), 1215–1234. https://doi.org/10.1080/030 66150.2017.1311868.

Lancione, M. (2017). Revitalising the uncanny: Challenging inertia in the struggle against forced evictions. Environment and Planning D: Society and Space, 35(6), 1012–1032. https://doi.org/10.1177/0263775817701731.

Lancione, M. (2020). Radical housing: On the politics of dwelling as difference. International Journal of Housing Policy, 20(2), 273–289. https://doi.org/10.1080/1949124 7.2019.1611121.

Lancione, M., & Simone, A. (2021). Dwelling in liminalities, thinking beyond inhabitation. Environment and Planning D: Society and Space, 39(6), 969–975. https://doi .org/10.1177/02637758211062283.

Larner, W. (2000). Neo-liberalism: Policy, Ideology, Governmentality. Studies in Political Economy, 63, 5–26.

Lefebvre, H. (1968). Le droit à la ville. Anthropos.

Lefebvre, H. (1970). La révolution urbaine. Gallimard.

Lefebvre, H. (1974). La production de l'espace. Anthropos.

Lewinson, T., Thomas, M. L., & White, S. (2014). Traumatic Transitions: Homeless Women's Narratives of Abuse, Loss, and Fear. Affilia – Journal of Women and Social Work. https://doi.org/10.1177/0886109913516449.

Lima, A. P. de. (2023). Chapter 9: Care, emotions, and public policies. Reflections from Portugal. In M. C. Coelho & I. Beleli (Eds.), Emotions and Public Policies (pp. 257–280). Etnográfica Press. https://doi.org/10.4000/books.etnograficapress.8491.

Lima, V. (2021). Urban austerity and activism: Direct action against neoliberal housing policies. Housing Studies, 36(2), 258–277.

Lira, M., & March, H. (2021). Learning through housing activism in Barcelona: Knowledge production and sharing in neighbourhood-based housing groups. Housing Studies, 0(0), 1–20. https://doi.org/10.1080/02673037.2021.1921121.

Lund, C. (2018). Predatory peace. Dispossession at Aceh's oil palm frontier. Journal of Peasant Studies, 45(2), 431–452. https://doi.org/10.1080/03066150.2017.1351434.

Lusa. (2016, August 24). Alterações à renda apoiada entram em vigor em setembro. Observador. https://observador.pt/2016/08/24/alteracoes-a-renda-apoiada-entram-em-vigor-em-setembro/.

Lusa. (2017, March 1). Moradores de bairros sociais queixam-se de 'injustiças' na lei da renda apoiada. Diário de Notícias. https://www.dn.pt/sociedade/moradores-de-bairros-sociais-queixam-se-de-injusticas-na-lei-da-renda-apoiada-5697755.html.

Luxemburg, R. (1951). The Accumulation of Capital. Routledge. https://doi.org/10.1093/cje/7.3-4.405.

Mack, J. (2013). Urban Design from Below: Immigration and the Spatial Practice of Urbanism. Public Culture, 26(1), 153–185. https://doi.org/10.1215/08992363-2346286.

Mahler, A. G. (2017). Global South. Global South Studies, 1–4. https://doi.org/10.1093/OBO/9780190221911-0055.

Mahmood, S. (2005). Politics of piety: The Islamic revival and the feminist subject. Princeton University Press. https://hdl.handle.net/2027/heb04721.0001.001.

Mahmood, S. (2006). Feminist theory, agency, and the liberatory subject: Some reflections on the Islamic revival in Egypt. Temenos, 42(1), 31–71.

Malheiros, J. M., & Vala, F. (2004). Immigration and city change: The Lisbon Metropolis at the turn of the twentieth century. Journal of Ethnic and Migration Studies, 30(6), 1065–1086. https://doi.org/10.1080/1369183042000286250.

Malheiros, J., Mendes, M., Barbosa, C. E., Brito Silva, S., Schiltz, A., & Vala, F. (2007). Espaços e expressões de conflito e tensão entre autóctones, minorias migrantes e não migrantes na Área Metropolitana de Lisboa. In R. Carneiro (Ed.), Observatório da imigração (Vol. 22). Alto-Comissário para a Imigração e Minorias Étnicas (ACIME).

Marcus, G. E. (1995). Ethnography in/of the World System: The Emergence of Multi-Sited Ethnography. Annual Review of Anthropology, 24(1995), 95–117.

Marcuse, P. (1985). Gentrification, Abandonment, and Displacement: Connections, Causes, and Policy Responses in New York City. Journal of Urban and Contemporary Law, 28(1), 195–240. https://doi.org/10.3868/s050-004-015-0003-8.

Marinas Sánchez, M. (2004). Derribando los muros del género: Mujer y okupación. In R. Adell Argilés & M. Martínez López (Eds.), Dónde están las llaves? El movimiento okupa: Prácticas y contextos sociales (pp. 205–226). Catarata.

Martínez López, M. A. (2017). Squatters and migrants in Madrid: Interactions, contexts and cycles. Urban Studies, 54(11), 2472–2489. https://doi.org/10.1177/0042098016639011.

Martínez, M. A. (2019). Bitter wins or a long-distance race? Social and political outcomes of the Spanish housing movement. Housing Studies, 34(10), 1588–1611. https://doi.org/10.1080/02673037.2018.1447094.

Martínez, M. A. (2020a). European squatters' movements and the right to the city. In C. F. Fominaya & R. A. Feenstra (Eds.), Routledge Handbook of Contemporary European Social Movements. Protest in Turbulent Times (pp. 155–167). Routledge. https://doi.org/10.4324/9781351025188-12.

Martínez, M. A. (2020b). Squatters in the capitalist city. Housing, Justice and Urban Politics. Routledge.

Martínez, M. A. (2020c). Urban commons from an anti-capitalist approach. Partecipazione e Conflitto, 13(3), 1390–1410. https://doi.org/10.1285/i20356609v13i3p1390.

Marx, K. (1976). Capital: A Critique of Political Economy, vol. 1. Vintage.

Matos, A. R. (2016). "Eu participo, tu participas … nós protestamos": Ações de protesto, democracia e participação em processos de decisão". O Público e o Privado, 27, 119–137.

Matos, A. R., & Sabariego, J. (2020). Collective mobilization, democratic transformation and resistance against the crisis and austerity in Southern Europe: The experience of Portugal and Spain. Revista Espanola de Sociologia, 29(1), 71–86. https://doi.org/10.22325/fes/res.2020.05.

May, T. (2014). Subjectification. In L. Lawlor & J. Nale (Eds.), The Cambridge Foucault Lexicon (pp. 496–502). Cambridge University Press. https://doi.org/10.1017/CBO9781139022309.087.

Mayer, M. (2013). Preface. In S. E. K. SqEK (Ed.), Squatting in Europe: Radical Spaces, Urban Struggles (pp. 1–9). Minor Compositions.

Mbembe, A. (2019). Necropolitics. Duke University Press.

Mbembe, A., & Roitman, J. (1995). Figures of the Subject in Times of Crisis. Public Culture, 7, 323–352.

McAdam, D. (1999). The Political Process and the Development of Black Insurgency, 1930–1970. University of Chicago Press.

McAdam, D., Tarrow, S. G., & Tilly, C. (2001). Dynamics of contention. Cambridge University Press.

McCarthy, J. D., & Zald, M. N. (1977). Resource Mobilization and Social Movements: A Partial Theory. American Journal of Sociology, 82(6), 1212–1241. https://doi.org/10.1086/226464.

McFarlane, C. (2019). Thinking with and beyond the informal – formal relation in urban thought. Urban Studies, 56(3), 620–623. https://doi.org/10.1177/0042098018810603.

Mendes, L. (2017). Gentrificação, financeirização e produção capitalista do espaço urbano. Cadernos Poder Local, 8, 56–86.

Mendes, L. (2018). Gentrification and the New Urban Social Movements in Times of Post-Capitalist Crisis and Austerity Urbanism in Portugal. Arizona Journal of Hispanic Cultural Studies, 22, 199–215.

Mendes, L. (2019). A «nova» Questão da Habitação (Debate "Políticas Para o Território – Desenvolvimento Equilibrado, Uma Visão Estratégica, Issue March). Partido Comunista Português. https://www.researchgate.net/publication/331828761_Mendes_L_2019_Da_nova_Questao_da_Habitacao_Seminario_Politicas_para_o_Territorio_desenvolvimento_equilibrado_uma_visao_estrategica_Partido_Comunista_Portugues_Auditorio_da_Uniao_das_Freguesias_da_Noss.

Mendes, L., Carmo, A., & Malheiros, J. (2019). Gentrificação transnacional, novas procuras globais e financeirização do mercado de habitação em Lisboa. In A. C. Santos (Ed.), A nova questão da habitação em Portugal. Uma abordagem de economica política (pp. 111–142). Conjuntura Actual Editora.

Meyer, D. S., & Staggenborg, S. (2012). Thinking about Strategy. In G. M. Maney & R. Kutz-Flamenbaum (Eds.), Strategies for Social Change (pp. 3–23). University of Minnes. https://doi.org/10.4135/9781483329536.n1.

Miraftab, F. (2004). Invited and Invented Spaces of Participation: Neoliberal Citizenship and Feminists' Expanded Notion of Politics. Wagadu: Journal of Transnational Women's and Gender Studies, 1, 1–7.

Miraftab, F. (2006). Feminist Praxis, Citizenship and Informal Politics. International Feminist Journal of Politics, 8(2), 194–218.

Miraftab, F. (2009). Insurgent Planning: Situating Radical Planning in the Global South. Planning Theory, 8(1), 32–50. https://doi.org/10.1177/1473095208099297.

Mitchell, W. J. T. (2012). Image, space, revolution: The arts of occupation. Critical Inquiry, 39(1), 8–32. https://doi.org/10.1086/668048.

Mohanty, C. T. (1991). Under Western Eyes: Feminist Scholarship and Colonial Discourses [1986]. In C. T. Mohanty, A. Russo, & L. Torres (Eds.), Third World Women and the Politics of Feminis (pp. 51–81). Indiana University Press.

Moleiro, R. (2019, June 26). 31.651 famílias pedem casa à Câmara em Lisboa and Porto. Expresso / Primeiro Caderno, 20–21.

Morais, L., Silva, R., & Mendes, L. (2018). Direito À Habitação Em Portugal: Comentário Crítico Ao Relatório Apresentado Às Nações Unidas 2017 Right To Housing in Portugal: Critical Comments on the Report Presented To the United Nations 2017. Revista Movimentos Sociais e Dinâmicas Espaciais, 7(1), 229–243.

Moreira, C. F. (2018, June 8). Isto é a necessidade da minha vida: Ter onde dormir com os meus filhos. Público. https://www.publico.pt/2018/06/08/local/noticia/isto-e-a-necessidade-da-minha-vida-ter-onde-dormir-com-os-meus-filhos-1833798.

Motta, S. (2016). Decolonizing Australia's Body Politics: Contesting the Coloniality of Violence of Child Removal. Journal of Resistance Studies, 2(2 Special Issue on Feminized Resistances), 100–133.

Motta, S. C. (2011). Notes Towards Prefigurative Epistemologies. In A. G. Nilsen & S. C. Motta (Eds.), Social Movements and/in the Postcolonial: Dispossession, Development and Resistance in the Global South (pp. 178–199). Palgrave Macmillan.

Motta, S. C. (2013). "We Are the Ones We Have Been Waiting For": The Feminization of Resistance in Venezuela. Latin American Perspectives, 40(4), 35–54. https://doi.org/10.1177/0094582X13485706.

Motta, S. C., & Nilsen, A. G. (2011). Social Movements and/in the Postcolonial: Dispossession, Development and Resistance in the Global South. In S. C. Motta & A. G. Nilsen (Eds.), Social Movements in the Global South. Dispossession, Development and resistance (pp. 1–31). Palgrave Macmillan. https://doi.org/10.15713/ins.mmj.3.

Motta, S. C., & Seppälä, T. (2016). Feminized Resistances. Journal of Resistance Studies, 2(2 Special Issue on Feminized Resistances), 5–32.

Muñoz, S. (2017). A look inside the struggle for housing in Buenos Aires, Argentina. Urban Geography, 38(8), 1252–1269. https://doi.org/10.1080/02723638.2017.1349988.

Muñoz, S. (2018). Urban Precarity and Home: There Is No "Right to the City". Annals of the American Association of Geographers. https://doi.org/10.1080/24694452.2017.1392284.

Murphy, M. (2020). Dual conditionality in welfare and housing for lone parents in Ireland: Change and continuity? Social Policy and Administration, 54(2), 250–264. https://doi.org/10.1111/spol.12548.

Nader, L. (1972). Up the Antropologist: Perspectives Gained From Studying Up. In Reinventing Antropology (pp. 284–311). Random House.

Neveu, C. (2011). Démocratie participative et mouvements sociaux: Entre domestication et ensauvagement? Participations, 1, 186–209.

Nielsen, M. (2011). Inverse governmentality: The paradoxical production of peri-urban planning in Maputo, Mozambique. Critique of Anthropology, 31(4), 329–358. https://doi.org/10.1177/0308275X11420118.

Nomisma. (2016). Dimensioni e caratteristiche del disagio abitativo in Italia. http://www.istitutodegasperi-emilia-romagna.it/pdf-mail/290_11052016a3.pdf.

Nunes, J. A., & Serra, N. (2003). 'Casas decentes para o povo': Movimentos urbanos e emancipação em Portugal. In B. de S. Santos (Ed.), Democratizar a democracia. Os caminhos da democracia participativa (pp. 213–245). Edições Afrontamento.

Nunes, J. A., & Serra, N. (2004). 'Decent housing for the people': Urban movements and emancipation in Portugal. South European Society and Politics, 9(2), 46–76. https://doi.org/10.1080/1360874042000253483.

Nygren, A. (2016). Socially Differentiated Urban Flood Governance in Mexico: Ambiguous Negotiations and Fragmented Contestations. Journal of Latin American Studies, 48, 335–365.

Nygren, A. (2018). Inequality and interconnectivity: Urban spaces of justice in Mexico. Geoforum, 89(October 2016), 145–154. https://doi.org/10.1016/j.geoforum.2017.06.015.

Nygren, A., & Wayessa, G. (2018). At the intersections of multiple marginalisations: Displacements and environmental justice in Mexico and Ethiopia. Environmental Sociology, 4(1), 148–161. https://doi.org/10.1080/23251042.2017.1419418.

OHCHR. (1997). CESCR General Comment No. 7: The Right to Adequate Housing (Art 11.1): Forced evictions. UN Office of the High Commissioner for Human Rights. http://www.refworld.org/docid/47a70799d.html.

Oliveira, A. U. de. (2001). A longa marcha do campesinato brasileiro: Movimentos sociais, conflitos e Reforma Agrária. Estudos Avançados, 15(43), 185–206.

Osterweil, M. (2013). Rethinking public anthropology through epistemic politics and theoretical practice. Cultural Anthropology, 28(4), 598–620. https://doi.org/10.1111/cuan.12029.

Osuoka, I. (2018). Niger Delta: Community and Resistance. In M. Lang, C.-D. König, & A.-C. Redelmann (Eds.), Alternatives in the World of Crisis (pp. 18–45). Rosa Luxemburh Stiftung; Universidad Andina Simon Bolívar.

PAH. (2020). Qué es la PAH? https://afectadosporlahipoteca.com/que-es-la-pah/.

Palma, T., & Bourgard, J. (2018, November). Mães Ocupas. Quando viver com os filhos na rua não é opção. Renascença. https://rr.sapo.pt/maes-ocupas/.

Palomera, J., & Vetta, T. (2016). Moral economy: Rethinking a radical concept. Anthropological Theory, 16(4), 413–432. https://doi.org/10.1177/1463499616678097.

Patel, S., Arputham, J., & Bartlett, S. (2016). "We beat the path by walking": How the women of Mahila Milan in India learned to plan, design, finance and build housing. Environment and Urbanization, 28(1), 223–240. https://doi.org/10.1177/0956247815617440.

Paulo, L. (2017). A Questão da Habitação. Portugal 2017. Cadernos Poder Local, 8, 11–25.

Peake, L. (2016). The Twenty-First-Century Quest for Feminism and the Global Urban. International Journal of Urban and Regional Research, 40(1), 219–227. https://doi.org/10.1111/1468-2427.12276.

Peck, J. (2012). Austerity urbanism: American cities under extreme economy. City, 16(6), 626–655. https://doi.org/10.1080/13604813.2012.734071.

Peck, J., & Tickell, A. (2002). Neoliberalizing Space. Antipode, 34(3), 380–404.

Pereira, A. M., & Pereira, R. M. (2016). Investimentos em Infra-estruturas em Portugal. Fundação Francisco Manu.

Perlman, J. E. (1979). The Myth of Marginality. Urban Poverty and Politics in Rio de Janeiro. University of California.

Pinto, L. (2018, October 16). Governo destina 156 milhões a Políticas de Habitação e Reabilitação. Público. https://www.publico.pt/2018/10/16/economia/noticia/orcamento-de-estado-destina-156-milhoes-de-euros-a-politicas-de-habitacao-e-reabilitacao-1847718.

Pinto, L., Barros, R., Jorge, S., & Oro, A. V. (2021, February 21). Porque falha a mala de ferramentas para a crise da habitação? Público. https://www.publico.pt/habitacao-do-protesto-a-proposta/porque-falha-mala-ferramentas-habitacao.

Pinto, P. R. (2015). Lisbon Rising: Urban Social Movements in the Portuguese Revolution, 1974–75. Manchester University Press.

Pinto, T. C. (1998). Modelos de habitat, modos de habitar: O caso da construção clandestina do habitat. Sociedade e Território, 25/26, 32–44.

Pinto, T. C., & Guerra, I. (2013). Some structural and emergent trends in Social Housing in Portugal. Rethinking housing policies in times of crisis. CIDADES, Comunidades e Territórios, 27(27), 1–21. https://doi.org/10.7749/citiescommunitiesterritories.dec2013.027.art01.

Piotto, M., & Sanches, D. (2019). A resiliência do MSTC e a Ocupação Nove de Julho.

Pleace, N. (2015). How to Cause Homelessness. Homeless in Europe, Summer, 21–22.

Pleace, N., Culhane, D., Granfelt, R., & Knutagård, M. (2015). The Finnish Homelessness Strategy – An International Review. Ministry of the Environment.

Pleace, N., Fitzpatrick, S., Johnson, S., Quilgars, D., & Sanderson, D. (2008). Statutory Homelessness in England: The Experience of Families and 16–17 Year Olds. Department of Community and Local Government.

Podlashuc, L. (2011). The South African Homeless People's Federation: Interrogating the myth of participation (p. 38). ACCEDE, University of Western Cape.

Podlashuc, L. N. (2007). Class for itself? Shack/slum Dwellers International: The praxis of a transnational poor movement. University of Technology, Sydney.

PORDATA. (2018). Employees with national minimum wage by sector of economic activity – Mainland (%) [data set] [Dataset]. https://www.pordata.pt.

PORDATA. (2019a). Agregados domésticos privados monoparentais: Total e por sexo [data set] [Dataset]. https://www.pordata.pt/.

PORDATA. (2019b). At-risk-of-poverty rate after social transfers: Total and by household type [data set] [Dataset]. https://www.pordata.pt.

PORDATA. (2019c). Portugal: National minimum wage [Dataset]. pordata.pt.

PORDATA. (2021a). National minimum wage [data set] [Dataset]. https://www.por data.pt/.

PORDATA. (2021b). Salário médio mensal dos trabalhadores por conta de outrem: Remuneração base e ganho [data set] [Dataset]. https://www.pordata.pt/.

Portas, N. (1986). O processo SAAL: entre o estado e o poder local. Revista Crítica de Ciências Sociais, 18-19-20, 635–644.

Porteous, D., & Smith, S. E. (2001). Domicide. The Global Destruction of Home. McGill-Queen's University Press.

Pöysä, A. (2018). Portugalin pimeä puoli. Vastapaino.

Pozzi, G. (2019). Expulsionscapes. Logics of Expulsion and Economies of Eviction in Milan (Italy). Archivio Antropologico Mediterraneo, 21(2). https://doi.org/10.4000 /aam.2126.

Pozzi, G., & Rimoldi, L. (2017). Marginal Uncertainties. EtnoAntropogia, 5(1), 95–108.

Pradel-Miquel, M. (2017). Crisis, (re-)informalization processes and protest: The case of Barcelona. Current Sociology, 65(2), 209–221. https://doi.org/10.1177 /0011392116657291.

Provedor da justiça. (2016). Programa Especial de Realojamento das Áreas Metropolitanas de Lisboa e do Porto. Bairro de Santa Filomena e 6 de Maio: Vol. 003/B/.

Pruijt, H. (2003). Is the institutionalization of urban movements inevitable? A comparison of the opportunities for sustained squatting in New York City and Amsterdam. International Journal of Urban and Regional Research, 27(1), 133–157. https://doi .org/10.1111/1468-2427.00436.

Pruijt, H. (2013). The Logic of Urban Squatting. International Journal of Urban and Regional Research, 37(1), 19–45. https://doi.org/10.1111/j.1468-2427.2012.01116.x.

Queirós, J., & Pereira, V. B. (2018). Voices in the revolution: Resisting territorial stigma and social relegation in Porto's historic centre (1974–1976). The Sociological Review, 66(4), 857–876. https://doi.org/10.1177/0038026118777423.

Rancière, J. (1999). Disagreement: Politics and philosophy. University of Minnesota Press.

Raposo, I., & Valente, A. (2010). Diálogo social ou dever de reconversão? As Áreas Urbanas de Génese Ilegal (AUGI) na Área Metropolitana de Lisboa. Revista Crítica de Ciências Sociais, 91, 221–235. https://doi.org/10.4000/rccs.4480.

Raposo, O., Alves, A. R., Varela, P., & Roldão, C. (2019). Negro drama. Racismo, segregação e violência policial nas periferias de Lisboa. Revista Crítica de Ciências Sociais, 119, 5–28. https://doi.org/10.4000/rccs.8937.

Reis, C. (2019, July 26). Rendas altas levam famílias a ocupar casas vazias. "Era isto ou ficar na rua". Diário de Notícias. https://www.dn.pt/edicao-do-dia/26-jul-2019/rendas-altas-levam-familias-a-ocupar-casas-vazias-era-isto-ou-ficar-na-rua-11150984.html.

Robinson, J. (2003). Postcolonialising geography: Tactics and pitfalls. Singapore Journal of Tropical Geography, 24(3), 273–289. https://doi.org/10.4324/9781315236285-28.

Rodrigues, Anabela Fernandes, A., Fernandes, C., Roldão, C., Insali, I., Pereira, J., & Ba, M. (2017). A urgência de um combate real às desigualdades étnico-raciais e ao racismo. Le Monde Diplomatique (Versão Portuguesa), 6–7.

Rodrigues, C. (2012). O envolvimento dos moradores nos programas de realojamento no Portugal democrático. Configurações – Revista de Sociologia, 9, 1–12. https://doi.org/10.4000/con.

Rodrigues, J. (2018). Na sombra de 1989: Economia política internacional depois do fim da história. Revista Crítica de Ciências Sociais, Número especial, 189–216. https://doi.org/10.4000/rccs.7834.

Rodrigues, J., Santos, A., & Teles, N. (2016). A financeirização do capitalismo em Portugal. Actual.

Rolnik, R. (2013a). Late Neoliberalism: The Financialization of Homeownership and Housing Rights. International Journal of Urban and Regional Research, 37(3), 1058–1066. https://doi.org/10.1111/1468-2427.12062.

Rolnik, R. (2013b). Report of the Special Rapporteur on adequate housing as a component of the right to an adequate standard of living, on the right to non-discimination in this context: Vol. A/HRC/22/4 (Issue December, pp. 1–27). UN Human Rights Council.

Rolnik, R. (2019). Urban Warfare: Housing under the empire of finance. Verso.

Rolnik, R., Amadeo, C., & Rizzini Ansari, M. (2022). Territorial dispossession under financialised capitalism and its discontents: Insurgent spatialities and legal forms. City, 26(5–6), 929–946. https://doi.org/10.1080/13604813.2022.2126192.

Roy, A. (2003). City requiem, Calcutta: Gender and the politics of poverty. University of Minnesota Press.

Roy, A. (2009a). The 21st century metropolis – New geographies of theory. Regional Studies, 43(6), 819–830. https://doi.org/10.1080/00343400701809665.

Roy, A. (2009b). Why India cannot plan its cities: Informality, insurgence and the idiom of urbanization. Planning Theory, 8(1), 76–87. https://doi.org/10.1177/1473095208099299.

Roy, A. (2011). Slumdog Cities: Rethinking Subaltern Urbanism. International Journal of Urban and Regional Research, 35(2), 223–238. https://doi.org/10.1111/j.1468-2427.2011.01051.x.

Roy, A. (2015). Governing the Postcolonial Suburbs. In P. Hamel & Keil (Eds.), Suburban Governance: A Global View (pp. 337–349). University of Toronto Press.

Roy, A. (2017). Dis/possessive collectivism: Property and personhood at city's end. Geoforum, 80, A1–A11. https://doi.org/10.1016/j.geoforum.2016.12.012.

Roy, A., Oldfield, S., McElroy, E., Malson, H., & Graziani, T. (2019). Housing Justice in Unequal Cities (A. Roy & H. Malson, Eds.). Institute on Inequality and Democracy – UCLA.

Roy, A., & Rolnik, R. (2020). Methodologies for Housing Justice. In A. Roy, R. Rolnik, T. Graziani, & H. Malson (Eds.), Methodologies for Housing Justice Resource Guide (pp. 12–29). Los Angeles: Institute on Inequality and Democracy.

Rutland, T. (2013). Activists in the Making: Urban Movements, Political Processes and the Creation of Political Subjects. International Journal of Urban and Regional Research, 37(3), 989–1011. https://doi.org/10.1111/j.1468-2427.2012.01110.x.

Saaristo, S.-M. (2015). Favela Associations. Between Repression, Violence and Politics. Suomen Antropologi: Journal of the Finnish Anthropological Society, 40(2), 28–49.

Saaristo, S.-M. (2019). Asociaciones de residentes de las favelas: Entre represión, violencia y política. In A. Nygren, L. Durand, & A. C. de la Vega-Leinert (Eds.), Naturaleza y neoliberalismo en América Latina (pp. 385–422). Universidad Autónoma de México. https://doi.org/10.22201/crim.9786073022231e.2019.

Saaristo, S.-M., & Silva, R. (2024). Struggles against financialisation of housing in Lisbon – the case of Habita. Housing Studies, 39(6), 1467–1494. https://doi.org/10.1080/02673037.2023.2190958.

Salgueiro, T. B. (1972). Bairros Clandestinos na Periferia de Lisboa. Finisterra, 12(23), 28–55. https://doi.org/10.18055/finis2281.

Sanches, D., Stevens, J., & Piotto, M. (2019). Ocupações e Urbanismo Insurgentes: Área Central de São Paulo. ICHT III Colóquio Internacional – Imaginário: Construir e Habitar a Terra, 3, 553–569.

Sandercock, L. (1998). Introduction: Framing Insurgent Historiographies for Planning. In Making the Invisible Visible: A Multicultural Planning History (pp. 1–33). University of California.

Santos, A. C. (2019a). A nova questão da habitação e a nova geração de políticas em Portugal. In A. C. Santos (Ed.), A nova questão da habitação em Portugal. Uma abordagem da economia política (pp. 293–323). Conjuntura Actual.

Santos, A. C. (2019b). A nova questão da habitação em Portugal. Uma abordagem de economica política (A. C. Santos, Ed.). Conjuntura Actual.

Santos, A. C. (2019c). Habitação em tempos financeiros em Portugal. In A. C. Santos (Ed.), A nova questão da habitação em Portugal. Uma abordagem da economia política (pp. 15–52). Conjuntura Actual.

Santos, A. C., Teles, N., & Serra, N. (2014). Finança e habitação em Portugal. Centro de Estudos Sociais, Universidade de Coimbra.

Santos, B. de S. (2003). Orçamento Participativo em Porto Alegre: Para uma democracia redistributiva. In Democratizar a democracia. Os caminhos da democracia participativa. Edições Afrontamento.

Santos, B. de S. (2014). Epistemologies of the South. Justice Against Epistemicide. Routledge, Taylor & Francis Group.

Santos, B. de S. (2017). The Resilience of Abyssal Exclusions in Our Societies: Toward a Post-Abyssal Law. Tilburg Law Review, 22(1–2), 237–258. https://doi.org/10.1163/22112596-02201011.

Santos, B. de S., & Nunes, J. A. (2004). Introduction: Democracy, participation and grassroots movements in contemporary Portugal. South European Society and Politics, 9(2), 1–15. https://doi.org/10.1080/1360874042000253465.

Santos, J. H. (2014). Sem mestres, nem chefes. O povo tomou a rua ... Lutas dos moradores no pós-25 de Abril. Letra Livre.

Santos, R. (Ed.). (2016). Cidada Participada: Arquitectura e Democracia. Operações SAAL – Oeiras. Tinta-da-china.

Sapo. (2018, November 29). Com 'milhares' a pedir ajuda, Igreja quer resposta do Governo contra 'a indiferença e o descarte'. Sapo. https://rr.sapo.pt/noticia/132482/com-milhares-a-pedir-ajuda-igreja-quer-resposta-do-governo-contra-a-indiferenca-e-o-descarte.

Sapo. (2019, May 30). Lisboa é a cidade europeia com mais casas convertidas em alojamento turístico. Sapo. https://sol.sapo.pt/artigo/660279/lisboa-e-a-cidade-europeia-com-mais-casas-convertidas-em-alojamento-turistico.

Sassen, S. (2000). Women's Burden: Counter-geographies of Globalization and the Feminization of Survival. Journal of International Affairs, 53(2), 503–524.

Sassen, S. (2009). Cities Today: A New Frontier for Major Developments. Annals of the American Academy of Political and Social Science, 626, 53–71.

Sassen, S. (2014). Expulsions: Brutality and complexity in global economy. Belknap Press of Harvard University.

Sassen, S. (2018). Who owns the city? In United Nations Human Settlements Programme (Ed.), The Quito Papers and the new urban agenda (pp. 48–51). Routledge.

Scanlon, K., Fernández Arrigoitia, M., & Whitehead, C. M. (2015). Social Housing in Europe. European Policy Analysis, 17(July), 11–19. https://doi.org/10.1002/9781118412367.

Scheba, S., & Millington, N. (2023). Occupations as reparative urban infrastructure: Thinking with Cissie Gool House. City, 1–25. https://doi.org/10.1080/13604813.2023.2266192.

Schilling, H., Blokland, T., & Simone, A. (2019). Working precarity: Urban youth tactics to make livelihoods in instable conditions in Abidjan, Athens, Berlin and Jakarta. Sociological Review. https://doi.org/10.1177/0038026119858209.

Schipper, S. (2014). The financial crisis and the hegemony of urban neoliberalism: Lessons from Frankfurt am main. International Journal of Urban and Regional Research, 38(1), 236–255. https://doi.org/10.1111/1468-2427.12099.

Scott, J. C. (1985). Weapons of the Weak: Everyday Forms of Peasant Resistance. Yale University Press.

Secretaria de Estado da Habitação. (2017). Para uma nova geração de políticas de habitação. Sentido estratégico, objetivos e instrumentos de atuação. Government of Portugal. https://www.portugal.gov.pt/download-ficheiros/ficheiro.aspx?v =95621259-fdd4-4099-82f3-2ff17c522882.

Seixas, J., & Guterres, A. B. (2019a). Political evolution in the Lisbon of the digital era. Fast urban changes, slow institutional restructuring and growing civic pressures. Urban Research & Practice, 12(1), 99–110. https://doi.org/10.1080/17535069.2018.150 5272.

Seixas, J., & Guterres, A. B. (2019b). Unbalanced Lisbon. Local movements, municipal governments, national politics and global finance in a swiftly changing metropolis. In L. Fregolent & O. Nel·lo (Eds.), Social Movements and Public Policies in Southern European Cities (pp. 189–202). Springer International Publishing.

Seixas, J., Tulumello, S., & Allegretti, G. (2019). Lisboa em transição profunda e desequilibrada. Habitação, imobiliário e política urbana no sul da Europa e na era digital. Cadernos Metrópole, 21(44), 221–251. https://doi.org/10.1590/2236-9996.2019-4410.

Seixas, J., Tulumello, S., Corvelo, S., & Drago, A. (2015). Dinâmicas sociogeográficas e políticas na Área Metropolitana de Lisboa em tempos de crise e de austeridade. Cadernos Metrópole, 17(34), 371–399. https://doi.org/10.1590/2236-9996.2015-3404.

Selmeczi, A. (2014). Dis/placing political illiteracy: The politics of intellectual equality in a South African shack-dwellers' movement. Interface: A Journal for and about Social Movements, 6(May), 230–265.

Sendra, P., & Sennett, R. (2020). Designing Disorder: Experiments and Disruptions in the City. Verso books.

Sennett, R., Burdett, R., & Sassen, S. (with United Nations Human Settlements Programme). (2018). The Quito papers and the new urban agenda. Routledge, Taylor & Francis Group.

Seppälä, T. (2016). Feminizing Resistance, Decolonizing Solidarity: Contesting Neoliberal Development in the Global South. Journal of Resistance Studies, 2(1), 12–47.

Sequera, J., & Nofre, J. (2018). Urban activism and touristification in Southern Europe: Barcelona, Madrid & Lisbon. In J. Ibrahim & J. M. Roberts (Eds.), Contemporary Left-Wing Activism Vol 2: Democracy, Participation and Dissent in a Global Context (pp. 88–105). Routledge. https://doi.org/10.4324/9781351047401-6.

Serpa, F., Fonte, M. M. da, Allegri, A., Arenga, N., & Monteiro, M. L. (2018). Habitação de promoção pública: Da construção nova à reabilitação, uma leitura dos projetos.

In Habitação. Cem anos de políticas públicas em Portugal. 1918–2018 (pp. 407–464). Instituto da Habitação e da Reabilitação Urbana.

Serra, N. (2019). Quanto custa ser parente pobre? Do lugar periférico da habitação à sua centralidade no processo de financeirização. In A. C. Santos (Ed.), A nova questão da habitação em Portugal. Uma abordagem da economia política (pp. 275–291). Universidade de Coimbra.

Silva, Â., & Lima, R. P. (2008, September 30). 3.000 casas atribuídas por cunha em Lisboa. Expresso. https://expresso.pt/actualidade/3000-casas-atribuidas-por-cunha-em-lisboa=f412879.

Silva, R. (2019a). Crise e desigualdade habitacional. Como (não) se vive em Lisboa. In A. C. Santos (Ed.), A nova questão da habitação em Portugal. Uma abordagem de economia política (pp. 233–258). Conjuntura Actual Editora.

Silva, R. (2019b, July 1). A Nova Geração de Políticas de Habitação não é nova e não defende a habitação. http://habita.info/a-nova-geracao-de-politicas-de-habitacao-nao-e-nova-e-nao-defende-a-habitacao/.

Silva, R. (2021, September 23). Não há rendas acessíveis sem regulação das rendas. Público. https://www.publico.pt/2021/09/23/opiniao/opiniao/nao-ha-rendas-acessiveis-regulacao-rendas-1978428.

Simone, A. (2008). The politics of the possible: Making urban life in Phnom Penh. Singapore Journal of Tropical Geography, 29(2), 186–204. https://doi.org/10.1111/j.1467-9493.2008.00328.x.

Simone, A. (2010). A Town on Its Knees?: Economic experimentations with postcolonial Urban politics in Africa and Southeast Asia. Theory, Culture and Society, 27(7), 130–154. https://doi.org/10.1177/0263276410383708.

Simone, A. (2013). Cities of Uncertainty: Jakarta, the Urban Majority, and Inventive Political Technologies. Theory, Culture & Society, 30(8), 243–263. https://doi.org/10.1177/0263276413501872.

Simone, A. (2015a). Afterword: Come on out, you're surrounded: The betweens of infrastructure. City, 19(2–3), 375–383. https://doi.org/10.1080/13604813.2015.1018070.

Simone, A. (2015b). The Urban Poor and Their Ambivalent Exceptionalities. Current Anthropology, 56(S11), S15–S23. https://doi.org/10.1086/682283.

Simone, A. (2016). City of Potentialities: An Introduction. Theory, Culture and Society, 33(7–8), 5–29. https://doi.org/10.1177/0263276416666915.

Simone, A. (2018). Designing Space for the Majority: Urban Displacements of the Human. Cubic Journal, 1, 124–135. https://doi.org/10.31182/cubic.2018.1.007.

Simone, A. (2019a). Contests over value: From the informal to the popular. Urban Studies, 56(3), 616–619. https://doi.org/10.1177/0042098018810604.

Simone, A. (2019b). Improvised lives: Rhythms of endurance in an urban south. Polity.

Slater, T. (2006). The Eviction of Critical Perspectives from Gentrification Research. International Journal of Urban and Regional Research, 30(4), 737–757. https://doi .org/10.1111/j.1468-2427.2006.00689.x.

Sletto, B., & Nygren, A. (2016). Unsettling Neoliberal Rationalities: Engaged Ethnography and the Meanings of Responsibility in the Dominican Republic and Mexico. International Journal of Urban and Regional Research, 39(5), 965–983. https://doi .org/10.1111/1468-2427.12315.

Smelser, N. J. (1962). The Theory of Collective Behavior. Routledge & Kegan.

Smith, A. (2007). An Inquiry Into the Nature and Causes of the Wealth of Nations. In J. B. Wight & G. Osbourne (Eds.), Harriman House Publishing. Harriman House Publishing.

Smith, N. (2002). New Globalism, New Urbanism: Gentrification as Global Urban Strategy. Antipode, 427–450. https://doi.org/10.1002/9781444397499.ch4.

Smolen, A. G., & Harrison, A. (2013). Mothering without a Home: Attachment Representations and Behaviors of Homeless Mothers and Children. Jason Aronson.

Soederberg, S. (2016). Governing stigmatised space: The case of the 'slums' of Berlin-Neukölln. New Political Economy, 22(5), 478–495. https://doi.org/10.1080/13563467 .2017.1240671.

Soederberg, S. (2017). The rental housing question: Exploitation, eviction and erasures. Geoforum, 89, 114–123. https://doi.org/10.1016/j.geoforum.2017.01.007.

Soederberg, S. (2018). Evictions: A Global Capitalist Phenomenon. Development and Change, 49(2), 286–301. https://doi.org/10.1111/dech.12383.

Soederberg, S. (2019). Governing Global Displacement in Austerity Urbanism: The Case of Berlin's Refugee Housing Crisis. Development and Change, 50(4), 923–947. https://doi.org/10.1111/dech.12455.

Soederberg, S. (2021). Urban displacements: Governing surplus and survival in global capitalism. Routledge.

Souza, M. L. de. (2010). Which right to which city? In defence of political-strategic clarity. Interface: A Journal for and About Social Movements, 2(1), 315–333.

Spivak, G. C. (1988). Subaltern Studies: Deconstructing Historiography. In R. Guha & G. C. Spivak (Eds.), Selected Subaltern Studies (pp. 3–34). Oxford University Press.

Spivak, G. C. (2005). Scattered speculations on the subaltern and the popular. Postcolonial Studies: Culture, Politics, Economy, 8(4), 475–486. https://doi.org/10.1080 /13688790500375132.

SqEK. (2014). The squatters' movement in Europe: Commons and autonomy as alternatives to capitalism (C. Cattaneo & M. A. Martínez, Eds.). Pluto Press.

Stahler-Sholk, R. (2010). The Zapatista Social Movement: Innovation and Sustainability. Alternatives, 35(3), 269–290. https://doi.org/10.1177/030437541003500306.

Stavrides, S., & Travlou, P. (Eds.). (2022). Housing as commons: Housing alternatives as response to the current urban crisis (First Edition). Bloomsbury Academic, Bloomsbury Publishing.

Stevens, J. (2019). Occupy, resist, construct, dwell! A genealogy of urban occupation movements in central São Paulo. Radical Housing Journal, 1(1), 131–149.

Stryker, R., & González, R. J. (2014). Up, down, and sideways: Anthropologists trace the pathways of power (R. Stryker & R. J. González, Eds.). Berghahn Books.

Suzuki, N., Ogawa, T., & Inaba, N. (2018). The right to adequate housing: Evictions of the homeless and the elderly caused by the 2020 Summer Olympics in Tokyo. Leisure Studies, 37(1), 89–96. https://doi.org/10.1080/02614367.2017.1355408.

Swyngedouw, E., Moulaert, F., & Rodriguez, A. (2002). New Geographies of Power, Exclusion and Injustice Neoliberal Urbanization in Europe: Large-Scale Urban Development Projects and the New Urban Policy. Antipode, 34, 542–577. https://doi.org/10.1111/1467-8330.00254.

Tarrow, S. G. (2011). Power in Movement: Social Movements and Contentious Politics. Cambridge University Press.

Thompson, E. P. (1971). The Moral Economy of the English Crowd in the Eighteenth Century. Past & Present, 50, 76–136.

Tilly, C. (1978). From Mobilization to Revolution. Addison/Wesley.

Tilly, C. (1995). Contentious repertoires in Great Britain, 1758–1834. In M. Traugott (Ed.), Repertoires and Cycles of Collective Action (pp. 15–42). Duke University Press.

Tilly, C. (1997). Invisible Elbows. In Roads from Past to Future. Rowman & Littlefield.

Tilly, C. (2004). Social Movements, 1768–2004. Paradigm Publishers.

Tilly, C. (2005). Identities, boundaries, and social ties. Paradigm Publishers.

Tronto, J. C. (2013). Caring Democracy: Markets, Equality, and Justice (pp. xix–xix). NYU Press. https://doi.org/10.18574/9780814770450.

Trouillot, M.-R. (1995). Silencing the Past. Power and the Production of History. Beacon Press.

Tulumello, S. (2016). Reconsidering neoliberal urban planning in times of crisis: Urban regeneration policy in a 'dense' space in Lisbon. Urban Geography, 37(1), 117–140. https://doi.org/10.1080/02723638.2015.1056605.

Tulumello, S. (2019). Struggling Against Entrenched Austerity. From the housing crisis toward social movements for housing in post-crisis Lisbon and Portugal. In F. Othengrafen & K. Serraos (Eds.), Urban Resilience, Changing Economy and Social Trends. Coping with socio-economic consequences of the crisis in Athens, Greece (pp. 61–79). Leibniz Universität.

Tulumello, S., & Dagkouli-Kyriakoglou, M. (2021). Financialization of housing in Southern Europe: Policy analysis and recommendations. European Parliament office of MEP José Gusmão. https://doi.org/10.1080/13673882.2020.00001074.

UN DESA Statistics Division. (2023). Average number of hours spent on total work (paid and unpaid), by sex [Dataset]. https://gender-data-hub-2-undesa.hub.arcgis.com/datasets/0033dd733af84252a088ff5552bce323/explore.

UN-HABITAT & OHCHR. (2014a). Assessing the Impact of Eviction. Handbook. UN-Habitat. https://doi.org/10.1111/j.2151-6952.2000.tb01155.x.

UN-HABITAT & OHCHR. (2014b). Fact Sheet No. 25 (Rev.1), Forced Evictions, No. 25/Rev. 1. UN Office of the High Commissioner for Human Rights. https://www.refworld.org/docid/5566d6744.html.

UNODC. (2018). Global Study on Homicide 2018. United Nations Office on Drugs and Crime. https://www.unodc.org/documents/data-and-analysis/GSH2018/GSH18_Gender-related_killing_of_women_and_girls.pdf.

Vale de Almeida, M. (2000). Um Mar da Cor da Terra: Raça, Cultura e Política da Identidade. Celta Editora.

Varley, A. (2013). Feminist Perspectives on Urban Poverty. De-essentialising difference. In L. Peake & M. Rieker (Eds.), Rethinking Feminist Interventions into the Urban (pp. 260–293). Taylor & Francis Group.

Vasudevan, A. (2015). The makeshift city: Towards a global geography of squatting. Progress in Human Geography, 39(3), 338–359. https://doi.org/10.1177/0309132514531471.

Vilaça, E., & Ferreira, T. (2018). Os anos de crescimento (1969–2002). In Instituto da Habitação e da Reabilitação Urbana (IHRU) (Ed.), Habitação. Cem anos de políticas públicas em Portugal 1918–201 (pp. 317–364). Imprensa Nacional-Casa da Moeda.

Wacquant, L. (2008). Urban outcasts: A comparative sociology of advanced marginality. Polity.

Wacquant, L. (2009). Punishing the Poor: The Neoliberal Government of Social Insecurity. Duke University Press.

Wacquant, L. (2016). Revisiting territories of relegation: Class, ethnicity and state in the making of advanced marginality. Urban Studies, 53(6), 1077–1088. https://doi.org/10.1177/0042098015613259.

Wacquant, L., Slater, T., & Pereira, V. B. (2014). Territorial stigmatization in action. Environment and Planning A, 46(6), 1270–1280. https://doi.org/10.1068/a4606ge.

Wardhaugh, J. (1999). The Unaccommodated Woman: Home, Homelessness and Identity. The Sociological Review, 47(1), 91–109. https://doi.org/10.1111/1467-954X.00164.

Watts, M. (2005). Baudelaire over Berea, Simmel over Sandton? Public Culture, 17(1), 181–192. https://doi.org/10.1215/08992363-17-1-181.

Wayessa, G. O., & Nygren, A. (2016). Whose Decisions, Whose Livelihoods? Resettlement and Environmental Justice in Ethiopia. Society and Natural Resources, 29(4), 387–402. https://doi.org/10.1080/08941920.2015.1089612.

Wilde, M. (2019). Resisting the rentier city: Grassroots housing activism and London. Radical Housing Journal, 1(September), 63–80.

Wilde, M. (2020). Eviction, Gatekeeping and Militant Care: Moral Economies of Housing in Austerity London. Ethnos, 0(0), 1–20. https://doi.org/10.1080/00141844.2019.1687540.

Wilhelm-Solomon, M. (2020). The City Otherwise: The Deferred Emergency of Occupation in Inner-City Johannesburg. Cultural Anthropology, 35(3). https://doi.org/10.14506/ca35.3.03.

Young, I. M. (1990). Justice and the Politics of Difference. Princeton University Press.

Zhang, Y. (2017). It Felt Like You Were at War's State of Exception and Wounded Life in the Shanghai Expo-Induced Domicide. In K. Brickell, M. Fernández Arrigoitia, & A. Vasudevan (Eds.), Geographies of Forced Eviction: Dispossession, Violence, Insecurity (pp. 97–119). Palgrave Macmillan.

Appendix

TABLE A.1   Biographical interviews

Nº	Pseudonym	Date	Age	Gender	Family	Current housing	Origin
1	Anabela	Oct-18	40–49	F	Living alone	Occupying	Born in Guinea-Bissau (GW), parents from GW and Portugal (PT)
2	Maria	Oct-18	40–49	F	Single-parent	Occupying	Born in Angola (AO), parents from AO
3	Cláudia	Oct-18	40–49	F	Single-parent	Occupying	Born in PT, parents from CV
4	Miriam	Nov-18	20–29	F	Single-parent + grandmother	Council home	Born in PT, parents from CV
5	Ema	Jan-19	30–39	F	Single-parent	Occupying	Born in PT, parents from São Tomé and Príncipe (ST)
6	Francisca	Mar-19	40–49	F	Living alone	Rental room	Born in PT, parents from PT
7	Carla	Mar-19	20–29	F	Nuclear	Occupying	Born in PT, parents from AO
8	Sara	Apr-19	30–39	F	Single-parent	Occupying	Born in PT, parents from PT
9	Célio	Apr-19	50–59	M	Nuclear	Staying with relatives	Born in CV, parents from CV
10	Cátia	Apr-19	40–49	F	Single-parent	Occupying	Born in Mozambique (MZ), parents MZ/PT
11	Francisco	Apr-19	30–39	M	Living alone	Council home	Born in AO, parents from AO
12	Nina	Apr-19	30–39	F	Single-parent	Occupying	Born in PT, parents from CV
13	Paula	Apr-19	40–49	F	Nuclear	Council home	Born in Germany, parents from PT

TABLE A.2 Interviews with local politicians and municipal employees

Nº	Interviewee code	Date	Organisation	Position
1	ME1	Jun-18	City Council of Loures	Municipal employee
2	LP	Sept-18	City Council of Loures	Local politician
3	ME2	Oct-18	City Council of Loures	Municipal employee
4	ME3	Oct-18	City Council of Loures	Municipal employee
5	ME4	Nov-18	Gebalis, Lisbon	Municipal employee
6	ME5	Nov-18	Gebalis, Lisbon	Municipal employee
7	ME6 + ME7 (group interview)	Dec-18	Gebalis, Lisbon	Municipal employee
8	ME8	Feb-19	City Council of Loures	Municipal employee
9	ME9, ME10, ME11 (group interview)	Apr-19	City Council of Loures	Municipal employee

TABLE A.3 Interviews with activists and NGO workers

Nº	Interviewee code	Date	Organisation	Position
1	A1	Feb-18	Habita	Activist
2	A2	Mar-18	APPA	Activist
3	NGO1	Mar-18	AIL	NGO worker
4	NGO2	Mar-18	Renovar a Mouraria	NGO worker
5	A3	Apr-18	Rede da Solidariedade	Activist
6	A4	Apr-18	SOS Racismo	Activist
7	NGO3	Jun-18	Pastoral dos Ciganos	NGO worker
8	NGO4	Jun-18	Pastoral dos Ciganos	NGO worker
9	NGO5	Jul-18	Projeto Escolhas	NGO worker
10	NGO6	Oct-18	Projeto Dá-te ao Condado	NGO worker
11	A5	Apr-19	Habita	Activist